THE COLLECTED WORKS OF

ERIC VOEGELIN

VOLUME 2

RACE AND STATE

PROJECTED VOLUMES IN THE SERIES

THE COLLECTED WORKS OF

ERIC VOEGELIN

VOLUME 2

RACE AND STATE

TRANSLATED FROM THE GERMAN BY

RUTH HEIN

EDITED WITH AN INTRODUCTION BY

KLAUS VONDUNG

LOUISIANA STATE UNIVERSITY PRESS

BATON ROUGE AND LONDON

Originally published in 1933 as *Rasse und Staat*
by J. C. B. Mohr (Paul Siebeck), Tübingen
Translation and Introduction copyright © 1997
by Louisiana State University Press
Manufactured in the United States of America
First printing
06 05 04 03 02 01 00 99 98 97   1   2   3   4   5

Designer: Albert Crochet
Typeface: Trump Mediaeval
Typesetter: Impressions Book and Journal Services, Inc.
Printer and binder: Thomson-Shore, Inc.

The Editorial Board wishes to give grateful acknowledgment to those who have
contributed to support publication of this book and series and especially to the
Earhart Foundation, the Foundation for Faith in Search of Understanding, the
Windway Foundation, the Liberty Fund, Inc., Robert J. Cihak, M.D.,
and John C. Jacobs, Jr.

The translator wishes to acknowledge use of Thomas Heilke's study *Voegelin on
the Idea of Race: An Analysis of Modern European Racism* (Baton Rouge, 1990)
in adopting some of the terminology used in this book.

Library of Congress Cataloging-in-Publication Data

Voegelin, Eric, 1901–
    [Rasse und Staat. English]
    Race and state / translated from the German by Ruth Hein ; edited
with an introduction by Klaus Vondung.
        p.   cm. — (the collected works of Eric Voegelin ; v. 2)
    Includes index.
    ISBN 0-8071-1842-7 (alk. paper)
    1. Race. 2. Philosophical anthropology. 3. Racism—Germany.
4. Germany—Race relations. 5. Europe—Race relations.
6. Totalitarianism. 7. State, The. I. Vondung, Klaus. II. Title.
III. Series: Voegelin, Eric, 1901– Works. 1989 ;v. 2
B3354.V88   1997
[GN269]
193 s—dc21
[305.8]
                                                        97-19444
                                                           CIP

The paper in this book meets the guidelines for permanence and durability of the
Committee on Production Guidelines for Book Longevity of the Council on
Library Resources. ∞

Contents

vii

CONTENTS

Editor's Introduction

The German edition of *Race and State* was published in 1933 by the renowned academic press J. C. B. Mohr (Paul Siebeck) in Tübingen, which had already published Voegelin's first book, *On the Form of the American Mind,* in 1928. *Race and State* forms a unit with *The History of the Race Idea,* which appeared only a few months later, still in 1933 and again within the borders of the German Reich. It was published by Junker and Dünnhaupt in Berlin.[1] Voegelin was at that time lecturer in political science and sociology (Privatdozent für Staatslehre und Soziologie) at the University of Vienna, Austria.

When and where these two books were written and published are critical to a full understanding of *Race and State* and *The History of the Race Idea.* On January 30, 1933, Hitler was appointed chancellor of the German Reich, which opened the way for establishing the dictatorial regime of the National Socialist Party during the following two years. In March, 1933, Austrian chancellor Engelbert Dollfuss overthrew, by means of a coup d'état, the parliamentary constitution of Austria and introduced an authoritarian regime. This was an attempt to overcome the parliamentary stalemate in Austria, to rein in the strong Social Democratic Party, and, at the same time, to ward off the growing threat of the National Socialist movement, which had become very active and successful in Austria, especially after Hitler came to power in Germany.[2] The pre-

1. See my introduction to *The History of the Race Idea: From Ray to Carus,* Vol. 3 of *The Collected Works of Eric Voegelin* (forthcoming).
2. Dollfuss' situation was as precarious as his politics. His attempt to prevent potential Socialist upheavals as well as to secure Austria's independence against Germany and German-influenced National Socialism resulted in an alliance be-

ceding years, when *Race and State* and *The History of the Race Idea* were still being written, had been characterized by economic crisis, mass unemployment, social unrest, and political destabilization in Germany as well as in Austria and, above all, by the rise of National Socialism. In the German national elections of 1930 the National Socialist party for the first time won a major victory and could appoint one-sixth of the representatives of the Reichstag. From then on Hitler's party grew constantly. Even though "one could not yet foresee that it would come to power," as Voegelin remarks in his *Autobiographical Reflections,* "the debate about races, the Jewish problem, etc., went on all the time."[3]

This situation must have presented a compelling motive to an alert and critical young scholar like Eric Voegelin to take a closer look at race ideas and race theories. Race ideas played an important role in various political ideologies of the time; in National Socialism they were essential for the project of a renewed political and social community. Race theories had been developed, some of them in close proximity to the National Socialist movement, to claim a scientific status for the discourse on race. Voegelin's two books on race can be viewed as a grand test of the discourse on race. As "theory," its scientific validity is scrutinized; as "idea," its history is traced, and its motives, functions, and consequences in the realm of politics and society are analyzed. The result of Voegelin's investigation was devastating. He ascertained the aporias of race theories in general and proved the insufficiency of National Socialist race theories in particular, thereby attacking the very center of National Socialism. And he demonstrated that the National Socialist race ideas, which masked themselves as theories, were basically rooted in an inferiority complex, and that they served to reduce the mind-body unit of human beings to animal categories. Thus Voegelin's grand test dismissed the discourse on race for good. This was of lasting importance, not only for any future attempt to develop a race theory, but also for Voegelin's own intellectual biography. He had cleared the way for himself to advance the analysis of National

tween his conservative and Catholic Christian-Social Party and fascist forces (which leaned towards Mussolini's fascism, not German National Socialism). See Erika Weinzierl's introduction to *The Authoritarian State,* Vol. 4 of *The Collected Works of Eric Voegelin* (forthcoming).

3. Eric Voegelin, *Autobiographical Reflections,* ed. Ellis Sandoz (Baton Rouge, 1989), 38.

Socialism with new categories, especially that of the "political religion" he established in 1938. Even more important were the general theoretical insights offered by Voegelin's analysis of the philosophical problems involved in race theories. For Voegelin was not compelled exclusively by "political stimuli"[4] to embark on investigations of race theories and race ideas. There was an additional reason why he took up these studies, a reason he mentions in the very first sentences of *Race and State* and that he explains again in his *Autobiographical Reflections.*[5]

After finishing *On the Form of the American Mind,* Voegelin began to develop a system of *Staatslehre.* Usually, the German word *Staatslehre* is translated into English as *political science* or, more literally, *theory of the state.* Neither term, however, captures what the German academic discipline *Staatslehre* really was, in contrast to the Anglo-Saxon tradition of political thinking. As Voegelin indicates in his introduction, since the founding of the German Reich in 1871, *Staatslehre* had been treated as an appendix to the theory of constitutional law, which, in its turn, usually formed a branch of jurisprudence. Insofar as philosophical reasoning was needed at all to categorize and justify constitutional and legal norms, it remained in the tradition of the philosophy of idealism, mostly in its neo-Kantian form.[6] The goal of this type of *Staatslehre* was to subsume all propositions on law and government in a logically consistent system of thought forming a "normative sphere," independent from the realm of contingent political phenomena. This meant "to purge *Staatslehre* of everything that does not pertain to positive law," as Voegelin points out in the introduction to *Race and State.* The most consistent type of such a "positivist *Staatslehre*" had been achieved by Hans Kelsen, who had turned it into a "pure theory of law" (*reine Rechtslehre*).[7]

Voegelin had been partly educated in the tradition of *Staatslehre,* and he had studied it under Kelsen. The influence of this school of thinking is still visible in his project to develop a "system of *Staats-*

---

4. See Voegelin's comments on the "Political Stimuli" of the time in his *Autobiographical Reflections,* 24–25.

5. *Ibid.,* 38–39.

6. For neo-Kantianism and the intellectual background of Voegelin's early works, see Jürgen Gebhardt's introduction to Vol. 1 of *The Collected Works of Eric Voegelin.*

7. P. 7 herein. Cited parenthetically in the text hereafter.

lehre" (1); the use of this phrase reveals also that the notion of a "system" of thought—in the sense of the idealistic tradition—still had weight. In the course of his project Voegelin actually wrote sections dealing with the theory of law and the theory of power, as he tells in his *Autobiographical Reflections*.[8] But by that time he was already aware that this would not suffice. He criticized Kelsen for having excluded the realm of contingent political phenomena, especially the "ideas of the state," or political ideas, from *Staatslehre*, although he acknowledged that Kelsen's "purification" at the same time clearly showed which "topics from the pre-positivist sphere" had to be reintroduced in order to make *Staatslehre* a really comprehensive system of thought (7). In the third part of his projected system of *Staatslehre*, Voegelin therefore wanted to deal with political ideas, because he was aware that the state with its laws and norms had its roots in "ideas of the state" or "ideas of community." Among these ideas "body ideas" (*Leibideen*), in particular race ideas, as elements that produce political communities drew his special interest for well-known historical reasons. Hence there was, apart from the political stimuli, also a systematic reason for working on the political ideas of race.

In his introduction Voegelin explains why he published his studies on race ideas and race theories separately from the theoretical sections of his *Staatslehre*, which he had begun earlier. He does not say, however, that by that time he was about to give up the project of a "system of *Staatslehre*," or explain why he had to abandon it, although one can infer the reason from his introduction and from the way he deals with the race question in these two books. When Voegelin began his study of what he then called "ideas of the state" or "political ideas," concentrating on race ideas first, he discovered that there was no analytical access from the "normative sphere" of *Staatslehre* to the political and social reality of ideas. The relationship had to be reversed; the task was to develop "a system of *Staatslehre* out of the theory of human nature" (7). To accomplish this task one had to recur to "the fundamental human experiences that give rise to the phenomenon of the state" (5).

Although Voegelin still used the term *Staatslehre* for a comprehensive science of politics, it is obvious that he had acquired a new

8. Voegelin, *Autobiographical Reflections*, 38.

theoretical perspective that would have changed the meaning of *Staatslehre* altogether if he had maintained this notion. At that time he had already formulated the principle to which he adhered until the end of his life, that one has to uncover and analyze "existential experiences" (4) in order to understand and judge the norms of a society and its system of government. The phenomena reflecting these experiences and producing social and political norms and institutions Voegelin later called "symbols," or "symbolizations of experiences," or "symbolic forms of political order," depending on the perspective from which he saw them. In 1933 he still used the term *ideas*, although he was already aware of the foundation of ideas in experiences. However, he had not yet fully developed the theoretical basis for adequately analyzing this correlation, so that "ideas of the state," or "body ideas" and "race ideas" respectively, still appeared as a comparatively independent body of political phenomena. On the other hand, Voegelin realized the importance of political ideas for understanding the overall political and social reality, and he saw that such ideas form a part of this reality and must not be mixed up with theories of a scientific status.

It is from here on that Voegelin's major project of the 1940s comes into view, his multi-volume *History of Political Ideas*, which broke up, as it were, from the inside his original project of a "system of *Staatslehre*," dissolving the systematic parts of the "normative sphere" completely. Yet this new project of a history of political ideas, although almost completed, was abandoned again—and not published during Voegelin's lifetime—in favor of *Order and History*, which dealt with the correlation between phenomena of political order and disorder, ideas—now "symbols"—and experiences on a more differentiated philosophical basis. But Voegelin knew already when he wrote *Race and State* and *The History of the Race Idea* that this correlation had to be taken into account by all means and that a theory had to be developed for its adequate analysis. Thus one can rightly say that these two books were important steps on Voegelin's way to reconstitute political science in the sense of his seminal study of 1952, *The New Science of Politics*.

The task Voegelin set himself in the introduction to *Race and State*, to develop "a system of *Staatslehre* out of the theory of human nature," meant that a philosophical anthropology was necessary as a basis for a renewed and comprehensive science of politics, especially for the adequate treatment of political ideas, in particular race ideas. In the 1920s several efforts were made in Germany to develop a new philosophical anthropology; Voegelin in his introduction lists Scheler, Plessner, Groethuysen, Jaspers, and Heidegger. Since Voegelin was soon to develop his own philosophical anthropology on the basis of classical philosophy, which he began to study at that time, he looked for theoretical stimuli for his race books in the works of the scholars mentioned above. Although their ideas could not be applied directly to the race problem, he found Max Scheler's philosophical anthropology, as expressed in the late work *Die Stellung des Menschen im Kosmos*,[9] sufficiently useful to be adopted for the purpose at hand.

What appealed most to Voegelin in Scheler's work, and what furthered his own analysis of the race problem, was Scheler's endeavor to develop a "coherent idea of the human being" (*eine einheitliche Idee vom Menschen*) with which to bridge the gap between physical anthropology, philosophical anthropology, and theological anthropology.[10] In a similar attempt Voegelin lays the foundation for his investigation of race theories and race ideas by analyzing first the interrelationship of body, soul, and mind. Most race theories of the time assumed that one part of the human being (most often the body) dominates or even determines the others. It was obvious for Voegelin that such "super-power constructions" were theoretically inadequate. Thus he starts out, before embarking on his specific investigation, with an extensive philosophical discussion, including theoretical and methodological problems.[11]

The analysis of the actual subject matter is divided into two parts, race theories and race ideas, in accordance with Voegelin's conviction that theories of a scientific status must not be mixed up with ideas. Theories, which try to describe and explain reality, must be tested under the terms of theory, *i.e.*, with respect to the

9. First published in 1928, in the year of Scheler's death. Reprinted in Max Scheler, *Gesammelte Werke*, Vol. 9: *Späte Schriften*, ed. Manfred S. Frings (Bern, 1976), 7–71.

10. *Ibid.*, 11.

11. A detailed exegesis of Voegelin's two books on race has been presented by Thomas W. Heilke in *Voegelin on the Idea of Race: An Analysis of Modern European Racism* (Baton Rouge, 1990).

validity of their premises, the logic of their reasoning, the rationality of their argumentation. Ideas, however, present a different
task and have to be treated in a different way. Since ideas form a
part of political, or social, reality itself, they have no place within
theoretical reasoning. The task is rather to find out how they originate, how they function, and how, for instance, they contribute to
the formation of groups and societies. It is not the theoretician's
concern to express moral indignation and pass value judgments. He
can uncover the implications of ideas and demonstrate their possible consequences; more cannot be done within the realm of serious scholarship. Obviously, this is Max Weber's position, which
Voegelin adopted at that time as the soundest epistemological
stand in the philosophical and ideological turmoil of the time.

The chapter entitled "Race as Biological Unit" reveals the specific quality of Voegelin's method of examining the various biological theories from Darwin to his time and of demonstrating, on the
basis of the preceding philosophical reflections, their intellectual
shortcomings and theorctical fallacies, up to the point where such
concepts substitute an apparatus of demanding terminology for a
real explanation of the problem. This does not mean that Voegelin
is an opponent of physical anthropology, but he makes clear that
physical characteristics do not suffice to distinguish different races
among human beings, and he concludes that biological theories of
heredity and of the transformation of species (variations, mutations) do not contribute to a race theory of explanatory value.

The discussion becomes more complicated when Voegelin proceeds to the analysis of what race theories tell us about the problem
of the intellectual traits of races. He examines the theories of five
major authors: Lenz, Scheidt, Günther, Clauss, and Spann. Fritz
Lenz (1887–1976) had studied medicine; in 1923 he became professor at the University of Munich on the first chair of "Race Hygien-
ics" in Germany. Apart from his anthropological works on race
and eugenics, he also published essays with direct political impact,
including several on the biological foundations of education. In
1933 he became professor at the University of Berlin and director
of the Anthropology, Human Genetics, and Eugenics department
in the Kaiser Wilhelm Institute. Walter Scheidt (1895–1976) was
professor of anthropology at the University of Hamburg; his special
field was the interrelationship between race and culture. Hans

Friedrich Karl Günther (1891–1968) was professor of social anthropology at the University of Jena (during the Third Reich at the Universities of Berlin and Freiburg); he was the most famous theoretician of race of the time and exerted a strong influence on the racist ideology of National Socialism, especially with his major work *Rassenkunde des deutschen Volkes* (1928). Ludwig Ferdinand Clauss (1892–1974), an anthropologist who spent most of his life as a private scholar traveling in the Islamic world, was a student of the philosopher Edmund Husserl; renouncing biological methods, he used Husserl's phenomenology for developing a *Rassenseelenkunde,* which tried to advance the understanding for other races. During the Third Reich he was regarded as deviating from the official ideology. Othmar Spann (1878–1950) was professor of economy and social sciences in Brünn and, after World War I, at the University of Vienna; he was a prominent speaker of the so-called Conservative Revolution, and advocated an organistic model of society rooted in German idealism and Romanticism. In 1938, when Hitler occupied Austria, he was dismissed from his professorship. Voegelin studied under Spann before he began to work with Kelsen.

In examining the theories of these scholars, Voegelin again demonstrates his singular ability to take them at their own premises, and to reason out these premises in order to test their consistency and validity. Lenz's, Scheidt's, and Günther's theories are dismissed as inadequate. Voegelin shows that the premise of the physical foundation of the mind leads to absurdities when it comes to the question of how intellectual traits are inherited. These theoreticians of race, Voegelin concludes, do not understand what is at stake when the human mind, or rather, the spirit (*Geist*), is concerned; they treat the interrelationship of body, mind, and soul in a pseudo-scientific manner. Clauss comes off better because he views the human being as a comprehensive totality. The theory of Spann, finally, is valued as "the only major philosophical attempt to get to the heart of the race problem" (102). Voegelin agrees with Spann that one has to recur to fundamental experiences, although he assumes more than the two Spann accepts (spirit and matter). Nonetheless, the problem of race can be seen as a special case of the general problem of how the connection between spirit and matter works. Voegelin shares Spann's position that race, not to mention something like the "purity of race," is not determined biologically, but created and evaluated by the mind, which, of course, has to be seen in its social and historical dimension. Thus, the physical basis of how the spirit or, in individuals, the human mind presents itself is to be viewed as a subsidiary problem within the greater context of the sociality of the spirit.

The discussion of Spann's theory serves as an apposite transition to the second part of the book, in which Voegelin analyzes the race idea and the structuring of community. Race ideas—this is Voegelin's major insight, which every analysis of such ideas must take into account—are never biological ideas in the strict sense; they are always spiritually transformed. "The body, that, as an idea, contributes to constructing the community, is not the body of biology; it is not an animal body but always a body of the mind. The idea of this body may be pictured in objective animal ideas, but it can never coincide with them and may stray very far indeed from this image" (128).

Again Voegelin embarks on careful philosophical considerations in order to build up a reliable basis for his analysis. He shows first that the modern race idea is just one body idea among others, and he presents the classical tribal state and the Kingdom of Christ as two other major body ideas. Second, he reiterates the special character of an "idea," in contrast to a theory, and its function to structure community. In his essay "The Growth of the Race Idea" of 1940, in which he summarized some results of his investigations for the American reader, he brought this characterization to the point even more clearly, now using also the term *symbol* in its description. Political ideas, he says here, are neither theories nor "instruments of cognition"; they do not represent an "attempt to describe reality as it is," but set up "symbols . . . which have the function of creating the image of a group as a unit."[12] Third, Voegelin distinguishes between the different body ideas as symbolic images of communities, between the universal pretension of, for instance, the body idea of the Christian empire and the idea of a particularist community. Finally, he shows that the rise of the modern race idea must be seen in the context of the modern process of historicization.

12. Eric Voegelin, "The Growth of the Race Idea," *Review of Politics,* II (1940), 284.

If the idea of a community is particularist, it tends to compete with other particularist ideas and to interpret itself by way of devaluing the others. Thus the rise of the race idea is closely linked with the formation of the idea of an "anti-race." In modern Europe, especially in Germany, the idea of the Aryan, Teuton, German, or Nordic race creates, as its counterpart, the anti-race of the Jews. Voegelin expresses surprise that, of all possible races and peoples, the Jews became the anti-race for the Germans, given that they represented only 1 percent of the population. Although there is no exhaustive explanation for this phenomenon, Voegelin points out the functions of the anti-race within the German race idea. He shows that the anti-Semitic race ideas are not primarily concerned with understanding the Jewish character but use the idea of the Jewish anti-race in order to contrast it to the character of the German race. The stereotyped characterizations of the Jews serve as a means to build up the German community idea. Thus Voegelin uncovers, as motive of the German race idea, a lack of "intellectual rootedness." He concludes that for the German formation of ideas, this intellectual rootedness "is such a burning question . . . because there is no natural and immediately sure political rootedness in reality [*Wirklichkeitsboden*] for the German ideas of community as there is for the world of ideas of France, England, and America" (206).

Race and State did not provoke, as Voegelin probably had hoped, an extensive debate among political scientists and theoreticians of race. For that it came out too late. The book was not on the market for very long, for obvious political reasons; after some time the publisher discontinued its sale.[13] Nevertheless, it received a considerable number of reviews up to the beginning of 1934.[14] There were reviews, of course, criticizing Voegelin's book from a National Socialist viewpoint. Norbert Gürke, for instance, lecturer in international law and constitutional law and a faithful National Socialist who, ironically, became full professor at the University of Vienna in the year after Voegelin's emigration, commented that

13. In the 1970s, more than forty years after its publication, some thirty copies were still found in the stacks of the press.
14. A collection of reviews can be found in Box 54, Eric Voegelin Papers, Hoover Institution Archives.

Voegelin's book "contradicts, in its general thought, the National Socialist concept of the people and the state. It is neither a scholarly nor a politically meritorious book, but a collection of intellectual constructions that serves to question the basic ideas of race."[15] Other reviews, however, tried to give a comparatively objective account of the book; this was still possible during the first year of Hitler's regime. The philosopher Arnold Gehlen even praised *Race and State* as an "important work" that undertakes a "first decisive approach to a philosophical analysis of the race problem," although he criticized the parts bearing on political problems of the day, not without bows to Rosenberg and other representatives of the National Socialist race ideology.[16]

The longest and most interesting review was published by Helmuth Plessner, who was a major contributor to the development of a modern philosophical anthropology. He had been professor of philosophy at the University of Cologne before he emigrated in 1933 to the Netherlands, where he became lecturer in sociology at the University of Groningen. The journal in which his review appeared was published in Vienna. Plessner's review is a congenial appraisal of the philosophical distinction and the political significance of Voegelin's book. He sees it as part of the endeavor of modern philosophy to develop an anthropology aimed at a "concept of the human being that does justice to its multi-layered existence as a physical, vital, psychic, and intellectual being, without making one of these layers the measure and explanatory basis for the others." Plessner, who shares with Voegelin the Weberian epistemological position, points out the philosophical range of Voegelin's theoretical endeavor as well as the political consequences visible in his analysis of the race ideas: the objection to Marxism as degrading the spiritual realm to a "super-structure" of the economic-material conditions is even more true when applied to race theories, which derive spirit and state from biological facts and turn them into a super-structure of the blood. But any attempt—thus Plessner summarizes the essence of Voegelin's analysis of race theories and race ideas—to subsume the human being under animal

---

15. *Deutsche Literaturzeitung,* Heft 46 (November 12, 1933), col. 2198.
16. *Die Erziehung* (January 4, 1934), pp. 201–204, copy in Box 54, Folder 2, Voegelin Papers.

categories has to be paid for by the human being and by the categories that are to confine him. "If the human being voluntarily renounces his spiritual existence, he will indeed bestialize and cannot complain if he is treated in accordance with Mendel's Law."[17]

17. *Zeitschrift für öffentliches Recht*, Vol. XIV (1934), 407–14; copy *ibid.* Quotations from 408, 414.

RACE AND STATE

Introduction

§1. Man and the State

The following study grew out of my work on a system of "theory of the state" [*Staatslehre*]; in a section on the various ideas about the state, I intended to discuss also body ideas [*Leibideen*] as one of the elements producing political communities. In the course of my work, however, it became clear that precisely these questions—which are of comparatively minor significance in the overall system—to be comprehensible at all would have to be discussed so extensively as to lead to a serious quantitative disproportion among the parts of the system. I therefore separated out the problem of body ideas, with special attention to the race idea, which is of paramount importance at the present time. I present its systematic treatment here, under the title *Race and State.* A further volume, dealing with the race idea's foundations in intellectual history is finished and, provided that economic conditions allow it, will also be published in the near future.[1] These remarks concerning the ori-

1. Since my exploration of the race idea (the second part of the present study) is based on the result of my work on the history of ideas, and since I wish to assure the reader that none of the historical judgments presented as givens in that second volume lack documentation in the most specific sources, I will cite here the table of contents of the proposed second volume:

gin of the present volume are necessary to explain the book's systematic intent and to draw out its lines of thought to their focal point in the fundamental idea of the system of *Staatslehre*, namely, that the roots of the state must be sought in the nature of man.

This statement poses the challenge of developing the problems of *Staatslehre* on the basis of a philosophical anthropology. Here I will name only the essential themes of such a *Staatslehre* in order to present a rough idea of what is meant by this challenge. An essential problem, as yet posed only inadequately in *Staatslehre*, is

---

the justification of the phenomenon of law [*Rechtserscheinung*]. The phenomenon of law is to be traced to its origins, one of which is to be found in the moral experience of the individual, while the other resides in the experience of the community. From the moral experience of the individual future real states of affairs (actions and their consequences in the environment) receive the index of "what should be done";[2] from communal experience, it seems to me, emerges that universality of the norm that renders it obligatory for a majority of persons. Individual and community are the fundamental human experiences from which the "norm" in the sense of an anticipatory design for the future actions of people as members of a community arises. At every level of the legal system there is the idea of the "norm" in the succinct sense of a model for the realization of the community in the actions of its members.

The general phenomenon of norm (which includes not only the law but also community ethics) becomes particularized as the norm phenomenon of the political community through its relationship to a particular community rooted in other fundamental human experiences, namely those of ruling and serving. Systematically speaking, the *Herrschaftslehre* is the second part of a *Staatslehre*; it serves to delimit the specific action by which the community constitutes itself as having political existence (Carl Schmitt).[3] Sociology offers significant contributions to a *Herrschaftslehre* (for example, Alfred Vierkandt, Egon Freyer, Max Weber), but a complete restoration of this great theme, it seems to me, is possible only by returning to Nietzsche and Fichte and especially to the *Herrschaftslehre* of antiquity.

The "legal order" arising at the intersection of the general phenomenon of norm and the governmental organization of the community, has two typical complexes as regards content: regulating the actions of the community's members in relation to each other and regulating the actions of the community as a political entity. The first thematic cluster is the one probably most neglected today—it was handled in its classical form in the great systems of

2. I have published a preliminary study on this question: "Das Sollen im System Kants," in *Gesellschaft, Staat und Recht: Untersuchungen zur reinen Rechtslehre,* ed. Alfred Verdross (Vienna, 1931).

3. See my essay "Die Verfassungslehre von Carl Schmitt: Versuch einer konstruktiven Analyse ihrer staatstheoretischen Prinzipien," in *Zeitschrift für öffentliches Recht,* XI (1931).

natural right (with the principal themes of freedom and property), though in dogmatic form. We need a transformation of the dogmatic system of natural right into an analysis of existential experiences that make regulation of certain institutions (property, obligation, family) the inevitable component of any legal order. Attempts at such an undertaking are evident today even in the German literature, but I believe the English and American writings offer better points of departure since they have treated these themes continuously ever since the classical natural-rights doctrine.[4]

The second cluster of legal contents—regulating the actions of the community as a political entity—comprises the problems of the idea of the state and the form of the state. Concerning this question I support the thesis that the so-called forms are ideas, once again with the trenchant sense of *models*, and indeed models with a specific content, in which the reality of the political community is built up for the members of the political community. These ideas of the state are not a science of the state but an essential part of the reality of the state itself. The contents of these state ideas essentially originate in the fundamental human experiences already mentioned—they are ideas pertaining either to persons or to communities. The class of ideas about persons contains all formations of ideas that nourish the experience of political reality from the figure of a great ruling person (ideas of caesars, dictators, kings, priest-kings, leaders, and the like); the class of ideas about communities includes all ideas that draw from the experience of the community the certainty about the state's reality (for our Western Christian world, these are significantly the experiences of the Christian communities which since the beginnings of Christianity have supported the empire and passed over into the nation-states; they are most strongly felt today in American political ideas but very significantly also, for example, in French solidarism. The last resonances of this idea are the communist doctrines of the free association of free individuals; but Germanic ideas of community

4. For a German attempt I draw the reader's attention to Wilhelm Schapp, *Die neue Wissenschaft vom Recht* (1930, 1932). For an American one, most particularly John R. Commons, *Legal Foundations of Capitalism* (1924). The full implications of the idea that, for example, "property" is a pre-legal and pre-economic category (Yorck von Wartenburg)—that is, grounded in human nature—have, however, barely been recognized.

also figure alongside the Christian ones).[5] The problem of the body idea as co-constitutive of the reality of the state, which gave rise to the present study, is also part of this thematic complex. Person and community are grounded essentially in the body, and therefore body ideas will always share significantly in the structure of the reality of the state, as the idea of dynasty, blood lineage, or as the idea of blood kinship, the mystical body of Christ, or race.

A system of *Staatslehre* must include as a final part a depiction of the structure of the legal system (the levels [*Stufenbau*] of the legal system, forms of legal principles [*Rechtssatzformen*], theory of institutions [*Organlehre*]) and a constitutional theory [*Verfassungslehre*], meaning a theory of the foundation of the ideas of the state in terms of the contents of positive law.

This cursory overview of a system of *Staatslehre* directly indicates a stance toward the prevailing theory. Against German *Staatslehre* since the founding of the Reich the general objection must be raised that because of the history and organization of academic disciplines, it is treated as an appendage to the theory of constitutional law, so that its systematic center is located not in the fundamental human experiences that give rise to the phenomenon of the state but in the final part of *Staatslehre* that presupposes all the other parts (general theory of norms, *Herrschaftslehre*, theory of the personal spheres of community members, theory of the ideas of the state). The basic problems are dealt with not on their own ground but only as they are reflected in the contents of positive law, and therefore they are *of necessity* seen in a distorted way. Georg Jellinek's *Staatslehre*, today still the most comprehensive treatment of the subject and absolutely indispensable to any overview of the problems, is not a system but a loose series of individual treatments of topics that traditionally belong to the stock of a *Staatslehre*. The work contains chapters, such as those on the purposes of the state and the justification for the state, that were included only because in the history of theories of the state these topics have been addressed over and over. But *why* the problem of purpose, or the problem of evil, *necessarily must* be part of a theory of the state is a question that (aside from hints at "psychological

---

5. I have made an initial attempt at solving the problem of the form of the state in this context in my essay, "Zur Lehre von der Staatsform," in *Zeitschrift für öffentliches Recht*, VI (1927).

necessity" and the necessity of institutions to justify themselves as reasonable to the consciousness of each generation) is not explored systematically by this *Staatslehre*. The systematic problem of the prevailing *Staatslehre* can be seen most clearly in Hans Kelsen's work.[6] The idea that *Staatslehre* is a theory of law, a theory of the validity of law and the positive content of law, is adhered to with the utmost consistency. This fundamental stance is, to varying degrees, an advantage for the various topics of *Staatslehre*. It works excellently in those parts where a simple principle, hardly needing further analysis, is presupposed for the articulation of legal contents, as for example in the case of the state's spatial organization—it is a matter of describing the typical legal contents by which specific partial legal orders that have emerged historically in the modern European states in relation to particular spaces and settlements are distinguished. The typology of the theory of governmental forms does not fare so well, because in this case the presuppositions are numerous and complicated (the total theory of the ideas of the state), and this difficult circle of problems cannot possibly be made transparent by its embodiment in the contents of positive law. As the principle of the formation of forms Hans Kelsen accepts only the eruption of freedom, which softens domination. Now the demand for freedom certainly is an agent in the formation of political institutions, but it is only one in a very complicated web of such operative causes and surely not the first—more likely the last—since control of rule by narrower or wider circles of the ruled presupposes a political existence that encompasses the rulers and the ruled, and it is only within this that political struggles for a share of the power can be carried out. Thus Kelsen's theory of governmental forms lacks a theory of the ideas of the state—and necessarily so, since with the assumed identity between *Staatslehre* and theory of the content of law, a theory of ideas transcends the scope of *Staatslehre*.[7] The link of *Staatslehre* to the theory of

6. Hans Kelsen, *Allgemeine Staatslehre* (1925), in *Enzyklopädie der Rechts- und Staatswissenschaft*, Vol. 23. [*General Theory of Law and the State*, trans. Anders Wedberg (New York, 1945; repr. 1961)].
7. On the critique of pure jurisprudence [*Rechtslehre*], see my essays "Reine Rechtslehre und Staatslehre," *Zeitschrift für öffentliches Recht*, IV (1924); "Kelsen's Pure Theory of Law," *Political Science Quarterly*, XLII (1927); "Die Souveränitätslehre Dickinsons und die Reine Rechtslehre," *Zeitschrift für öffentliches Recht*, VIII (1928); "Die Einheit des Rechtes und das soziale Sinngebilde Staat," *Internationale Zeitschrift für Theorie des Rechts* (1930).

constitutional law is even more blatantly expressed in the fact that the second principal topic of governmental legal order, the regulation of the personal spheres of the community's members in their interrelations, is made the subject of investigation merely to conjure it out of existence by declaring it a sham problem. Just as there is no analysis of government and ideas of the state, the "private" legal sphere is never traced back to its roots in human nature. And finally, the "normative sphere" is accepted as a reality without pointing to its origin in man.

In his attempt to purge *Staatslehre* of everything that does not pertain to positive law, Kelsen was in fact consistent. I think the great achievement of this purifying work is the elevation of positivist *Staatslehre* to a level from which the other thematic areas not of a positive law nature and their autonomous laws have come into view with a clarity they never had before. *Staatslehre* was in fact "syncretistic," as Kelsen put it, in the sense that the problems connected with the structure of the legal order and the reflection of ideas in the content of the law were grouped in an inadmissable way with the problems of the person and the community, of rule and service, and of the ideas of the state. The purification of one cluster of problems simultaneously purges the others. So far, however, little use has been made of the opportunities opened up by this purgative work. The most significant attempts to reintroduce topics from the pre-positivist sphere into *Staatslehre* did not move beyond the initial phase. With his theory of integration Rudolf Smend undertook a first step into the reality of the state though seriously handicapped by Theodor Litt's theory of community, which is important in itself but hardly suitable to this purpose. Carl Schmitt dealt with the problem of the "political" at length, and his constitutional theory posed the problem of the political "existence" of a state; however, these attempts were not developed into a system. Dietrich Schindler advanced furthest—he called for the derivation of the reality of the state from human nature; yet his work on constitutional law and social structure satisfied this demand only in part. The task of developing a system of *Staatslehre* out of the theory of human nature has not yet been completed—it is given by the incontestable fact that man is the creator of the state.

§2. Race Theory and Race Idea

The body idea, as part of the structure of the ideas of state that in their totality build up the political community spiritually, manifests itself now as the race idea. As it is the most important idea for any understanding of the modern world of political ideas, we have made it the central point of our investigation; we have only alluded in one chapter to other instances of body ideas—those in the ancient tribal state and in the Christian empire—in order to remove from the race idea the character of the extraordinary, which it still has for many people today. Any study of this modern form of the body idea must necessarily be arranged in two parts, one of which deals with race theory and its scientific content, while the other traces the race idea as a political idea in its effectiveness in the construction of a community. The dual arrangement is necessary, since the race idea does not appear as simply a political idea (or rather, has not yet appeared as such) that shapes the lives of those who belong to it, uniting them while excluding all others; rather, beyond this it claims to result from scientific reflection. On this point it differs from the body ideas of other historical periods, which believe primarily in the mythical bodily unity of their community and largely or entirely forgo any scientific justification.

The first part of this book therefore deals with race theory insofar as it claims to be a science. A comprehensive humanistic analysis of this complex of problems is indispensable, since in spite of the hugely swollen literature on the race question (aside from two exceptions) neither the supporters nor the opponents of race theory have furnished a sufficient foundation or critique of this science. The race problem is a part of the body-soul problem; the former requires for its adequate understanding complete clarity about the latter and therefore about the nature of man. But in Germany today a theory on the nature of man is only just emerging, and in spite of outstanding work by Max Scheler, Helmut Plessner, Bernhard Groethuysen, Karl Jaspers, and Martin Heidegger, the ideas of these thinkers cannot be applied directly to the race problem because they arose from quite different philosophical impulses and must first be subjected to a thorough restructuring in order to be fruitful for the concrete field of race theory. If we ignore a few occasional remarks, race theory finds no support in contemporary philosophy, and this circumstance seems to me the decisive reason why (again with two exceptions) today the questions of the principles of race theory have not been addressed in depth by any of the scholars who deal with the subject.

Thus we have explained why race theory lacks any awareness of issues of principle and clarity concerning its foundations, but not why quite obviously there is no indication of any need for foundations. Anyone perusing the main works in the literature on race will be astonished by the self-satisfied, complacent tone prevailing on all sides and by the smug, self-satisfied pride in so-called significant achievements, which contrast oddly with the undemanding nature of these studies. The need for a critical foundation does not make itself felt because prevailing race theory works with a system of dogmas that, as we can see, is neither transcendentally shaken by philosophical anthropology nor deeply affected inherently by the course of biology and scientific anthropology. It is a system of dogmas that arose in the second half of the nineteenth century and that, in short, I will call the system of scientific superstition. Here I will limit myself to listing the two basic dogmas of the system; from them most of the phenomena relevant to our purpose follow: (1) The method of natural science is the only "scientific" one, and it alone is therefore qualified to solve all the problems within the human horizon. All other methods, especially those in the humanities, are remnants of a "metaphysical" period in the evolution of the human mind, a phase that has been virtually "outgrown" today. Problems that cannot be mastered by the scientific method are merely pseudo-problems. (2) Science progresses steadily; the researcher is sufficiently equipped for his work if he is aware of the problems currently facing his discipline, and he must proceed from this point on. The problems and ideas of earlier times are "antiquated," "overcome," irrelevant to the present, and need not be known.

These two dogmas form the comfortable basis of the clear conscience typical race scholars enjoy even though they remain ignorant of scientific developments outside their specialty and have no detailed understanding of the principles of their own science beyond Darwin or, at best, Lamarck.

The topics for the first part of the present work are determined by this situation in the history of science. We must present an outline of the systematic content of the race problem, beginning with an analysis of the relationships among body, soul, and spirit. We have found substantial help in this endeavor among contemporary philosophers, especially Scheler. For the rest these introductory investigations must observe the same procedure that characterizes all subsequent ones: the restoration of the problem through insertion of the classical formulations into the current thinking. The essential sources for an understanding of body-soul-spirit relationships are Aristotle, Descartes, Kant, and the anthropology of Immanuel Hermann von Fichte. We have not "adopted" theses from these thinkers but have used their ideas to illustrate the problem and its speculative range in order to get a basic understanding of what is meant by these things; the problems in this area are not to be "solved"; they need to be shown first of all and to be restored to their importance. First we had to create the basis from which an analysis of the race problem could be meaningfully approached.

Building on this basis we thoroughly explore the biological and anthropological significance of the concept of race in the second and third chapters of the first part and take a critical stance toward the most important theories in the fourth and fifth chapters.

The results of this systematic investigation can be summarized in the following theses:

1. According to his ontic structure, man belongs simultaneously to all realms of being; in spite of this multiple determination of his makeup, however, he is a unified whole, a totality.

2. As far as the possibilities of scientific studies of man are concerned, his ontic makeup means that he can be studied as belonging to each particular realm of being with the methods proper to that realm—he is a mechanical as well as a chemical entity and also an appropriate subject for biology and for the humanities [*Geistesforschung*].

3. The difficulties of a human race theory are due to the fact that the methods proper to one of the realms of being and applicable to a part of man are to be applied unjustifiably and impossibly to other partial spheres. Thus, it is possible to study man as an animal, and to that extent there is quite properly (but note the restriction in the following points) a physical anthropology; however, it is impossible to make meaningful statements about the mental sphere on that basis. Insofar as statements about racial types of souls are contained

in the literature of physical anthropology, they use the methods of the humanities (only, as a rule, very bad ones) and are, rightly or wrongly, independent of the questions of physical anthropology.

4. Within the field [*Gegenstandsbereich*] of physical anthropology, methodological difficulties exist (which the discipline itself has not so far addressed in principle) because the methods of biology cannot be directly applied to human societies (see Chapter 3 of Part I).

5. Within the biological method itself basic problems remain unclarified; attempts to achieve clarity on them have not progressed very far up to now (see Chapter 2 of Part I).

6. Because a scientific race theory, a science that catalogues human body types, can, due to philosophical-anthropological and epistemological reasons, achieve *nothing* for the problem of mental racial types, because the kind of connection among body, soul, and mind cannot be the subject of possible scientific judgments does *not* necessarily mean that such a connection does not exist. The human totality is the reality of this connection, experienced daily by everyone. Though the connection is not a possible subject of a *science,* it is the legitimate basis for forming *ideas* of the body— whose analysis is offered in Part II.

It is particularly important to me that these topics and their implications are correctly understood. To this day there exists among scholars of political and social science a certain timid mistrust toward race theory and the race idea. In part this mistrust is rooted in the prevailing world of political ideas, which rejects any discussion of the race problem because it must of necessity lead to a shake-up of the political dogma of equality. I have said all I have to say as a scholar about this political mistrust by characterizing it—that is, by describing it as unobjective and unscientific. In part, however, this mistrust is very much justified by the scientific level on which arguments for and against race theory operate. The proponents of race theory enjoy the great advantage of championing a real, crucially important problem. That a thorough elaboration of the foundations is lacking is shown with as much clarity as can be wished for in my critiques in Chapter 4 of Part I—but in spite of such a lack, race theoreticians could always counter each objection by resorting to the sure conviction that they were fundamentally in the right against all opponents, that there was "something to" their cause. Unfortunately, they have seriously and utterly unnecessarily jeopardized their excellent position and opened it up to cheap attacks by proceeding with, let us say, a generosity that is rare in the German history of science regarding particular issues (i.e., the listing of mental types, the theory of mental traits, and the like). Only the works of Ludwig Clauss have raised race theory to a level on which no one need be ashamed to operate. The case of the opponents of race theory—I will name Jean Finot and Friedrich Otto Hertz—is just the reverse; their critique of individual historical judgments made by race theorists is frequently well-founded in contrast to their overall attitude, which is opposition to race theory and to the intellectual problem of race in general and is not in any way well-founded. If we can accuse the past and current forms of race theory of having failed in all its basic questions, the same accusation can be leveled even more strongly against the works of its opponents. The attacks on race theory are in fact of such low-grade character that they could not persuade its proponents but only annoy them even though they did not have much to say in response.

The fact that the controversy over race theory is played out in forms that fall short of the standard of German scholarship and that neither side in this conflict has ever said anything that was well-founded in terms of the theory of science, has led to a situation which this book wants to help bring to an end. Contemporary race theory is an offshoot of biology, a so-called natural science, and as a result, its adherents see this idea and its opposition in terms of a contrast between the natural sciences and the humanities. There is no evidence justifying the assumption of such a contrast since when anthropologists claiming to be adherents of the scientific method establish mental or psychological racial types, the makeup of the subject under investigation compels them to use methods that have no relation whatsoever to those of biology or any other natural science; they must work with what is today conventionally identified as the methods of the humanities, namely with the formation of types [*Typenbildung*] based on historical material. Thus it is not a matter of an opposition between the methods of the natural sciences and those of the humanities but only one of whether the humanistic method is being applied correctly and thoroughly or—generously. We do not need to raise the question here now, since Clauss already posed it within race theory itself. His analyses must be understood as an attempt to refine the still somewhat primitive methods of race theorists and to advance to the epistemological presuppositions of a typology of races. Both the types he proposed and his epistemological explications represent an enormous step forward in reforming race theory from within; though many details still need to be improved (see Chapter 4 of Part I), he nevertheless furnished a new beginning for race theory from which it can continue on the scientific path. Clauss's race theory and Othmar Spann's (these are the two exceptions I mentioned above) offer the first indications that within race theory the system of dogmas proper to scientific superstition, as I have called it, is being overcome and the significant idea of race theory is gaining its appropriate form.

But we must surely distinguish between race theory and the race idea. The theory claims to be a science and we can test the correctness of its judgments and the solidity of its foundations. The idea belongs to politics, and it is our task to interpret it as a human phenomenon and to fit it into the context of our experiences of the reality of the state as a human creation. Therefore our study must take as its starting point the widest range of the idea problem and gradually approach the historically concrete particular phenomenon of the Nordic idea. We will first study the problem of the ideas of community (Part II, Chapter 1), then within the framework of the ideas of community the body ideas (Part II, Chapter 2), and then we will examine two historical cases of body ideas to show that the race idea is not a unique phenomenon among political ideas but is a body idea like any other, and as such appears in the community's total network of ideas as co-generator of community. At the same time, we will also briefly touch on the profoundly important insight that body ideas, insofar as they help in building up the intellectual reality of the community (that is, insofar as they are not objective animal ideas), are *never* scientific judgments concerning matters in the biological sphere through which their correctness could be tested; rather, the idea of the community as a body is *always* a "mythic" idea, and it *always* (not only in the case of the Christian community) establishes a *corpus mysticum*. After these three steps, we develop in the chapter on the particularist community (Part II, Chapter 4) the type of the network of ideas within

13

which the body idea of race finds its place. The next chapter, on the expansion of the historical horizon (Part II, Chapter 5), finally addresses the race idea itself and shows how it has gradually grown out of the older eighteenth-century race theories into the form of the political race idea of the nineteenth century as elaborated by Gustav Klemm and Count Arthur de Gobineau. The chapter on race and state (Part II, Chapter 6) develops the classical dogmas of the race idea and their ramifications for the naturalistic *Staatslehre* of the second half of the nineteenth century. The final two chapters, about the Jews as a counteridea and about the Nordic idea, show the new development of the race idea since the 1890s (Part II, Chapters 7 and 8).

In the final chapter, dealing with the Nordic idea, I have included in the discussion on typology those branchings of ideas that seemed to me still to derive directly from the impulses at work in the scientific race theory of the last few decades. On the other hand, I have no longer discussed those recent developments in the Nordic idea that have their origin in the nationalist movement itself and only marginally use the arguments of scientific race theory but indeed oppose a concept of organic truth to that of scientific truth— I am primarily thinking here of the myth of blood as it appears in Alfred Rosenberg's work.[8] To the extent that we can already evaluate this development, which is only a few years old, it seems to me that a sharp line separates the older form of the race idea, represented by such men as Hans F. K. Günther, Fritz Lenz, and Eugen Fischer, from the one Rosenberg and the more recent generation of the nationalist movement represent. While the older form of the race idea characteristically takes its justification from an anthropology understood as a natural science, the new one deliberately presents itself as a "myth"—or, as we would prefer to say in the sphere of science, as a body idea and specifically *an idea of the total nature* of Nordic man, which takes for its model an intellectual type of Nordic man. Body and soul are no longer two separate realms, connected by an untenable metaphysics, but a unity. Here the mind is not dependent on the body, but blood and soul are merely different ways of expressing the unity of the Nordic image

8. Alfred Rosenberg, *Der Mythus des 20. Jahrhunderts: Eine Wertung der seelisch-geistigen Gestaltenkämpfe unserer Zeit* (2nd ed.; 1931).

of man. Here the talk is of the new experience of "the consonance of body-soul-mind" that had found its "symbol" in the awareness of "blood."[9] Out of the political movement itself there evolved the idea of the unity of the total human nature, an idea that is still categorically rejected by the older theorists working within race theory in the form Clauss gave it. This seems to me a welcome indication that the last remnants of Darwinism in race theory will also disappear in time.

As far as the relevant materials and the cited literature are concerned, in both parts of the book—the part dealing with race theory and the part on the race idea—the determining criterion was that the problems should be presented *systematically*. Ludwig Schemann, in his great work on race in the humanities, assembled outstanding materials on the *history* of thinking about race. The work at hand intends to be an exposition of human nature both as it is treated as an object in race theory and when, as a subject, it is a creator of body ideas in the community. Part I must therefore outline a theory of human nature and indicate in their inherent lawfulness the speculative problems that arise from the makeup of this nature; thus, materials and works will be cited only to the minimal degree that they are essential for a concrete illustration. Part II is designed to develop the problem of the body idea and of the particular community and to demonstrate how the essentially inherent speculative possibilities were realized in historical reality. Of course, many more sources could be cited for each question—in every instance I have limited myself to the most necessary and selected those materials that seemed to me most illustrative of the speculative possibility in question.

In conclusion, a word on the question that is always posed anew in discussions of the race problem and perhaps also in view of our choice of materials: why have race theory and the race idea developed so vigorously particularly in Germany, while the other great nations have not undergone any intellectual movement of similar social magnitude? A detailed answer to this question would lead us deep into the problems of German political history as contrasted with those of the Western nation-states—here I must limit myself

9. Werner Haverbeck, "Aufbruch der jungen Nation: Ziel und Weg der nationalsozialistischen Volksjugendbewegung," *Nationalsozialistische Monatshefte*, No. 35 (February, 1933), 16.

to one point. Since the decay of the old monarchic ties, the German community has become such an excellent soil for the blossoming of new political movements—for liberalism and socialism in their day as well as for dictatorial nationalism today—because the new movements were not opposed by an established political idea shaping the entire community. Compared to the Western nations, the German nation is young in the sense that an idea of German political man shared by the entire nation does not exist in the way such an idea has existed in France and America since the eighteenth century and in England even longer. There are race ideas in the other nation-states as well (the chapter on the Nordic idea draws a few comparisons); to this day they have hardly become socially relevant as a mass phenomenon (except perhaps in America) because the old idea of nationalist politics, with its essential roots in the Christian doctrine of community [Gemeinschaftslehre], in which there is no room for the race idea, opposes the latter in comparatively undiminished force. We were therefore compelled to draw primarily upon German historical materials to provide persuasive proof for our study, supplementing them only occasionally with French, English, and American examples.

PART I

THE SYSTEMATIC CONTENT
OF RACE THEORY

1

Body—Soul—Mind

Man's nature is an eternal topic of philosophical speculation—eternal because the fundamental experiences that drive us on to speculation are always the same: the same typical situations present themselves as essential to the image of man, and though our knowledge of them increases in particulars, and speculation must absorb this knowledge, the scope of these situations itself is not enlarged. Our current study of man, anthropology, has no other materials to take as a starting point than those already available to Aristotle when he embarked on his investigations, and Aristotle had no materials but those the myth-forming imagination of earlier times concretized into mythical figures. But the topic is also eternally presented as a problem to be solved because the forms through which the speculative course of thought moves are few in number and closely interrelated, so that the same types of problems and solutions must always recur. And finally, the topic remains eternal because the basic experiences in interpreting it with the help of speculative forms inevitably lead to mental situations that cannot be resolved; thus, there need be no fear that one day the topic might disappear from the group of problems that a philosopher takes pride in having solved. The fundamental experiences mentioned belong in part to the domain of human existence as such and in part they are experiences of conditions in inorganic, vegetable, and animal nature, which are placed in a comparative relation with our experiences of human existence. Within the domain of human existence itself these are primarily the fundamental experiences of death, sleep, dream, illness, fear, and skill (power), the purposeful control of actions, depersonalizing [*entselbstend*] Dionysian ecstasy, mystical submersion in God [*Gottversenkung*], the spiritual self-involvement of meditation, all of which serve as points of departure for reflecting on man's nature and inner organization.

A few examples will show how these fundamental experiences [*Grunderfahrungen*] become the starting point for a set of problems.

In the external phenomenon of death human existence moves from the mode of being [*Seinsweise*] we consider complete to one in which the bodily form is preserved for a short time but in which functions of soul and mind are no longer discernible. For speculation the difference between these modes of being becomes the reason for constructing a differential theory of man according to which man's nature is a composite, consisting of essentially dead matter and principles, forces, or substances that are called soul, intellect, reason, mind. The composite of the two can be imagined more externally as a material mechanism that is connected at only one point with the soul (Descartes), or it can be envisaged as a complete parallelism between all mechanical processes in the body and the life processes proper to the soul as it is in the occasionalistic type of constructions. Alternatively, one can assume an active, ensouling principle that for a time shapes dead matter into a life form, then abandons it again to the laws of its material structure, and so forth. All these are distinctions in the interpretation of a fundamental experience that depend in part on the larger context of the metaphysical system within which the speculation on man takes place and in part on the contemporary state of knowledge of biology. For our investigation now only the basic element in the speculative interpretation of the experience of death is important, namely, that the difference between the modes of being of the living man and the dead body are reinterpreted into an internal differentiation of the human being.

Similar speculations are prompted by others of the above-cited fundamental experiences of human existence. The rhythm of sleeping and waking leads us to isolate one level of human existence in which a life force or *élan vital*, cutting through this rhythm, continues to maintain the fire of life while waking consciousness and the higher mental processes are temporarily suspended. Dream research has shown that during sleep the imagination of the instinctive sphere produces images and image associations that are not present during the waking state when we are under the control of reason, character, and mind of the healthy person (however, certain illnesses, in their turn, are even in the waking state structurally related to dream fantasies), so that we see ourselves compelled to distinguish between an instinctive state of human existence on the one hand, which follows its own structural laws when it is not under the supervision of a center of will guided by the mind, and these higher centers themselves on the other. Various essential possibilities of man as a totality, such as sleep, dream, and illness, all of which appear in the individual life, as well as differences between these modes of being in various periods of human history (similarity of the inner life of so-called primitive peoples to the structures of dreams and neuroses) are reinterpreted in speculation on the nature of man into a hierarchical differentiation of human nature, with the rank of each level being determined by the extent to which it is shaped or controlled by another. Dead matter is subject to organization by the life principle; the vital instinct [*Lebensdrang*], which cuts through the waking and sleeping states, lies below the faculty of practical intelligent guidance that determines a living person's waking, purposeful actions. The instinctive sphere, with fantasies and intentions of its own, is subject to the intellectual power of the will, which can restrain its formative force in order to provide the space where the creations of the mind are constructed.

The inner experiences of success and defeat are further sources of speculation that arise from the domain of human existence. In the case of ideas or difficult decisions, when we find ourselves left entirely to our own resources, without any counsel from outside, we experience the spontaneity of our thinking or acting. Then our thoughts and decisions cannot be traced back to previous ideas and prior decisions but seem to issue from ourselves as from substances capable of thinking and acting. We experience ourselves then as starting points, not merely transitional points, of an event, of initiating something new and thus affecting the course of the world. In addition, we have the experiences of failing in the face of tasks, of the weakness of our body, of illnesses, and the eventual defeat of our total life, with its willed deeds and plans, in death. We experience ourselves now as powerful points of origin and transition, now as powerless beings impotent against the lawful course of natural processes in which we are merely disappearing particles. The experiences of spontaneous activity and of helpless surrender to a transcendent force are the reasons for the interpretation of human nature as powerful, active through the higher faculties of intelligence and spirit and, at the same time, as powerless by virtue of the body's participation in a series of events that seemingly run their course independently of our mental experiences of will.

The hub of fundamental experiences from which the spokes of speculation radiate can be enlarged beyond human existence by comparing it with the other great classes of being—inorganic, vegetable, and animal. While in the examples above the differential theory of human nature is based on the different conditions of human existence itself and the differences are synchronized as parts of a whole being, in any comparison with other ontic classes the similarities and differences between human nature and the basic facts of these classes serve as points of departure for an ontology. Once again the human being is interpreted as composed of parts, each of which can appear in a particular form of being and only thus become discernible as separate parts, but their forms of being appear not as human modes but as self-enclosed forms without immediately visible essential relation to human existence. In relation to man the dead body is a remnant; as matter, it belongs to the class of inorganic nature, whose independent manifestations in themselves show no indication of the possibility of their assimilation and organization by a vital principle. The simple animation of matter without the higher psychic forms of instinct, memory, and purposefully acting intelligence has taken on independent form in the plant kingdom. In the animal kingdom we find the psychic forms of instinct and perhaps also simple acts of intelligence, but not anything of the mind. Only in human beings does the mind join the other mental functions as a formative principle. None of these classes of being points to the next higher one as a necessary next step in development, and none provides any basis for prophecies concerning further forms of being. Each of these forms of being is complete in itself and differs from the others in such a way that each also contains the elements of the others plus one more, namely the element that uniquely characterizes it. Plants show themselves to be inorganic matter animated by the vital instinct or *élan vital;* animals have higher mental functions in addition to the elements of animated matter of the plants. In human beings the animal elements are augmented by the mind unique to man. Thus, a comparison with the other classes of being leads to a picture of a structured organization of the human being that is similar to the one resulting from the examination of the fundamental experiences in the sphere of human existence.

Studying the components in the picture of the human being as they are assembled from experiences is relatively unproblematic. There are no disagreements about the fact that experiences of the sort cited here serve as the point of departure for the classification of nature. What is uncertain, however, is the extent to which these experiences are used in the speculative elaboration of the picture, and—aside from the general level of knowledge of the day and from the individual philosopher's personal level of knowledge—the decision on this issue depends on the principles of construction by which the unity of being is to result from the multiplicity of elements. In applying the principles of construction we are dealing with the general problem of creating a unified whole of a being that consists of several parts, and this problem is as evident in the speculative understanding of plant and animal forms as in that of human existence—and perhaps even in the constructive understanding of the formation of matter out of the movement of electrons. Nevertheless for us all that is important is the exceptional case, in which the principles are applied to the composition of a unified whole out of a part considered specifically human and others considered subhuman. Whether these principles can be arranged in a final a priori system may remain an open question here; the following remarks are merely intended to describe some examples of construction types.

1. The *isolation* of one part, considered uniquely human, from the other parts constituting the whole human being. I have spoken of the nature of the human being as a totality consisting of several parts. The isolation construction defines as human only that part that must be recognized as uniquely human, differentiating human beings from other forms of being. The human being is imagined as a form originally not human in itself, which only through the addition of a specific, essential element becomes a whole human being. For now it does not matter whether this additional element is called soul, reason, or mind. The rigid separation of substances Descartes established between the extensive mechanistic substance and the soul is the classical case of this type; the subhuman mechanism and the soul, which makes up the human being, are con-

nected quite externally by the fact that a specific, rather small organ of the human body is assumed to be the seat of the soul.

Scheler has superbly criticized the shortcomings of this construction and pointed out that the functions of the soul are not at all localized in a particular part of the body, but they are spread out in all their variety over the whole body; thus, ontologically we should speak of a strict identity between the physiological and psychological life processes. The pure mechanism, Scheler noted, cannot be found anywhere; rather, the physical-mental functions must be regarded as two sides of one and the same life process. Scheler therefore replaces the isolation construction with another fundamental type of construction, which will be presented in more detail below: the transformation of the substratum through the addition of the new element into a new unity in which the substratum loses the specific character it had as long as it existed separately. However, Scheler interwove his analysis and criticism of this fundamental type of construction so densely with other trains of thought that the fundamentals are obscured, and he himself proposed a construction that also belongs to the type of isolation construction he criticized. In addition to isolation, another shortcoming of Descartes' theory is that it cuts off the inanimate physical form from the soul and takes the soul as the essence of man. Today we extend the concept of animate nature, as Aristotle already did, to the plant kingdom, and we find higher mental functions in the animal world and perhaps even the beginnings of intelligent actions. Therefore, after touching on the problem of isolation, Scheler directs the full force of his criticism against the desouling of subhuman nature and opposes it with the theory of the mind as the characteristic distinguishing man from the animal. The human mind is added to physical-mental subhuman nature to complete man's total being.

However, in this addition Scheler cuts off mind from the body and soul even more rigidly than Descartes isolated the soul from the mechanism. Descartes established the connection between the two substances in the shared site of the pituitary gland; Scheler made the concept of the connection between mind and body-soul more dynamic by removing all possibilities of localization and allowing as connection only the fact that the mind diverts the energy it needs for its activity in the world from the submental [*untergeistigen*] sphere of drives. The mind, he suggested, is powerless in itself and can be realized only through the drive, which the mind guides along its own paths. Mind and drive are thus the primal elements in the being of the world [*Welt-Sein*]. The same basic argument Scheler raises against Descartes' dualism applies also to his own isolation of a powerless mind devoid of space-time, body, and soul, that is, inherently unrelated to the animal-vital sphere. Just as in Descartes' system the separation of the mechanical from the mental function had to be negated and the physiological and psychological phenomena were shown to be different aspects of the same process, so in Scheler's system the isolation of the mind from the vital sphere must be negated. On the contrary, it must be asserted that the reality of the mind in all its power is so closely connected with the vital reality that here, too, applying image of two aspects of the same process is justified. Nor does Scheler deny the close connection between the two spheres; yet he still attempts constructively to maintain the isolation of the mind by defining its power as derived from the deeper levels. However, this attempt founders on his explanation of why instinctual energy, instead of satisfying its instinctual aims, allows itself in part to be diverted into realizing formations of the mind. Scheler can explain this phenomenon of displacement and sublimation (for the same reason the crux of psychoanalysis as well) only by assuming volitive acts of the mind by which the mind seductively holds out intellectual objectives to the instinctual energy, as it were—or, to put it differently: assuming that the will is the guiding function of the intellectual sphere locates in this very sphere, though under another name, a power center whose energy is superior to that of the instincts. In addition to the instinct as the animal-vital source of energy, the will emerges as the energy source of the mind. Though by definition the mind is powerless, it has will. Since the power of the will is able to affect the instinctual sphere directly and repress the instinct's formative drive, introducing the will thus restores the connection to the subhuman sphere that had been removed by the isolating construction in the interest of the special position of the human being compared to the other kingdoms of being. The approach of the mind to the vital sphere characterized by the vital drive is not entirely clear in Scheler's construction because (1) the will is not integrated as an autonomous link in the scheme of world structure [*Weltaufbau*] consisting of inorganic matter, the vital drive of the plant kingdom, instinct, associative memory, practical intelligence, and mind, and because (2) the drive as the fundamental element of the world, and as such already present in the formation of matter, is not clearly differentiated from the vital drive supposedly unique to the plant kingdom.

2. The difficulties and byways of the isolation construction lead to a further typical principle of construction in this speculative realm—the construction principle of the *intermediate link* between the parts that were contrasted as heterogenous and must now be linked again into the unity of total human existence. In the theories of Descartes and Scheler we have already seen examples for this type of construction. In Descartes' philosophy the pituitary gland as the organ of the soul was the common site of body and soul, the space where the two realms intersected and thus generated a neutral entity that belonged to *both* the parts it was to link. (A more detailed analysis would also have to elucidate the role of the "animal spirits" as mediators between the body and the seat of the soul, that is, between the two substances.) In Scheler's energy theory the intermediary link was not a place; rather the function was carried out by the volitive acts which belong to the mind but at the same time are distinguished from all other forms of acts of the mind in that they are energy sources affecting the vital sphere and for this reason are of the same kind. The models for this construction, however, are found in the great speculative psychologies—I am thinking especially of the Aristotelian one. Aristotle developed a system of animate nature and arranged the functions of the soul—from bottom to top—from the nourishing soul, in which the plants share, through the sensitive soul, which is inherent to animals, to the thinking soul, which is unique to human nature. The thinking soul, or reason, is not mingled with the body as are the lower soul functions; it has no sensory constitution, no bodily organs like the other faculties, and it is real only in the acts of its working. Thus, it is completely cut off from the lower faculties. Now in order to establish the bridges to the transitory character of life, Aristotle divides the thinking soul into active and passive reason. Active reason is essentially without substance, imperishable, unadulterated, and purely real and active, while passive reason is connected to human existence and perishes with it. Active reason can affect only passive reason but not the other soul functions; it

26

is itself indeterminate and therefore has no memory. Anamnesis in the Platonic sense is therefore impossible for this part of the soul. But anamnesis is equally impossible for passive reason precisely because it is connected to human existence and transitory. The intermediate link, passive reason, is the thinking soul and therefore differentiated from the lower psychic functions; at the same time it belongs to the individual human existence; and for the duration of that existence passive reason is the place where active reason can affect human life. We might also consider whether this Aristotelian division echoes the older Greek distinction between *thymos* and *psyche* (about which we will have more to say below); in its function active reason is closely allied to *thymos,* which escapes at death but has nothing of the dying personality; in this view death is an end to self [*Entselbstung*] rather than an end to physical existence [*Entleibung*], in which a personal soul leaves the body. In Aristotle this corresponds to the absence of memory in active reason, by which a continuum between the form of existence of the soul in human life and its preexistence would be produced.

Kant works out a quite similar intermediate-link construction to combine subhuman sensory nature with pure reason, which is the essence of man, into the whole of human existence. Arbitrariness [*Willkür*] is inserted between these autonomous parts of the human totality; this arbitrariness is a faculty that takes its capacity for spontaneity and the direction of human existence from reason but that can at the same time be affected by the world of the senses. Arbitrariness is not completely determined (necessitated) by sensibility but only "moved" (affected) by it to such an extent that the phenomenon of the unity of mind and body is explained without relinquishing the freedom and spontaneity of the will. In this as in the other examples, a faculty or part of the soul is constructed that simultaneously belongs and does not belong to each of the two, it is meant to unite. These constructions have no epistemological value; here they serve merely to illustrate the problems resulting from the fundamental experiences: the philosopher is forced (1) to reinterpret the contrasting components of experience as functions of the human totality, and (2) to posit a relationship between functions strictly and inherently separated from each other. Here I refer to Plessner's recent attempt to characterize the co-existence [*Zusammen-Sein*] of the inherently unrelated parts of the human totality precisely by pointing out that they have no other recogniz-able connection to each other except their common occurrence. He therefore calls human nature an "and-combination" of its ele-ments; it is at once mental power and powerless nature—it is the one "and" the other, and no further details about this connection can be presented.

3. In their system of thought the intermediate-link construc-tions of the Aristotelian and Kantian types serve the function of preserving the autonomy of the parts they unite—that is, of ac-knowledging the reality of the mind [*Geistwirklichkeit*] as such, unaffected by the natural sphere while, conversely, also maintain-ing the possibility of experiencing the inorganic and vital sphere by itself, without reference to an intellectual reality. Alternatively, a third type of construction attempts to establish a causal relation-ship between the parts of the whole human being. The phenomena of the essentially human sphere of the mind and those of the sub-human sphere are acknowledged in their reality, but the manifes-tations of the one realm are considered dependent variables of those of the other realm. The knowledge of one is the key to knowing the other, and ontically one is determined by the other. The causal relationship can be assumed both from the intellectual sphere to the natural one (this is the Romantic type of construction) and—more common today and more important for race theory—from natural sphere to that of the mind. Insofar as the power inherent in the lawful structure of a segment of existence [*Seinsausschnitt*]—whether mind or nature—is part of the fullness of its reality, this construction leads to a diminishing of the reality of the sphere de-clared dependent, and, as a corollary, to a strengthening of the re-ality of the sphere declared determinative. The determinative being can reach beyond itself and have an immediate effect on a being of another kind; it becomes powerful beyond itself, super-powerful, and the being that is acted upon becomes sub-powerful [*unter-mächtig*]. These ontological premises concerning the realms of be-ing are the major premises of every metaphysics of man claiming that one part of the human being affects another within the human totality. In this case, human existence is merely the site where the claimed superiority of the one sphere of existence over the other becomes evident. Concerning the speculative problem of under-standing the unity of the total human being, this super-power con-

struction comes into various conflicts with the fundamental experiences it has to deal with. The problem to be resolved is the
development of unity out of phenomena of realities of being
[*Seinswirklichkeiten*], each of which has its own inherent lawfulness. The super-power construction abolishes the autonomy of the
classes of being, which appears real in the fundamental experiences,
and replaces it with the heteronomy of one realm of being. The
claim to heteronomy is partially legitimated by another empirical
fact, namely, that in some way—and formulating this way is precisely the problem to be resolved—human existence is given as an
unquestionable unity, and as a whole it can be subject to only *one*
lawfulness, the lawfulness that constitutes its unity. The super-
power construction finds this lawfulness by declaring only one of
the several spheres experienced as autonomous as truly autonomous and treating the phenomena of the others as epiphenomena.
The experience of the inherent lawfulness of each of the parts of
being is not included in the interpretation. That the ontological
major premises and the anthropological constructions of this type
are articulated on a rather primitive level is borne out by the fact
that any part of being can arbitrarily be declared the super-powerful
one without any of these claims creating an essentially worse or
better speculative situation than any other.

Constructions of this type encounter further epistemological difficulties. If each of the classes of being that appear as parts of the
total human being is acknowledged as a reality existing separately
and independently of the others, there are just as many theories for
understanding these realms of being and methodologies of their
experience. On the object side, the unity of these realms of being
is given by the unity of the object's structure [*Gegenstandsstruk-
tur*], on the subject side, by the unity of the system of the method's
fundamental assumptions. But if the lawfulness of one sphere of
being is claimed to be dependent on that of another, the objective
and methodological unity is lost since statements about the relationships of these two realms of being are interpolated that cannot
be handled by the epistemology of either realm. In fact, there is in
general no conceivable theory for knowing them since the relationship of the one realm to the other—that is, the overarching unity
of both—is precisely the non-datum; indeed, precisely because this
cannot be experienced in an intelligible way it is the problem for

whose sake the constructions characterized here have been developed. The problem of unity cannot be solved by positing the *pars* for the *totum*—no matter which *pars* is selected to play the role. Statements about the phenomena of one class of being by their nature cannot have any meaning for the understanding of the phenomena of another class, since the meaning of one for the other is precisely the *terra incognita* that proves inaccessible to knowledge. The statement that it is impossible to penetrate with intellectual or natural experience from one of these realms of research to the other or to explain the connections between them does, of course, not mean that those connections do not exist and that the modes of being coexist within the human being without any interconnections. Claiming that would contradict the fundamental experience of the indispensability of each of the parts of being for human existence; this existence is not made up of parts that have come together merely externally and can be separated again without harm; rather, together they form a unified form of being, which can exist only as a whole. The unity of the parts therefore exists, and they can enter into a close connection, which presupposes that in their substance they are not totally alien to each other but can easily flow into each other and be amalgamated—regardless of what mechanical, organic, or dynamic images we use to imagine such an amalgam—but the kind of connection is not a possible subject for a science.

4. As the fourth and in this enumeration last construction we will outline the construction of the intellectual unity. Of all the historical systems, the anthropology of I. H. von Fichte comes closest to it. I refer to it for this reason and also because, in spite of more recent attempts—especially those of Scheler and Plessner, who had much more material from biology and physiology available—Fichte's is still the most comprehensive and most profound presentation of this complex of problems, which is so difficult to master. This type of construction also fails to solve our problem in the sense of providing a self-contained, rational systematization of the fundamental experiences—nor, as I have already noted, can such a solution be given—but it is nevertheless superior to the other constructions for our special problem of the unity of the human being because it has speculation start from the fundamental experience of this unity rather than from the experiences of the

autonomy of the parts, as the other constructions did. This may at first seem surprising, perhaps even inadmissible, since the point to be explained by these constructions is assumed as a given. However, this is not so surprising if we again recall the situation that gave rise to speculation. After all, it is not the separate experiences of the autonomous parts of the human totality as such [*Teilhaftigkeit*] that now have to be reinterpreted into a unity for the sake of some abstruse whim. Rather, these fundamental experiences become a problem only because they are all contradicted by the experience of the original unity of human existence. The differential theory of human nature is based on the fact that the differences between the whole and its elements are experienced. Only because we experience the unity of human existence with the same degree of valid understanding as we do the autonomy of its parts (which is incompatible with the former) does the interpretation of these latter experiences become a problem. And if the experience of unity is taken as the point of departure for speculation, we should not see this as a trick intended to solve what the other constructions could not achieve. On the contrary, the problem those constructions could not master is not solved either by the construction of the unified form; it remains just as open as in the other cases. However, the speculation starting from the experience of unity draws a different line through the experiential complex, a line that cuts through the circle of experience in a more favorable way for the purposes of a race theory of man than any other.

To elucidate our intention, we must recall Scheler's critique of Cartesian dualism. Isolating the soul from the body was inadmissible because the functions of the organism are completely of the nature of the soul; the soul is not poorly housed in some nook of the body but permeates all parts of it, down to the last fiber. Every detail of the body is a gesture of the soul. Immanuel Hermann von Fichte developed this theory in all its implications. The soul is a real, effective, powerful substance, that establishes space and fills it. In contrast to the mechanical concept of space, in which the real is infinitely divisible, Fichte advocates a dynamic concept, in which the real overcomes the divisive sense of space and is present in every part of its spatial existence with equal and full effect. The soul does not exist *in* space; it engenders space. It does not exist *in* time; but by existing, it establishes its own duration. And this space- and duration-establishing soul corporealizes itself and becomes perceptible to the senses through the organization of inorganic matter into its body. But its "body" as soul body, as inner or pneumatic body, must again be differentiated from the external body, the body composed of inorganic matter that enters the inner body and leaves it again. The inner body is the spatial-durational dimension of the soul; organizing this body through the processing of inorganic substances is the first and fundamental instinctive action of the soul substance, which perdures throughout life and becomes empirically manifest in many ways in all processes of nourishment, restoration, and self-healing. The animal organism, down to the last detail of its development, this theory holds, is the outwardly realized image of the animal's unique soul. Its tools for feeding, hunting, and locomotion are as characteristic of its soul as the body's physiognomical *habitus*. "The animal body is the physical symbol of the animal soul, which consequently finds the organ suited to carrying out its functions only in this characteristic body." Thus, to characterize the body-soul unity of the animal the following categories are juxtaposed:

mechanical space—dynamic space
time—duration
external body (physical body)—inner or pneumatic body

In analogy to this theory of the body as the one indivisible field of expression [*Ausdrucksfeld*] of the soul, human existence in the totality of its functions must be understood as the field of expression of the personal mind. The mind is not simply a characteristic added to the animal form, giving man superiority over the animal, but it is a substance that is just as originally active as the animal soul: as the animal body is the complete expression of the soul proper to the species of the animal in question, so man's physical and psychological functions are the complete expression of the active mind. The unique features of human organization as opposed to that of the animal, especially the upright gait (about the intellectual-physiognomical significance of which Herder said such excellent things) are precisely those appropriate to man's active relationship [*Wirkensverhältnis*] to his environment. The reduction of reflexes and instinctive actions to a minimum and the malleability of all given predispositions to action [*Aktionsanlagen*] through education, either by others or by the self, to forms at the service of the shaping of the mind [*Geistgestaltung*]—these are the empirical symptoms of the intellectual unity of *man* all the way down to the sphere of the senses. Man's physical and psychological functions, which seem to be the same as those of the animals, are in fact structurally different from the latter; they are directed to the organizing center of the mind.

The personal mind generates its space and its duration just as the animal soul does. It does not settle down unchanged in matter but develops in the process of development of its visible body. It undergoes phases of development, which are studied by child and adolescent psychology; it permeates the body, leaving its visible imprint in the intellectual aspects of physiognomy and gesture. It differs from the animal soul in that it is not merely a specimen of a genus; it is not purely and simply an ever-new revelation of the same soul type (although it is this *as well*), and its function is not exhausted in the preservation of the species (although this is *also* one of the human functions). Rather, the personal mind in its existence becomes conscious of itself as the unity of its acts; it is person.

This is not the place to justify and explicate a philosophy of the mind, and therefore we will note only the essential elements of the personal mind for a better understanding of the term: (1) The mind is a self-aware center; (2) it has the faculty of abstract, discursive thinking (as distinct from animals, whose ability to think—to the extent that it presumably exists—does not go beyond simple achievements of concrete, situation-bound, inventive intelligence); (3) it is capable of perceiving primal phenomena; (4) and it can create mental worlds (works of art, philosophical systems, and so forth), including its own mental life; (5) and it is the center of the will. The personal mind (in this sense of the word) is given to itself as a singular creative source for intellectual connections between actions [*Aktzusammenhänge*], and through the *singularity* of its *person* it is raised above the mere *species individuation* characteristic of animals.

For the body-soul problem in general and the race problem in particular, the construction of the unified form of the mind gives us an intelligible insight into the inevitability of ideas about the relation between mind and body. Every form of society and state has produced its typical ideas about the physical basis of its existence, and from the experiences that have prompted us to the construction under discussion here we know that this complex of ideas belongs to the intellectual world of a state. In characterizing this construction, I have strictly limited myself to an elucidation of the mental substance existing as a unity in space and time and have avoided all statements about the dependence of physical existence on the mind (or vice versa) since such statements would only lead us back to the other construction types, whose shortcomings we have already discussed. The construction of intellectual existence made visible in the body cannot therefore serve as a foundation for scientific attempts at inferring from somatic types of man the mental ones belonging to them; it merely legitimizes the emergence of the idea of the mind's somatic existence in the sphere of the mind itself, and in addition it can legitimize our attempt to clarify the structure of this intellectual idea of the body in the historical forms most important to us. It assures us that body and mind are connected and that the mind is justified in penetrating speculatively, as far as possible, into the mysteries of its physical existence, but it does not prepare the ground for a natural science of the body that could also disclose to us to the phenomena of the mind.

I want to point out again that this construction does not "solve" the body-soul problem but leaves untouched the experiences of the isolated existence of the parts of human totality and the possibility of experiencing each of these parts in itself with the means adequate to it. Physical anthropology exists as a natural science, and to dispute its potential in view of its existence and its brilliant results would be absurd; the classification of man into racial types according to groups of traits and the study of the transmission of physical traits and predispositions through heredity is a completely legitimate scientific endeavor because a part of total human existence is undoubtedly of animal nature and can be isolated as such. Yet on the basis of our doctrine of construction types we have to deny vigorously the claim that the findings of this anthropology could be in any way scientifically relevant to facts of the mind. The question of this relevance is not a scientific question but one of metaphysical speculation, and (whether positively or negatively) it must be decided on the grounds I am endeavoring to develop here.

To clarify the problem of the constructions in rational metaphysical speculation I want to refer to the form of the body-soul relationship in mythical thought. Primitive and mythic thought sees the same fundamental experiences as does philosophical thought in its narrower sense; the former differs, however, in interpretation from the speculative form, which begins in the West with Plato's doctrine of the soul. Mythical thinking lets the fundamental experiences stand in their full contradictory nature without attempting the "solutions" that by reason of their necessary one-sidedness in their construction conceal rather than reveal the true facts. Therefore, we find side by side concepts designating one or the other part of the total nature legitimated by one fundamental experience as well as a well-developed terminology for the totality of being itself according to the two fundamental modes of this-worldly and otherworldly life. The belief about death of the Homeric period distinguishes, for example, between *thymos* and *psyche*, the vivifying soul and the shade. *Thymos* leaves the body at death, and is therefore the part of the total that is certified as independent by the differences between the modes of being of life and death—typically it is a concept based on the differences between these modes of being. *Psyche*, on the other hand, is the "shade," the image of the total being transposed into the otherworldly; it is the lifeless being but not a disembodied soul or person, but rather human form as a whole that has simply found another reality status. The shade of Patroclus appears to Achilles with all his physical characteristics and is recognizable in shape, size, eyes, and voice. In the older meaning of *psyche*, ancient Greece had a concept designating the unified human form in its shadow existence. As a consequence of these distinctions, the conflicting fundamental experiences lead to similar difficulties in primitive thought as they do in philosophical speculation; however, these difficulties are not expressed as contradictions within a system but rather as variations in meaning. In antiquity the shade is the bearer of the self, but occasionally the inanimate corpse, the dead remnant, also appears as the self; the dead body is seen as contrast to the living body since it lacks the animating *thymos*, and therefore is like the shade. Thus, total existence minus the *thymos* is at one time interpreted as complete being in another dimension and at other times as deficient being in the dimension of the living.

We find very similar difficulties of interpretation in the Egyptian doctrine of the soul: in addition to the actual physical substances there are finer soul substances that make up the various souls—the *ka* is the double of the living person, it lives in his body and does not leave it even in death; another soul, the *ba*, flees at the moment of death, wanders about freely in space, and only occasionally visits the *ka* and the corpse in the grave. Only a third soul, the *khu*, possesses the qualities of immutability, indestructibility, and immortality. The second and third souls, *ba* and *khu* together, combine in themselves the functions of the soul as a concept in contrast to the dead body. The *ka*, on the other hand, the double that remains with the body, shares with the body functions similar to those of the Greek shade. The Greek vacillation concerning the bearer of the self between shade and corpse is dissolved in the Egyptian belief about death since there the body itself is the corporeal substrate of the soul after death and must be conserved by all means in order to make life after death possible.

2

Race as Biological Unit

We begin the analysis of the systematic content of contemporary race theory by determining the scientific concept of race the current theory claims to be based on. The term *race* is to be understood as a biological subunit of the species *Homo sapiens;* here morphological and physiological groups of traits allegedly typical of the subgroups called races are added to the general traits of the human species. The attempt to classify humanity according to physical traits is reasonable because there are constants—that is, traits and groups of traits hereditary in the sequence of generations—that follow Mendelian laws of heredity in their combination and separation when individuals of different types interbreed. The theory of the constants of racial traits, their combinations and Mendelizing in the course of interbreeding is the foundation of the historical-philosophical thesis that the mental qualities connected with particular groups of traits in the pure case are permanently effective causes of history and that the spread or suppression of one or the other race is related to significant consequences for the history of society, the state, and the spiritual worlds.

If we wish to get to the core of the problem of the species and its subgroups, the races, we best begin by specifying the time period implied when we speak of "contemporary" race theory and race theory "of the present time." The essential point for us, which we want to clarify, is the relationship of political race theory, which we call contemporary because its authors wrote in recent decades and their influence pervades the political life of our time, to the scientific and biological theory of race and species in the narrower sense of the term. Is race theory also "contemporary" in the sense that its basic theoretical concepts derive from the current theoretical biology, or are its leading concepts not rather drawn from the theories of earlier periods, and if this should be the case, which ones? To answer this question, we must as briefly as possible familiarize ourselves with the current status of the problem of species and race in theoretical biology.

In its basic features the current discussion of the species problem does not go farther back than Darwin's doctrine of the origin of species. Now as then the task of theoretical investigation is to explain how the constancy of species can be reconciled with their evolution from earlier forms all the way back to the abiogenesis of the simplest one-celled organic forms. The presuppositions of the Darwinian problem are therefore (1) the largely unfounded assumption of species in the Linnaean sense, and (2) the notion of the development of the organic world through history from simple to more differentiated forms, that is, the idea of what Darwin called the "Tree of Life," the phylogenetic tree. Thus formulated, the problem is essentially solved (we will here of necessity disregard all secondary constructions) by the following three theses: (1) slight personal variations distinguish all organic individuals from their parental individuals; (2) because of pressure from outside circumstances, among which we must count climatic conditions as well as the pressures caused by members of the same species, only the best adapted individuals, those fittest for the struggle for existence, have a chance to survive and reproduce; and (3) the individually acquired traits of the survivors that prove most useful in the struggle for existence are passed on to their descendants. Thus the titles of the three problems of variation, selection, and heredity are established.

This theory owes its well-known overwhelming success not to Darwin's outstanding qualities as a naturalist studying nature and collecting his observations but rather to the inadequate, badly thought-out dogmas that appealed to the emotions of the liberal era. The first thesis, the theory of variation, relies on everyday experiences, familiar to all, of children who resemble their parents but are not entirely like them, displaying some parental traits to a greater and others to a lesser degree. A family consists not of individuals who are all alike but of persons with a greater or smaller aptitude for various tasks. The second thesis is extracted from classic English economics: Malthus contrasted the geometric progression of population increase to the arithmetic progression of increase in the food supply and concluded that population growth is to a certain extent limited by shortage of the food supply; a struggle for existence erupts, and only the fittest survive. Darwin depicts the organic world according to the model of the harmony of liberal society which constantly reproduces and maintains itself by eliminating what is unfit and retaining what is fit and useful. The third thesis, finally, is also a basic liberal demand, namely, that what has been acquired be preserved and passed on to descendants. All three theses, offered by Darwin as solutions to the problem he took over from the preceding period, were soon—in fact, already in the period of unscientific and vulgar enthusiasm for Darwin—reformulated by critical minds as problems, with the result that we can today make the following statements:

1. The differences between living beings that are merely due to the individuation of a type (fluctuating variations) are irrelevant to the species problem.

2. The selection of useful traits by the environment is probably not without significance for the evolution of the species because individuals unfit for survival are eliminated and cannot reproduce, but it is not decisive since the premise of the theory of selection, namely, that organisms are completely adapted to their environment, is not correct. Of course they must be adapted sufficiently to survive in it at all and to reproduce, but there is a gaping chasm between this minimum of adaptation and the empirically found species, and it is so wide that the major part of all traits and particularly those relevant for speciation find room in it. The great majority of speciation traits is indifferently related to adaptation and fitness for survival—indeed, even slightly harmful traits can occur without endangering a species' survival.[1]

3. Heredity does not accomplish what it is said to accomplish in Darwin's theory, since precisely traits acquired by individuals and perhaps due to adaptation are not transmitted to the offspring. As best we can determine today, all that can be inherited are certain variations, the so-called mutations, that are due to a change of genetic structure, that is, a change in the genotype structure.

The situation is correctly summarized in the following sentences by Friedrich Alverdes:

1. On this question, see Carl Detto, *Die Theorie der direkten Anpassung und ihre Bedeutung für das Anpassungs- und Deszendenzproblem: Versuch einer methodologischen Kritik des Erklärungsprinzipes und der botanischen Tatsachen des Lamarckismus* (1904), particularly pp. 193, 195ff.

It is Darwin's achievement that he helped the idea of descent to break through—it seems for good. The decades following Darwin were filled with cheerful optimism and carefree building on his ideas. But the work that grew out of these efforts was not made for eternity, for today the edifice that is the theory of evolution looks more like a field of rubble than an inhabitable house. There is no up-to-date theory of the origin of species, and therefore a scientist such as Wilhelm Johannsen can speak of the problem of evolution as a completely open question. . . . It seems that the time has come when we approach the problems we have noted on the whole with greater respect than used to be common in many quarters.[2]

The turn away from Darwinian theory toward criticism of it seems reasonable. The theory of evolution is meant to explain the origin of species out of other species, but even if we accept the theory of natural selection as correct, natural selection does no more than select fit variations; it does not explain why variations develop and which ones will come about. The first step in criticism therefore turned from the external selective factor to the internal factors of the organism, through which the constancy of its traits throughout the generations (which in itself is not self-evident, but we habitually focus on it) and their variations are conditioned. The phenomenon of an *interior* and *exterior* peculiar to the world of the living reveals itself: life is an existence centered in itself, basically confronting the rest of the world as external to itself. The situation of interior and exterior appears relatively simple and clear if we picture one of the more highly evolved animals, such as a horse; we see before us the clearly outlined figure in its structure, enclosed by the covering of skin that marks the boundary between interior and exterior. In this case we have a static picture to which the concepts of interior and exterior can immediately be applied; a spatial figure at rest with an interior is clearly set off against the remaining space, i.e., the exterior. However, when we consider the living form not as a block standing in space but as a unified development from embryonic beginnings to mature and full growth, the earlier clear picture is obscured. For the development of the organism is a constant interplay between the interior and the exterior, a process in which the exterior is always assimilated into the interior and the interior in turn is excreted as exterior. And if in our search

2. Friedrich Alverdes, "Rassen- und Artbildung," in *Abhandlungen zur theoretischen Biologie,* ed. Julius Schaxel (fascicle 1, 1921), 1–2.

for the true interior we return to the beginning, where we must find an interior that has not yet been an exterior, we find the germ cell. Consequently, the theory of heredity locates the internal determinants of the organic forms in the germ cells. However, the germ cells, too, are not the final resting place, for they—in one of various methods of reproduction—derive from other cells in other individuals. Thus, in this quest for origins we cross the boundaries of the individual and penetrate to the parental individuals; as a result, the image of interior and exterior, which is based on the single individual taking up space, becomes meaningless. The "inner" determinants of a living form are pushed back into the formative laws of an organic substance without a determinate, permanent form, and characterized only by a periodically swelling and shrinking continuum of form throughout the course of its existence, and from this continuum we isolate certain forms as individuals. Individuals are thus not self-enclosed units but periodic knots in the continuous string of organic substance. The term "heredity" in the sense taken from the social world of transmitting an "amount" of dispositions, characteristics, abilities, and so on from one individual to another therefore loses its meaning, and biologists who are careful in their methods consider the phenomena of heredity nothing more than the existential persistence of a substance with a particular chemical and physical structure.

To prevent misunderstandings, I want to point out emphatically that pursuing the image of interior and exterior to its logical conclusion, in which it is dissolved, is not intended to imply that the concept of the individual and the problem of interior and exterior it gives rise to are meaningless. Rather, the logical dismantling of the image until it disappears in the existential continuum of organic substance, among whose ever changing forms the single individual no longer has the position of a center but merely that of a link in a chain, is intended to show where the train of thought taking the interaction between the individual's interior and exterior as its point of departure must necessarily lead us by virtue of its structure. The intention here is not to prove that the concept of the individual is wrongly formed, but that already with this concept—even before we have moved on to the further complications of the problem of race and species—we find ourselves in a sphere of speculative theorizing. And calling the concept of the individual a speculative one is not an accusation but merely the assertion of something inevitable; in our occupation with theoretical biology, we are from the outset moving in a system of speculations. Our movements will become clearly focused and successful only if we know the field's laws thoroughly and keep them carefully in mind at every step. If at this point we hide the reality of concept formation under the false theory that the concept of a living being or organic form is an empirical concept, faithfully designating some conditions or traits that can easily be looked at in isolation, then we ruin from the outset our chances of understanding the laws of theory formation of this sphere in its higher-level forms. The concept of the individual is therefore justifiably formed; it is based on the understanding of the living form as a primal phenomenon: the living being placed in an environment, the subject in its medium, is an undeniable reality.[3]

Henri Bergson expressed this slightly differently when he stated that the individual is not completely a separate individual but, depending on its position in the hierarchy of living beings, its boundaries are more or less fluid toward its ancestors and descendants, beginning with the simplest organisms propagating by cell division so that all individuals are seemingly parts of one and the same substance all the way to the most highly evolved forms, in which the fully formed individuals are connected by the thin threads of germ plasm. Even in these highest forms the individual is not completely self-contained, for parts of it can separate and live on independently—in other words, the individual is not a unit of life.[4]

The concept of the organic individual is a speculative-dialectical one because the individual, too, is not what it is supposed to be, namely, an indivisible entity. And the dialectic of the concept reflects the primal phenomenon of life, i.e., that the discontinuous forms are simultaneously also a true continuum. Thus in the concept of organic individual entity—the center of a world—with an interior and an exterior, the additional problems of the formation of race and species are already inherent, since theoretically the race and species types, as "seen" phenomena, contain the same prob-

---

3. See Jakob von Üxküll, "Der Organismus und die Umwelt," in *Das Lebensproblem im Lichte der modernen Forschung,* ed. Hans Driesch (1931), esp. pp. 220, 224. See also von Üxküll, *Theoretische Biologie* (1920).

4. Henri Bergson, *Schöpferische Entwicklung* (trans., 1921), 19–20.

lematic as the "seen" individual. The same continuously existing organic substance that carries the determinants of the individual also contains those of the varieties, races, and species. The schema of inside-outside speculation described above is repeated for each separate variation problem of the substance. Attempts have been made to separate, for example, the paratypical variations of the individuals—those determined by the environment—from the genotypical ones—those determined by structure. But speculation had to go beyond this and state that paratypical variations, though brought forth by environmental influences, are nevertheless also determined by the structure of the genotype. For if the genotype were not structured in such a way that the environment can affect it—and do so in precisely the way it does—then these particular modifications and adaptive phenomena would not be possible. Conversely, the emergence of genotypical changes that lead to inheritable mutations is quite evidently connected to conditions in the environment: good nutrition favors the occurrence of beneficial mutations while unfavorable conditions such as alcoholic poisoning can lead to hereditary pathological changes in the genotype.[5] The difference between hereditary and nonhereditary variations can therefore not be traced back to the interior-exterior antithesis as its ultimate explanation; rather, it is supported by the "seen" phenomena of constants, fluctuation, and variation of the "seen" types. If, as some biologists would have it, the varieties (races) and species developed from an accumulation of transmitted mutations, the same speculative schema would recur. Species could evolve from a prior form only under specific environmental conditions, but the conditions would avail nothing if the substance they affect were not prepared to be transformed under their influence into the determinant of a new species in precisely the way it is transformed. Using this schema, we could trace the origin of species back to the primordial cell, which already would have had to contain all the determinants of its later evolution, including those of the present multiplicity of forms in the living, visible world.

The progression of individuals, the expansion of the organic substance after its passage through the bottleneck of procreation,

5. On the problem of interior-exterior and the individual, see Julius Schulz, "Die Grundfiktionen der Biologie," in *Abhandlungen zur theoretischen Biologie*, No. 7, esp. Chapters 9–12.

shows the two phenomena of great similarity between ancestors and descendants and only small differences between them. Both the constancy of the type and its variation are functions of the structure of the organic substance in its development within an environment. Post-Darwinian biology studied both these functions with very unequal results. Since the end of the nineteenth century, exact research into heredity using Mendel's experiments and their continuation on the part of experimental zoologists and botanists has led to outstanding results concerning the laws of heredity— that is, the laws of type constants. On the other hand, efforts to discover the laws governing variations remained, if not unsuccessful, yet so insufficient that the problem of the evolution of species seems now farther than ever from being solved. The Darwinian assumption of general variation among individuals turned out to be untenable; though individuals vary from each other, their variations are not arbitrary or follow this or that direction by accident from which a particular variation could then be fixed upon by natural selection. Instead individuals vary only in very few directions and always in the same ones. Moreover, the great majority of these variations fluctuates—that is, they appear in only one individual and do not show up in the next generation; they are not transmitted. Only a very few variations, occurring suddenly and unpredictably, the so-called mutations, represent genuine structural changes in the organic substance (this term is to be used with the caution called for in the above analyses) and are preserved in further individuation. The occurrence of mutations can only to a very slight degree be influenced from outside through the creation of special conditions—for example, through ample nutrition. But it is not in the experimenter's hands to bring about the appearance of mutations at will.[6] Some species show very little tendency to mutate while others are more promising in this regard, and for purposes of research species must be chosen that tend to mutate in greater numbers and in shorter periods of time. Various theories have been proposed to explain the laws of mutation, and the differences between them, in spite of their significance for the interpretation of particular biological facts—and in spite of their even greater general

6. On the possibilities of experimental creation of mutations, see Richard Goldschmidt, *Einführung in die Vererbungswissenschaft* (5th ed.; 1928), 447–48. See also Goldschmidt, *Physiologische Theorie der Vererbung* (Berlin, 1927), 90 ff.

44

theoretical significance ascribed to them by their respective authors—for the analysis of theoretical structures all of them can basically be subsumed under a single type: in contrast to Darwin's theory, they put forth the thesis that it is the attribute of organic substance to mutate in a particular direction and only in that direction and that the existing species are stages in the process of mutation. Depending on the author's care for the methodological purity of his work and on the metaphysical outlook on which his thinking is based, various formulas have been found for this tendency of organic substance to evolve in a specific direction.

Carl Nägeli speaks of a principle of perfection of the organic substance that pushes its development from the primordial cell to the ever more complicated forms we see now in the organic world. Nägeli strongly criticizes Darwin's assumption of variations in all directions and limits the function of selection to the extermination of forms unfit for life, claiming that it can do nothing for the development of species. "The theory of perfection assumes that the organism has an inherent tendency to transform itself into a more complex one, and from this it follows that only some ascending evolutionary lines emerge from the original cells and that this process could not be reversed."[7] From the very beginning organic substance is determined in a specific direction; it can only evolve to higher forms, but not devolve. The abiogenesis of cells, from which higher forms evolve, is not, Nägeli continues, tied to a particular point far back in time, but it occurs constantly and therefore happens even now. Thanks to this recurring abiogenesis we now see the whole hierarchy of forms spread out before us. According to Nägeli, the highest forms have evolved from the oldest cells produced through abiogenesis, and the lower forms are, depending on their position in the hierarchy, the descendants of respectively more recent abiogenesis. What is remarkable in Nägeli's attempt is the effort, which we find frequently even nowadays among biologists under the pressure of physical-technical superstition, to present the teleoclinic character of organic formation as reconcilable with the laws of inorganic nature. As Nägeli emphasizes strongly, "No supernatural influence is needed to direct the process

7. Carl Nägeli, *Entstehung und Begriff der naturhistorischen Art* (2nd ed.; 1865), 29.

of modification."[8] Also characteristic here is the idea, taken as self-evident at the time, that natural phenomena could belong only to the physical class and that everything that could not be reduced to this class had to be "supernatural." Nägeli tried to show that the cells made up of carbohydrates and proteins could develop only in a specific direction, just as in inorganic nature only certain specific combinations can result from given elements. However, Nägeli had to concede that "precise analogies are lacking." This small imprecision is nothing less than the difference between inorganic nature and the phenomenon of life. This attempt to unite the two realms may be hopeless, but it is not unreasonable, for the problem of the origin of life lies in the transition from the organic realm through the primordial cell produced through abiogenesis to the inorganic.

The problem of beginnings is the boundary problem of the interior-exterior speculation: when we have pursued the determination of organic substance back to the primordial cell, the question of its origin arises. However we imagine this beginning—here speculation is a leap, an absolute end of the speculative continuum that is concealed by assiduous thinkers in various ways: through the assumption of divine intervention or the assumption that at some point inorganic nature following its inherent lawfulness suddenly stopped being inorganic and, for a change, became organic—and indeed immediately organic to such an extent that all the laws of the living world, humanity included, follow from this event. In this deeper sphere of scientific theorizing the problems of the body-soul relationship we analyzed in Chapter 1 recur. Though each of the two realms is governed by its own inherent laws but since the world of the living is based on the inorganic world, both are to be subject to a single set of laws. Therefore, according to the well-known construction type, the law of form of the one realm is construed as a byproduct of the other realm.

G. H. Theodor Eimer's attempt is extremely instructive for the problem of theory formation. He turns as sharply as Nägeli against the theory of general variation, particularly against the form it has taken in August Weismann's theory, but he opposes Nägeli just as vigorously. While the latter took as the point of departure for his theory the "interior" aspect of the speculative schema and posited

8. *Ibid.*, 129.

the principle of perfection as the inner determinant, ultimately construing this inner tendency as an exterior product because of his submission before the laws of the inorganic realm and because of his explicit denial of a "vital principle,"[9] Eimer on the other hand, begins with external influence: "According to my investigations, *organic growth* (*organophysis*), caused by continuous external influences, such as climate and nourishment, on plasma, which in turn is expressed in *specifically directed evolution* (*orthogenesis*), is the chief cause of transmutation, and its sporadic interruption, its occasional standstill (*genepistasis*) is the principal cause of the separation of the chain of organisms into species."[10] Here the expression *orthogenesis* is introduced to describe the variation in a specific direction toward the complexity of form; the term has survived in biological theory; however, the "direction" of genesis is not determined by a tendency of the organism but remains steady because the influences affecting growth and development are constant. Just as Nägeli moved from his "tendency" to constitution from outside, Eimer now finds himself compelled by the structure of his theoretical formation to move toward the inner determinant as a precondition for causative influences from outside. The constant influences on growth can only make their influence felt in a particular direction because an organic substance exists that by virtue of its inner constitution is susceptible to be influenced in the orthogenetic direction. "The causes of the specific direction of evolution," writes Eimer, "in my opinion lie in the effect of external influences on the *given constitution of the organism*." And even more explicitly, "In my view everywhere evolution can occur in only a few directions because the *constitution*, the material composition of the body, necessitates these directions and prevents changes in all directions."[11]

Now that both poles of the schema are given, the process of organic evolution can be played out, the given constitution continuously changing in its interaction with the external influences, and these ongoing changes leading to the variety of species. That the

---

9. *Ibid.*, 45.

10. G. H. Theodor Eimer, *Die Entstehung der Arten auf Grund von Vererben erworbener Eigenschaften nach den Gesetzen organischen Wachsens.* Pt. 2: *Orthogenesis der Schmetterlinge* (1897), 1.

11. *Ibid.*, 15.

process comes to a halt at specific points and stops at one species is explained by the principle of epistasis; that it sometimes moves ahead by leaps rather than causing only tiny variations is explained by the principle of halmatogenesis. Although nothing is explained by this, it is deeply reassuring to be able to name things.[12]

By contrasting Nägeli's and Eimer's theories, we could isolate the construction schema of the relationship between interior and exterior in its inherent lawfulness for theory formation; but it was not possible to isolate as completely the other line of construction, that of the speculative schema of inorganic-organic, even though the case of Nägeli showed that the two run parallel and are closely related. If the organism is considered only as a reactive substance interacting with other substances, the external ones, we need not give it a status different from the one we give to inorganic substances: Even the inorganic ones react only in the manner specific to them, and the "determinant" of the one is just as essential as that of the other in producing a reaction between two of them. The particular "seen" phenomenon of the organism that prompts us to distinguish between interior and exterior regarding this organism is the comprehensive unity of a complex of substances that seems inevitably to propel this organism into growth, metamorphosis, functional harmony, regenerative processes, and the like, which are characteristic of living forms. Observations of sea urchin eggs and of similar cases have shown that germ cell division does not impair the cell's ability to generate the entire organism, and they have given Hans Driesch the crucial concrete arguments (I use this term to distinguish between concrete and speculative arguments) to prove that the essence of the organic substance is not confined to its material structure but must lie in a non-material "potentiality," the "entelechy" that is capable of animating matter but is itself indivisible. Entelechy is an "integrating causal factor," "it makes whole in embryology, it transmits totalities in heredity, it restores damaged wholeness."[13] It is the subject of statements we make about the characteristics of an organism; it is the identical sub-

12. On the problem of interior and exterior, see also Detto, *Theorie der direkten Anpassung*, especially his formulation of the principle of "accidents," 190.

13. Hans Driesch, "Das Wesen des Organismus," in *Das Lebensproblem* (1931), 416. See also Driesch, *Die Philosophie des Organischen* (4th ed.; 1928), especially Section B, Introduction, and Part One; further, Driesch, "Der Begriff der organischen Form," in *Abhandlungen zur theoretischen Biologie* (1919), No. 3.

stance in morphological changes and the metabolic processes of the living being.

Even more instructive for the problem of theory formation than Driesch's theory of entelechy is Heinz Woltereck's doctrine of the reaction norm [*Reaktionsnorm*][14] because through this concept with its echoes of the conceptual world of chemistry and genetics the dialectical transition from concepts of a material structure as the carrier of the determinants to the concept of a potentiality or an "inextensive variety" of determinants is completed. As in most cases of biological theory formation, here too the line of construction is not an entirely pure one but follows to the vagaries of an actual concrete problem. Woltereck rejects the hypothesis that hereditary mutations can ever accumulate to the point where one species has developed into another. In fact only individual traits of the species type mutate, never crucial parts of the overall constitution. Furthermore, the overwhelming majority of mutations are extremely harmful, if not lethal, to the organism. A distinction must therefore be made between those hereditary changes in the genetic structure that occur within the framework of the species type and this species type itself; Woltereck calls such a species type a reaction norm. The reaction norm is "what persists as a complete and unchanged constant throughout the changes of the bodily substances and the determining substances. Without it the continuation of the species characteristics, which remain the same for such a long time in spite of constant changes, would be not only incomprehensible, but also impossible."[15] "Because everything that happens in the very complex processes and structure of the organism falls under the collective term of 'reactions,' this lawfully constant and therefore really identical element is probably best designated as the *specific reaction norm* of the various species and races."[16] The logical site of the concept of the reaction norm is therefore determined (1) by a speculative schema, (2) by the gradation of the species phenomenon in contrast to mutation phenomena.

14. Heinz Woltereck, "Vererbung und Erbänderung," in *Das Lebensproblem* (1931). See also, Woltereck, *Variation und Artbildung* (1919); on page 228, note 4, of "Vererbung und Erbänderung," Woltereck refers for a detailed presentation of the subject to a work published at the same time: *Die Organismen als Gefüge, Getriebe, und Normen* (Stuttgart, 1931).

15. Woltereck, "Vererbung und Erbänderung," 276.

16. *Ibid.*, 277.

Concerning (1): The concept of an unchanging constant becomes necessary in this sphere when the analysis aiming at determining the unified self-identity of the organism in the change of the constitutive substances is pursued further. Driesch, for example, begins his attempt to determine the identity of the organism in its essence by distinguishing between a something, which either must be the unchanging identity itself or at least must contain it, and the facts of metabolism. "It [the organism's unchanging self-identity] shows us that the *material* components of the organism—with, perhaps, a few exceptions—at least in its adult state are *not* always the same."[17] From this it follows that the organism's self-identity is not simply the sameness of substances.

Let us recall here the parallel argument I cited in Chapter 1, in which I. H. Fichte isolated the changing material body in order to arrive at the concept of the pneumatic body. Beginning at another point of the biological phenomenon, namely, at the genetic structure, Woltereck continues this speculation, for, concerning attempts to find the constant of a type in the genotype, he has to concede that "in the strictest sense, however, even the material genes in the various individuals, stages, and generations are not identical. . . . They do not remain the same materially but are continuously recreated through assimilation. In no case is the living substance and any gene substance of any given organism *the same* as that in the germ cells of its ancestors, siblings, and descendants. Both the living basic substance of the organism and the substance of all its genes are continuously renewed and increased."[18]

The problem of metabolism recurs in connection with the analysis of genetic structure, and it would have to recur even if we were successful in finding additional substances that might be considered as carriers of determinants, such as the filiform structure of chromosomes, on which the genes are arranged, or other components of the germ cell. Whether the analysis is supported by concrete arguments, such as that an enormous increase in the hereditary factors of one organism as compared to another does not necessarily entail any perceptible quantitative enlargement of the genetic apparatus, or that the highly complex human organism has

17. Driesch, "Das Wesen des Organismus," 389.
18. Woltereck, "Vererbung und Erbänderung," 275–76.

by no means the greatest number of chromosomes (a kind of argument that already played a large role in Joseph Hyrtl's campaign against materialism)—whether, that is, such "supports" for the theory are available or not in the given case (as, for example, Driesch's sea urchin egg) is immaterial to the outcome, which, because of the structure of the speculative schema, can only be the displacement of the identity determinants from the inorganic sphere to another, the nonmaterial-vital, one. It seems to me important to highlight this transition in Woltereck's speculation because he was not wholeheartedly convinced of the result; his summarizing statement sounds very much like a forced concession to the logic of his own thinking: "Since the enormous diversity of the species constants cannot be conceived as co-existing extensively-corporeally, . . . we are compelled to see in the processes of heredity a fundamentally *immaterial* connection."[19]

Concerning (2): In Woltereck's theory the transition from the inorganic sphere to the nonmaterial-vital sphere is connected with the return from the phenomena of mutation to those of species constants. The reaction norm is the determinant of the species with all its mutations and modifications. The species is defined as the unity of all the individuals connected by the same mode of reaction, that is, as a group identical in reaction. Thus, the unit in the system of biology is not the pure line (about which we will have more to say below)—that is, a group of individuals distinguished from all others by a single hereditary factor—but a group of individuals that in addition to its constant constitution also exhibits a specific complex of plausible factors. These plausible factors are the changes in the constant character of the species that appear as variations in its developmental phases. Hereditary mutations and non-hereditary personal variations are thus interpreted as components of the constant character of the species. Accordingly, mutations are not the basis for biotypical units but are themselves lawfully constant possibilities of variation within the constant building plan of the species. The reaction norm comprises the constitution of the structural plan of the species, which cannot be varied, as well as the modalities—that is, the plausible, interchangeable hereditary (though sometimes reversibly mutating) traits—and finally the in-

19. *Ibid.*, 298.

dividual modifications that are not transmitted to the next generation.

Thus the concept of reaction norm brings the unit of the biological system very close to the Linnaean concept of species, since the frame encompassing all variable traits is the species seen as morphologically constant. Regarding the problem of species development and descent we can say nothing from this standpoint based on results of zoological experiments. After all, zoological experiments can only elucidate mutations, and these do not constitute a species. Thus, the path that seemed to lead to a theory of species development on the basis of mutation theory is cut off. Woltereck summarized everything that can be assumed about it in an analogy to chemical-physical processes: *"Species change is constitution change,* which follows *internal* laws just as the decay of radioactive substances or the construction of combinations out of basic elements, from electrons to atoms, does."[20]

Woltereck's theory of species as a group of reaction-identical individuals already goes one step beyond the question of the unit in the biological system as it has been formulated in biology in recent decades as well as beyond the formulation of the question "current" theory of the human races is still coming to terms with. For anthropological race theory, this formulation of the problem of the system unit is of secondary interest because at present there is general agreement that human beings are members of one species; problems and conflicts arise only with the question of the systematic rank of the subunits of the species, the hereditary variations or races. Since Hugo de Vries's studies of *Oenothera lamarckiana*[21] and the flowering of genetics following the Thomas Hunt Morgan school's research into *Drosophila* fruit flies,[22] the problem is covered in the exact study of heredity under the title of mutations and the biological units based on them, the pure lines, pure tribes, elementary or subspecies. The science of genetics limits the concept of species to groups of individuals unified because a hereditary factor makes them all different from other biotypes.

20. *Ibid.,* 308.
21. See Hugo de Vries, *Die Mutationstheorie: Versuche und Beobachtungen über die Entstehung von Arten im Pflanzenreich* (1901, 1903). See also de Vries, *Die Mutationen in der Erblichkeitslehre* (1912).
22. See especially Thomas Hunt Morgan, *The Physical Basis of Heredity* (1919) and *Evolution and Genetics* (1925).

The pure line is the totality of all individuals descended from a self-fertilizing homozygotic individual. Individuals are homozygotic only if the two gametes (sex cells) combined into a zygote are homogeneous in regard to their genetic structure. The group of individuals thus determined is the smallest biological collective unit—but only as long as the genetic structure does not mutate. When a new mutation occurs, the pure line is broken, and a new subspecies or elementary species, as these units are called to distinguish them from Linnaean collective species, has emerged. As early as 1901 de Vries wrote: "As is well-known, the Linnaean species are groups of elementary species. What belongs to an elementary species can be determined in each given case by cultural analysis; how many such forms are to be combined into one Linnaean species is a matter of the so-called systematic tact, as is also the determination of the extent of the genera and families."[23] The experimental theory of the origin of species deals with the development of elementary species, or rather with the development of species traits. According to this theory, the Linnaean species develop when elementary species drop out of the continuing series, causing seemingly discontinuous forms. Every mutation of a trait constitutes a new exact elementary species. In 1909 Wilhelm Johannsen summarized the methodical significance of the elementary species in strong terms: It is now well known that the Linnaean species "in reality are not units but comprise several so-called 'small species' that can be characterized more or less clearly. And indeed today it is generally acknowledged that these small species must be considered the unit of systematic natural history."[24] In the third edition of his work he resignedly softens these strong terms by noting, "These small species *should* be the units of systematic natural history, *but this can hardly be implemented*."[25] Julius Schaxel again formulated in a fundamental way this postulate: "The taxonomists' species as collective names defined arbitrarily or by convention and the species occurring in nature whose genetic natural makeup has not yet been studied are both not appropriate subjects

23. De Vries, *Die Mutationstheorie*. Vol. I: *Die Entstehung der Arten durch Mutation* (1901), 43.
24. Wilhelm Johannsen, *Elemente der exakten Erblichkeitslehre* (1909), 7.
25. Wilhelm Johannsen, *Elemente der exakten Erblichkeitslehre: Mit Grundzügen der biologischen Variationsstatistik* (3rd ed.; 1926), 8 (emphasis added).

for research into the formation of species. The only appropriate subjects for this are the pure lines of the autogamous (asexually reproducing) organisms and the tribes of allogamous (sexually reproducing) organisms."[26]

On the basis of this concept of species, formulated with such methodological strictness, the possible answers to the question of species development are discouraging. The observed mutations are relatively few in number, and the mutational changes themselves are very small; that these small mutations could lead to the development of complicated organs and to the evolution from the lower life forms we know to the higher ones is so inconceivable that, as we have seen, attempts are made to reintroduce as a unit of biology a concept of species closer to the classical one. According to Friedrich Alverdes, a unified principle of the origin of species can never be found; rather, in each case special conditions of genesis prevailed. He suspects that the reaction changes crucial for evolution have not yet been discovered.[27] Based on the current status of mutation theory, he continues, evolution can be imagined only as a series of orthogenetic mutations—that is, of mutations directed toward the development of higher, viable life forms—although we do not know why precisely this mutational direction evolved instead of another harmful one that would have led to destruction. According to Alverdes, the answer to this question can be found only by experimental research, which gradually must become able to influence the genotype and through observation of series of mutations can determine whether there are in fact specifically directed series among them.

It hardly requires a concluding remark to make it clear that this exact concept of the subspecies cannot be the one on which the race theories of man are based. To purify the pure lines and tubes through several generations would require continuous cultivation and, once the pure line has been isolated, there would need to be additional experimental treatment for many generations in order to determine their traits exactly and to test their mutability. Indeed, even if observation shows that the pure line has been successfully cultivated, this purity remains always questionable be-

26. Julius Schaxel, *Grundzüge der Theorienbildung in der Biologie* (2nd ed.; 1922), 106.

27. Alverdes, "Rassen- und Artbildung," 104.

cause the purity of the hereditary factors can be assessed only by their effect on the external traits we can control. That they are actually identical in regard to all their genes cannot be proven. "Thus we arrive at the question: are there in the entire realm of organisms two individuals that can be called absolutely isogenic? Johannsen attributes the variations observed within a pure line to accidental differences in life situation; but could genotypical differences that have not yet been studied perhaps play a role here too? Most especially the *bloodlines*, which among cross-fertilizers comprise the species, would most likely not have any individuals that are identical with regard to all genes."[28]

With this qualification, that even under the most favorable experimental conditions the purity of the isolated material must remain doubtful, we have to evaluate the type of species that forms the basis of arguments in human race theory. Johannsen has already expressed the crux of the matter: human populations cannot be used for experiments. "Regarding man, we unfortunately must be content with making the best use we can of the insights that can be obtained from statistical data. But statistical studies are truly unsuited to properly elucidate the *fundamental biological problems* we encounter in questions of heredity. . . . In populations (stock) of animals or plants of any particular species or race where mating is more or less uncontrolled—as for example in human society— . . . it will be difficult or nearly impossible to carry out a closer analysis of heredity."[29]

28. *Ibid.,* 90.
29. Johannsen, *Elemente* (3rd ed.), 177–78.

3

Race as Anthropological Unit

In view of the impossibility of establishing pure lineages as the basis of the descriptive classification of man, the definitions of race given by anthropologists are more or less cautious in responding to the demand that only hereditary traits be included in the description of races. As an example of a cautious definition we may single out the standard work by Rudolf Martin.[1] Martin is primarily concerned with the craft and technical aspects of anthropology and remains relatively indifferent to theoretical issues. Therefore, he has a sharper eye for facts than authors who are intent on defending a position at all costs. For Martin races are the variations within the morphologically clearly differentiated species of *Homo sapiens*. According to his view, a definition of the groups of forms within the species must be based primarily on hereditary factors because "the true essence of man" is determined by heredity. However, for Martin race is not exclusively the embodiment of genetic traits since the characterizing traits also include paratypical ones—that is, those determined by the environment. For the definition of a race it suffices that its members share a complex of characteristics that distinguishes them from other groups of forms with other complexes of characteristics. The individual characteristic within this complex is not of crucial significance; it may vary to a very high degree provided that the combinations of traits remain otherwise constant. The groups of traits have merely empirical significance: "In any human population we examine we are primarily interested in those combinations of traits that have been realized most frequently and that are noticeable as 'types' because of this frequent occurrence."[2]

1. Rudolf Martin, *Lehrbuch der Anthropologie* (2nd ed.; 1928).
2. *Ibid.*, 9.

I consider these statements by Martin particularly important precisely because of their theoretical and methodological modesty (which seems unaware of the problems inherent in type theory, for example), because I believe they describe the process of type formation honestly and correctly. Combinations of traits "attract attention" because they are encountered more often, and they are then taken as the point of departure for the study. Generally, anthropologists know only very little about the significance of the characteristics used in defining the racial types. "Unfortunately we know very little about the classificatory significance of individual traits."[3] Looking at individuals, it is impossible to determine what part of the "attention-attracting" type is due to hereditary factors and what must be put down to environmental influences.[4] And such studies, I might add, are practically impossible, since experimental breeding and changes in the environment for the purpose of isolating these factors are out of the question. (More below about interesting attempts in this direction, especially Franz Boas's investigations.)

A more recent major work on the study of race, by Walter Scheidt,[5] is less modest. Scheidt understands race to mean a selected complex of hereditary traits. Reproduction from one generation to the next is shaped by a number of factors: heredity, changes caused by mixing hereditary characteristics, change in the genetic makeup itself, accumulation of hereditary changes, and natural selection. The genetic material is constantly being newly recombined; mutations alter its structure and physical-environmental and social processes of selection continually screen it in such a way that certain genetic elements are more frequently transmitted than others. When selective environmental conditions remain unchanged over a long period of time, a particular complex of traits will gradually become permanent in a population. Such a complex of traits resulting from natural selection is a race. Each group of influences has a corresponding race; the number of races depends on the number of selecting environments. The main emphasis of this position on race lies in selection, while the problematic fact, namely, the importance of the complex of traits as genetically uni-

3. *Ibid.*, 8.
4. *Ibid.*, 10–11.
5. Walter Scheidt, *Allgemeine Rassenkunde* (Munich, 1925).

fied [*erbeinheitlich*] complex is simply assumed as a matter of course. Scheidt does, however, admit that this concept of race should be related to the biological concept of elementary species; nevertheless, he passes over this question with only a brief gesture. If this species concept were accepted, he believes, "one can correctly designate the members of a family or a generation in their totality as a race although the similarity among these people is usually not due to race-forming selection processes but merely to their common descent."[6] It is not clear to me where the supposed difference between family and race is. After all, according to Scheidt's definition, is race not just as much a unit of descent as is the family—albeit a selected one—and is not the unit of the family selected by the social environment and the living conditions determined by the social stratum the family belongs to? Scheidt continues: "It is, of course, also clear that designating every family as a special race does not agree with the original meaning of the word 'race.' After all, a useful *definition of the race concept must be equally applicable in so-called systematics as in genetics.*"[7] I agree completely with the statement that the concept of elementary race and the designation of family as race are not compatible with the meaning originally assigned to the word *race* and it must have become clear by now that the anthropological concept of race does not agree with the biological one. The second statement, that a concept must be found that satisfies both genetics and the requirements of anthropology, is, however, without foundation, and indeed in the narrow sense this demand cannot be fulfilled because biology confines itself to the somatic sphere, but race theory distances itself from this sphere by taking the whole human being as its subject, and it thus enters a field that, as we discussed in Chapter I, cannot be treated with the way of thinking pertaining to the somatic sphere.

To fully clarify the situation of anthropology, I want to cite Eugen Fischer's treatment of the race problem. He defines race as a larger group of human beings sharing a common hereditary, innate physical and mental habitus that unites them and distinguishes them from other such groups. This view deviates from precise biological terms in the two determining elements of "larger groups" and "habi-

6. *Ibid.*, 331.
7. *Ibid.*

58

tus." Racial units are formed according to "attention-attracting" types in Martin's sense, and this requires that a larger number of traits characteristic for the race unit occurs in a larger number of individuals. Without further justification Fischer notes: "A single hereditary trait (perhaps appearing for the first time) does not (according to general linguistic usage [of all languages]) represent a race in anthropology. But modern scientists working with genetic experiments do use the word in that manner—and it is logically consistent."[8] The attempt to justify anthropology's formation of a unit thus does not go beyond the observation that the general linguistic usage of researchers has simply defined the unit this way. "Practical" considerations clearly determine the definition; "practical" experience determines how many traits must be present and how important they must be to justify calling a group a "race." And according to Fischer, the same holds true for the definition of species and genera: " 'Species' and 'genus' can be separated only on practical grounds (and sometimes not even then) but not in theory and not by definition. And anthropology must also use the concept of race as part of its conceptual system."[9] "Experience" decides which traits will be studied.[10] On this basis of "experience," in spite of the demand that a hereditary habitus has to characterize the group, it is difficult to decide which of the traits of the chosen habitus are really hereditary. Animal experiments, especially experiments with mice, have shown that very considerable differences in habitus, which would justify classifying the animals as belonging to different races, can be caused by environmental influences, and thus are merely variations in the phenotype, changes in outward appearance. "But this problem, needless to say, is of fundamental significance for human race theory! All older works about the purely anatomical differences between races lose much of their interest and all of their value for the system if those differences— perhaps all of them!—amount to nothing more than phenotype variations! While it is unlikely that this will be true for all those differences, it may be true for many!"[11] Even the shape of the skull,

8. Eugen Fischer, *Spezielle Anthropologie: Rassenlehre* (*Kultur der Gegenwart*, Pt. 3, Sec. 5: *Anthropologie*), 1923, 123.
9. *Ibid.*, 123–24.
10. *Ibid.*, 124.
11. *Ibid.*, 129.

considered so decisive, can to some degree be influenced. Boas' studies of European immigrants to America have shown that the skulls of children of brachycephalic East European Jews were less broad in America than those of their parents, that the skulls of descendants of dolichocephalic Neapolitans and Sicilians, conversely, are less narrow than those of their parents. That is, the American environment influences the shape of the skull in the direction of the mesocephalic type. Similar observations were made of Spaniards in Puerto Rico.

> We need hardly point out the enormous consequences the indisputable proof of the general validity of this phenomenon would have. For Europe, the question immediately arises: if somewhere—for example, in Central Europe—an earlier invasion of a population with long skulls (tomb findings) can be proven, and today a population with short skulls lives in the pertinent location, were those dolichocephalic immigrants eradicated and their descendants eliminated so that today's brachycephalics are not their descendants but the again increased offspring of the diminished old population spared by the immigrants? Or did the environment—some factors unknown to us—modify the long form of the skull into the short form, so that today's brachycephalics are still racially pure and the same (relatively) as the invading population except that they look different? For anthropologists to this time, for the systematicians, the very question seems almost absurd, the assumption of such environmental influences inconceivable—but that does not resolve the question—anthropology is faced with new challenges.[12]

Thus, it may well be that in future, under the pressure of findings like those of Boas, anthropology will turn away from the current method of classification, the so-called systematics, and arrive at a treatment of its subject that is better grounded in science and thus at a precise definition of the biological units in the human species. "Currently" the starting points are still "historical" groups—that is, units that pertain not to nature but to the realm of the mind. Units based on migration, settlement, marriage, and nations, which have led to the breeding of more or less fixed combinations of traits, of a more or less clearly defined habitus, "attract attention"; "ex-

12. *Ibid.*, 132. See also Fischer in Erwin Baur, Eugen Fischer, and Fritz Lenz, *Menschliche Erblichkeitslehre* (1927) I; 91–92. See further on the interpretation of these observations, which are such an embarrassment to political race theory, Günther, *Rassenkunde des deutschen Volkes* (15th ed.; 1930), 250–51, and *Rassenkunde Europas* (3rd ed.; 1929), 106.

perience" or "practice" determines the delineation of each group against others and their order in the system.

At this point we would do well to recall Kurt Hildebrandt's ideas on state and race because, in direct contrast to Scheidt's theories, they clearly take into account the distance separating the race concept from that of the pure line and give us a glimpse of the principles of the formation of the race concept. Hildebrandt, like Johannsen, points out that the pure line cannot be the systematic basic unit of a human race doctrine because it is obviously impossible to carry out experiments of inbreeding. When we speak of races as groups of individuals with identical hereditary traits or of "pure" races, the concept must always be understood as relative to the system of classification. According to race theory in Günther's sense, pure races are certain types (Nordic, Baltic, Alpine, and so forth) as opposed to mixed populations, in which those types can presumably be distinguished. Whether these races are also pure in the sense that they are immediate mutations of the still undifferentiated species of *Homo sapiens* or direct subsequent mutations of this primary mutation is impossible to ascertain. They *could* be pure in this sense, but it is just as probable that they are mixed races bred from such mutations by virtue of geographic isolation and social selection. Similarly, we cannot positively ascertain that cross-breeding of races we regard as "pure" leads to mixed races. Morgan, for example, points out that the yellow skin color of mixed Negroes and whites, mulattos, can be interpreted as the "pure" skin color, from which the black and white races have mutated away.[13]

In regard to the human species, therefore, "purity" means no more than an observed constancy of traits and their combinations, and today a combination of traits will essentially be a "practically" pure-bred mixture of original mutations. The "practically" pure mixed race is thus the unit on which Hildebrandt bases his thinking. "If two tribes merge in order to form a state that denies civil rights to later immigrants and their half-breed offspring, the original 'race mixture' comes ever closer and closer to the pure 'mixed race,' since new hereditary elements cannot enter but the existing ones can in part be eradicated."[14]

13. Thomas Hunt Morgan, *Evolution and Genetics* (2nd ed.; 1925), 183.
14. Kurt Hildebrandt, *Norm und Entartung des Menschen* (1923), 223.

The breeding of mixed races is a historical process, not in the sense of occurring over time but because orienting propagation according to a norm is a component of the state process. The historical structure of the state with its concomitant intellectual world requires the physical basis for its realization and, indeed, a basis suitable to it. Disturbances and mixtures arising from the physical realm can mar the harmony of the overall intellectual formation. According to this view, the physical phenomenon belongs no longer exclusively to the natural sphere, which as such is differentiated from that of the mind, but it is a process within the world of the mind, and the physical embodiment is part and parcel of this world's essence. Race is thus not an inescapable natural fact concerning the individual as it is in Günther's naturalistic race theory; instead it is a norm for the physical and mental development of the nation in its state. That is why, in contrast to the political theories making propaganda for the Nordic race, Hildebrandt calls for the breeding of a "German race"[15] as the body of the German nation and the German state, for the breeding of an increasingly purer and purer race out of the elements making up the German people. "The national idea is ranked higher than racial solidarity!"[16] Only when guided by a central idea of the state as a formation of the mind—and in the current world situation that means guided by the idea of the nation—is the formation of ultimate group units legitimate.

The basic elements of the difficult situation of anthropology as a natural science have no doubt become apparent from these juxtapositions. As a natural science, anthropology wants to use basic systematic concepts developed by biologists for the animal and plant world, but it gets into difficulties because, quite simply, human beings are not merely beings of nature, and their physical aspect in its group formation and selection is also determined by the higher principles shaping the formation of societies and states. Thus, we see anthropology moving from accurate attempts to order the multiplicity of biological phenomena of the human body by means of the mind-shaped body form—to the extent this is possible without conducting biological experiments and even though the value of such an order as system remains questionable in all its

15. Kurt Hildebrandt, *Staat und Rasse,* Veröffentlichung der schleswig-holsteinischen Universitätsgesellschaft, No. 19, p. 16.
16. *Ibid.,* 13.

details due to shortcomings of the available methods—to the questionable disputes between political race theoreticians and their opponents. In only one case, that of Hildebrandt, does an idea emerge that allows us to see that the question of the body as the basis of the community and the state must be answered on a deeper level than can be done by the misapplication of scientific categories in the realm of the human spirit: by breeding man to a norm of the body that can absorb, preserve and keep alive the spirit of community—to use Hildebrandt's language again.

4

The Soul-Characteristics of Races

Having developed the outline of race theory, let us in conclusion examine in detail a number of questions concerning the problem of the "soul-characteristics" and their "transmission." However, before analyzing the formulations of these questions in the contemporary literature, we will summarize for purposes of clarification the fundamentals of the problem.

§1. Review of the Premises

Man's total being [*Gesamtwesen*] is the unified form reaching from the apex of the mind through the layers of animal and vegetative animation down to inanimate matter. The question of the nature of man as a whole can therefore not be answered by saying that he is mind; he is mind and at the same time also animated body and inanimate matter. These relationships are difficult to understand because of the terms we have available for designating the various aspects of the human essence. We use the word "body" [*Körper*] to designate the human form we perceive with our senses in its material qualities; we also use the word "body" [*Leib*]—still more clearly with the qualifier "pneumatic"—to designate the human form as animated; but we lack a word for the human form as thoroughly permeated by the spirit. Animals have bodies in the sense of *Körper* and in the sense of *Leiber* and nothing more; human beings also have *Körper* and *Leiber*, and in addition they have the spiritual form [*Geistgestalt*] of the body. Similar difficulties arise when we try to define the various speculative moments of the spirit. When we speak of spirit without characterizing it further, we usually think of spirit as the element differentiating the whole human being from the animal, that is, we conceive of it as a body-less spirit. This is the sense in which Scheler understands spirit, as something lifeless and powerless. This is also the concept of spirit used in the isolating constructions presented above, and it typically leads to the construction of a connecting link between spirit and body, as in the case of Kant. There is no term in our language for spirit as tied to the body and permeating the body. Thus, the realities of matter, soul, and spirit can be experienced as parts of our whole being and at the same time have their status in this whole being as ensouled matter, as spirit-permeated matter and body. We must clearly see this peculiar speculative circumstance in order to understand the ramifications of the problem of heredity.

The idea that psychical or spiritual traits are hereditary has grown out of a number of fundamental experiences: the experience of spirit first of all, second, the experience that human beings come into existence through sexual reproduction as do the higher animals, and further from the experience that human beings despite all their variety are forms with the same structure, but that within this sameness individuals differ from each other physically and spiritually. Since the human spirit is human—that is, not a body-less spirit but joined with the body into a unified whole—we will always have reason to state that man as a whole is involved in the process of the succession of generations and that all his traits, including spiritual ones, are related to so-called hereditary transmission. However, it does not follow from this fact what race theorists deduce from it and what their opponents combat with unsuitable arguments, namely, the fatality, the inescapability of the structure and of the individual's development in the way it turns out for each one. With this statement I do not want to suggest in any way that the life of any individual could take a different course than it actually does if the person concerned only wanted it to, and I do not want to deny that man's physical nature and his coming into existence through procreation are an essential source of this experience of fatality or inevitability. I merely want to make it clear that this fatality cannot be the subject of a scientific judgment—such a judgment claiming the dependence of the phenomenon of spirit on bodily processes would, as we have seen, be a statement about the ontology of the real that can in principle not be supported by experiences. Nevertheless, the experience of being determined through blood can be an actual experience from a clearly definable aspect of the whole of human existence. In addition to the experience of being determined by our physical nature, which gives rise to the sense of fatality, there are the experiences of the activity of the spirit, from which, equally compellingly, we know our existence to be freely creative.

What follows from the possibility of seeing spiritual traits and processes as consistently parallel to physical ones if we think it through to the end? It follows that we would have to think of a series of bodily experiences running parallel to our entire experience of spirit and, nestling closely against the latter. The consequences of this idea are generally not clearly seen by race theoreticians. This idea would not only mean that for any of the popular prime examples of "psychical" traits, such as musicality or the like, there is a corresponding physical condition, but it would also mean that there is a physical condition for every work of the mind, down to its smallest details, that, for example, every bold stroke of scoring in each of Bach's fugues and the content of every statement in the *Critique of Pure Reason* down to the choice of words and sentence structure is, if not completely determined by race, at least in any case determined by the body. Each train of thought, every insight, every shaping of each insight is paralleled by a series of physical processes. If we draw this conclusion—and I think we must—we will find ourselves driven to the point we have already seen repeatedly in the first chapter: we are faced with a reality, here the reality of the human mind, that, because of the characteristic construction of the total human being, has two "sides." We have *one* reality of being with two aspects—that of the mind and that of the body.

This is the situation of thought that is dealt with in the third antinomy of the *Critique of Pure Reason*. The causal series of reality in which events occur according to inescapable laws is the side of phenomena behind which the reality of the thing-in-itself [*Ding an sich*] free from natural causality takes place. The realm of freedom and that of constraint of the law collide at every point along the line without the law becoming freedom or freedom becoming subject to the law of nature. At the end of the logical extension of the thought that the mind is conditioned by the body we see that though this idea is well grounded, pursuing it to its logical conclusion has not given us any new insights into the nature of the mind. We have direct knowledge of the mind, knowledge not mediated by physical conditions—that is, we experience our thinking, our insights, our inspirations, our self-awareness, our will to shape intellectual worlds in works of science, art, the experience of God, the state—and all these experiences are independent and do not require support from our knowledge of the body. A "science of experience" claiming that the mind is not as it presents itself to us in our direct experience of it does not add to our knowledge of the mind but presents merely a collection of false judgments that contradict our everyday experience of the mind.

The majority of modern race theories are characterized by their failure to take the idea presented above to its logical conclusion. For race theory, certain traits and dispositions forming the basic framework of the mental type concerned are inheritable, while other mental traits within this framework, under the heading of tradition of acquired traits or education, are invested with a more or less clearly defined element of freedom. The separation of inheritable elements tied to the body from those, which, though their essence is not clearly defined, appear, in contrast, to be independent of the body, creates the illusion that this theory covers both the experience of the ineluctable tie to the blood inheritance [Bluterbe] and also the experience of the creative powers of the mind. The two aspects of all mental events as free and determined at the same time are reinterpreted into two spheres within the realm of the mind itself: one, comprising the basic hereditary factors, is declared not free, while the other, comprising individual processes within the type that are conditioned by the environment, is declared free and open to being influenced.

Before we penetrate deeper into the tangle of questions concerning psychical traits and their transmission, I want to point out that in this context the problems of the relationship between body, mind, and spirit cannot be presented fully. For didactic reasons we must be content with a few simple ordering lines to be drawn through this field and I am well aware that this simplification will lead to imprecision and discrepancies that knowledgeable readers are sure to notice. I have therefore made a point of speaking of the tie to the body as only *one* source of a sense of fatality, of the inevitability of our human existence. We are not individuals in the sense of self-enclosed, self-empowered [selbstmächtig] points of existence; rather, we have our place in the chain of generations that

67

stretches behind us and ahead of us into what we call infinity. As physical beings we are woven into a world context. Nevertheless, it would be wrong to think that because of this tie, which has its counterpart in the inner personality and freedom, our whole being can be easily sorted out along the lines of determination and freedom, as was implied in the train of thought presented above. In each of these realms, that of the body and that of the mind, we have experiences of constraint and freedom each unrelated to the other. The body is not only constraint but also a place of freedom, the spirit is not only freedom but also law. With our body we, like all animals, are part of the chain of procreation, not just passively but also and essentially actively. Our body is not only a passive recipient of impressions from the environment but also an active center of gestures and actions; it is powerful in that it is a center from which we reach out into the world with our body and initiate changes in the world. Our body is open to the world not only passively, accepting intrusions, but also actively, reaching out.

Conversely, the human mind is not pure activity, not only a center and source of action and power working upon the outside, not merely a shaper of the world—it is also passive, receptive. It is open to the world not only by reaching out and acting but also open as the place for the eruption of the spiritual reality that lies beyond the person. The mind has insights and inspirations. It is directly connected to the world ground [*Weltgrund*] and is embedded in the spiritual communities of all levels: from humanity and the nation down to the circle of family and close friends. Just as the basic experiences of being tied to the body develop historically in the ideas of the family as blood community, of kinship groups, of races, so the experiences of the determination of the mind develop in ideas of the personal demon, of the narrower communities, and the national spirit [*Volksgeist*].

If we take as our premise this deeper insight into the essence of body and mind, it becomes very difficult, if not impossible, to illustrate the relationship between the two areas as two aspects of the same stream of events. The parallelism we outlined first roughly corresponds to Kant's antinomy; the causal series and spontaneous events occur side by side—one is the series of phenomena; the other is the thing-in-itself [*Ding an sich*]. From a methodological point of view one could say that it is the task of all sciences of causality to find the lawfulness of all phenomena; however, this requirement would not have any consequences for the reality as thing-in-itself. We can study the law of phenomena without running the risk of making any statements about the ontic dependence of the mind on matter or the body. On the other hand, if we enter into the ontology of man or, as it is called today, philosophical anthropology, then our experiences of human dependence on the body in its passive aspect have their equal counterpart in experiences of human dependence on the mind in its peculiarly passive, receptive mode. Both kinds of experiences arise independently of each other from different directions of the total human being. Here, too—as we want to point out—there are still possibilities for a connecting construction, but they lie far beyond the scope of the arguments of race theory.

Talk of inherited and acquired characteristics gains its primary sense from a comparison of the characteristics of two creatures [*Animalia*] one of which is a descendant of the other. In a sense that still needs to be defined more precisely, characteristics they share can be inherited, diverging characteristics can be individually acquired. A more precise definition of this statement leads to the dialectical tangles that, for the time being, have found their conclusion in Woltereck's theory of reaction norms. Separating traits into those that are conditioned by genotype and those determined by environmental influences has shown itself to be methodologically inadequate. All traits arise from the interaction of genotype and environment—the hereditary ones require the environment to develop, and the so-called acquired traits would not appear as they do without a genetic predisposition. The reaction norm becomes the firm framework within which traits are categorized according to their constancy, that is, according to their recurrence over generations. The most constant traits appear over and over again, defining the species in Linnaeus' sense; the next group, that of the mutations, comprises constant traits that, as our experience has shown, make way for other constant traits; and the third group, that of the modifications, includes traits of so little constancy that we call them individual because we cannot ascertain the laws of their recurrence. The theory of reaction norms entertains no doubts that all these characteristics—even those for which we cannot find a law of recurrence—are genetically co-determined. Nor can any doubt on this point arise, because we are not dealing with matters of perception that could be invalidated by contradictory perceptions; rather, we are dealing with the dialectical structure of theory formation. The group defined by the reaction norm, then, includes traits of varying persistence in the hereditary process [*Erbgang*], which is not equally well understood in all cases. Not included are any traits that are not transmitted through germ plasm and thus are not hereditary in the narrow sense of the term.

In its discussion of the contrast between inherited and acquired characteristics, the reaction-norm theory, logically consistent, arrives at the conclusion that there are *only* hereditary characteristics—that is, traits determined by the structure of germ plasm; in its discussion of the question of organic and inorganic substances, the theory arrived at the dissolution of the concept of heredity as a science speaking of plasm and genotype as material concepts. Reaction norm is an inextensive variety—that is, a law of the formation of life-forms that, as such, is not accessible to sensory perception. Germ plasm and genetic structure are not passed down materially from one individual to the next in the succession of generations because the germ cells, like the organism as a whole, are subject to the processes of metabolism. Thus heredity is not the transmission of identical matter with a particular structure but a process of propagating reaction-identical life-forms. Essentially, we simply know nothing about this process, our knowledge of cell division, chromosomes, their combinations and crossovers, and the like notwithstanding. Nor can we know anything about it because what the methods of the natural sciences can grasp always concerns only the mechanism of the process but never the "inextensive" law. Empirically speaking, we see, on the one hand, the traits recurring with various degrees of constancy and, on the other hand, the mechanism of reproduction down to the genetic structure—theoretically, everything is wide open: we can just as easily believe that all the traits of an individual are completely determined as that an unknown power intervenes at each moment of conception, as that a life force whose general mode of action is predetermined newly fills a sphere of freedom in the formation of every individual, or as many other possibilities. But we must not deceive ourselves into believing that any of these assumptions has anything to do with science.

After this preparatory clarification of the basic concepts, we now turn our attention to the problem of the hereditary transmission of mental traits as the problem is viewed today. For this purpose we present first the fundamental methodical stance of the standard work on this topic, that of Lenz.[1]

§2. Soul, Mind, Culture (Lenz)

Fritz Lenz takes as point of departure for his study the experience of mental differences among people. The cultural world in which we live, he asserts, is shaped by the human mind, and people's aptitude for the preservation and continuation of culture differs widely. From "the genius to the idiot," every level of "intellectual talent" can be observed, and this holds true similarly for the differences in temperament and character. What is the cause, we must ask ourselves, underlying these indisputable differences? Lenz unhesitatingly answers: "For those who are used to thinking in biological terms, it is entirely obvious that a person's mental characteristics just as the physical ones have their roots in hereditary predisposition and that external influences, including upbringing, effect only a further development or inhibition of these hereditary predispositions. Thus the fact that differences in mental predisposition are hereditary is certain from the outset; the question is only how far (nonhereditary) environmental influences are able to modify these predispositions."[2]

This is the extent of Lenz's comments on the fundamentals, and before we consider his further corollary thoughts on this topic, let us be clear on what his statement means. Most importantly, Lenz concedes that "culture" and the human "mind" as its "shaper" are facts of experience. I would not do that if I had to defend his position; instead, from the outset I would fall back on an ontology and epistemology according to which all experience of the mind is merely an illusion and the terms in which we speak of this experience are merely abbreviating expressions for material processes on a higher plane. But Lenz not only acknowledges that experience

---

1. Fritz Lenz, "Die Erblichkeit der geistigen Begabung," in Erwin Baur, Erich Fischer, and Fritz Lenz, *Menschliche Erblichkeitslehre und Rassenhygiene* (3rd ed.; 1927), I.
2. *Ibid.*, 471.

as real, but he also considers the mental (culture-shaping) differences between people "incomparably more significant" than their physical differences. "Thus, because of its crucial significance for human culture, the theory of psychological heredity is the focal point of the theory of heredity as a whole." Though Lenz does not say more on the subject, the explicit acknowledgment of the significance of the mind and its creation, culture, surely must be based on a philosophy—or, in the case of Lenz, let us call it a worldview— that considers mind and culture as the specific, indeed defining, human reality and the meaning of human existence. However, Lenz does not discuss the structure and laws of the mind in more detail in these introductory remarks; he lists briefly the levels of intellectual talent (that is all genius amounts to?), temperament, and character.

What Lenz has to say about heredity fits poorly with the recognition of the mind and its higher significance compared to the body. The mental characteristics are completely determined by hereditary predisposition and thus outside the sphere of the mind; environmental influences and upbringing can only promote or inhibit but not change the basic structure that is determined as though by a law of nature. However, if the mind is not mind but nature, and is subordinated to its laws, what then is the status of its dignity and its higher significance compared to the body? Is "mind" then nothing more than a phenomenon of nature, like colors, smells, minerals, planets, plants, and animals? And is one part of this nature set above the others and "more significant" than the others? Lenz does not say anything about this.

Let us proceed: the structure of the mind is subdivided into hereditary disposition and environmental influences; the individual mental characteristics of a person arise out of the interplay of genotype and environment (including upbringing). The basic mental experiences of activity in creating and of passivity in inspiration are swept away with a wave of the hand. "The idea that in the 'genius' creative activity without cause and independent of hereditary disposition and environment reveals itself cannot be supported by rational grounds or facts."[3] This does not amount to much, after all, and is, perhaps, a little bold in view of numerous

3. *Ibid.*, 473.

documents, reaching back through the millennia, in which mystics, poets, and philosophers have recorded their experiences of the mind. Plato's theory of ideas, Christ's mission, Paul's conversion, the confessions of Saint Augustine, Pascal's *mémorial*—all of it "irrational" prattle—of no interest to people as clever as we are today and at best something for scholars in the humanities [*Geisteswissenschaftler*] who, as we all know, are a bunch of con men: "While in the field of certain 'humanities' fame can on occasion still be attained, as it was at the time of Schelling and Hegel, by grand words and magical style, this danger hardly arises in the field of the natural sciences."[4]

Lenz is at least consistent; he must deny the essence of the mind, its activity and passivity, if he wants to pursue the idea of hereditary disposition and its reaction to environmental influences. Nonetheless, the opposing view that the mind has a higher value than the body remains intact—a view that, in my opinion, cannot be supported "by rational grounds and facts" if the mind is simply a natural phenomenon like any other.

Now how does a natural scientist deal with the characteristics of the mind? He is forced to concede with regret that, "unfortunately this [the theory of psychological heredity] is also the most difficult subdivision of it [the theory of heredity], because the traits and dispositions of the soul can hardly be measured and are also otherwise difficult to grasp." But for Lenz this is not a major impediment to their study because "aside from this, however, the method of the study of psychological heredity is exactly the same as that of the other studies of human heredity."[5] For example, mental characteristics are presented as follows: The philosopher: "The philosopher requires an unerring sense for truth that does not falter in the face of painful truths. The creative thinker must also have the strength to keep free of the prejudices of the day."[6] Thus, he must not, for instance, simply because he is "accustomed" to thinking in biological terms, cling to this favorite habit, but must— "free of the prejudices of the day" and above all free of his day-to-day scientific concerns—confront the phenomena of the mind. In this case, as Lenz so brilliantly remarks, "even the 'spirit of oppo-

4. *Ibid.*, 486.
5. *Ibid.*, 471.
6. *Ibid.*, 485.

sition,' which is generally, and not without reason, disliked by all authorities, can possibly be conducive to knowledge."[7]

But now we come to artists and their characteristics: "The creative artist and the poet must possess a lively imagination and creative power and the capacity to empathize with the souls of other people." This is perhaps not too felicitously put, but there is truth in it, thinks the reader; though the artist may not have to empathize with the souls of other people to create his works, he surely must have experienced the powers of soul and spirit to create his works from this material—some may even believe that the descriptions of these experiences are the only truly exact ones. But however that may be—it was not meant that way. When Lenz claims that artists must be able to empathize with the souls of others, he does so out of concern for the artist's external success. These considerations follow from the major premise of the entire subsequent discussions: "The beautiful is whatever pleases people." No one will dispute the conclusion: "That is why the artist must instinctively sense what will please the public." In order to sense this, the artist must be able to empathize with other people, who thus turn out to be the public for whom he creates his works. If the man, then, is sufficiently able to empathize, his artistic success is indeed assured; but in another way he once again falls short, since a man so constituted "can hardly also be a great thinker or researcher."[8]

After these basic discussions on the nature of the mind, an easier path is opened for a scientific treatment of the subject. What is the hallmark of the great man in the realm of the mind? Where must we look for material if we want to investigate whether and how outstanding talents are inherited? We have to look wherever we find major achievements actuated by the desire for recognition [Trieb zur Geltung]. The characteristics relevant to the art are not sufficient by themselves for cultural achievement: good physical health is necessary too, because "without it continuous mental work is hardly possible"; furthermore, "a lively interest in a subject" is indispensable, and finally the strong drive "to make one's name, kindled by a strong spiritual or material will to power." According to Lenz, it is not good to speak of "vanity" or "ambition"

7. *Ibid.*, 485ff.
8. *Ibid.*, 486.

in this context; it is better to use the neutral term "desire for recognition." Should someone object that achievements actuated by this desire, cannot be the expression of true greatness, then the exact scientist must counter: "Greatness in this sense is a value concept that cannot be defined in scientific terms. What we can determine is mostly only fame."[9] Apparently fame is not a value concept for Lenz. Consequently, he understands the ambiguous *fama* in the sense that it is greater or smaller in accordance with the number of people familiar with a man and his work. However, this would lead us to conclusions that perhaps even Lenz, the connoisseur of culture, might not approve of—how does the number of copies published of Paul Valéry's or Stefan George's works, for example, compare to those of Edgar Wallace's books? Does a great man automatically become greater simply because thirty years after his death his works are made available in cheap editions to a larger public? Lenz would object at this point, claiming that "greatness" is determined not merely by the quantity but also by the quality of those who make this judgment. This would bring us to the authorities—that is, in this case the experts, who are competent to pass a reasoned value judgment concerning mental characteristics. So something of value is present in fame after all? If it were not so, why would the scientist, indifferent to values, be so resentful of Hegel's and Schelling's indisputable fame? That fame should rather be an incentive for him to study precisely these men in his research on heredity, but Lenz actually and explicitly advises against this, recommending instead of these windbags men of more reliable fame, such as Gauss, Helmholtz, Boltzmann, Planck, and Einstein as proper subjects for genealogical research.[10]

After all these doubts we come to a statement that offers us the opportunity for a conciliatory conclusion: "Worldly success and fame do not, of course, depend only on objective achievement, but especially also on an impressive manner, an instinctive feeling for what will make an impression, and a knack for written expression or eloquence, as well as cleverness, a talent for acting, and lack of scruples."[11] As befits the scientist, this judgment is presented in the form of a general law, to which Lenz, with the philosopher's

9. *Ibid.*
10. *Ibid.*
11. *Ibid.*

75

"unerring sense for truth that does not falter in the face of painful truths," will surely not mind to subordinate himself. But at this point I want to contradict him in opposition to his authority and at the risk of becoming—and not without reason—unpopular. His fame is not quite so precarious. The parts of his work in which Lenz deals with the mind and its characteristics are of much smaller proportions than the others, in which he exhibits his extensive knowledge of the material.

§3. Characteristics and Traits (Scheidt)

The analysis of Lenz's thinking has shown in an exemplary way how the current theory of heredity views the problems of the mind and its characteristics. After all, the subject of our analysis was, as I want to stress once again the standard work of recent scholarship. Now we will go beyond the basics to analyze a specific question that is important in terms of method, namely, the question of characteristics and traits, best discussed by Walter Scheidt.

In Scheidt's methodologically very orderly inquiry, the expressions *characteristic, inherited characteristic, predispositions*, and *inherited predispositions* are all used as synonyms for the concept of the gene. "The something that is evidently transmitted from the parents to the children is called 'genes' (singular, 'gene') or hereditary factors."[12] The genes are the units of substance on the chromosomal threads of the germ cell, and they are considered the inner determinants of an organism's form in all its parts. Therefore the word "characteristic," strictly speaking, refers to a piece of matter or substance with particular reactions. And that is why Scheidt also offers the definition "that characteristics are merely reactions through which in response to particular external stimulation particular traits are formed."[13] Scheidt himself has fairly precisely outlined his position in the field of speculation. Hereditary factors or genes are for him the carriers of the supraindividual phenomenon of life. The individual consists, on the one hand, of parts that are truly individual, unrepeatable, and unique because due to environmental influences, and, on the other, of supraindividual parts that

12. Walter Scheidt, *Allgemeine Rassenkunde* (Munich, 1925), 97. See also pp. 99, 327.
13. *Ibid.*, 180.

are not only repeatable but basically repeatable arbitrarily, namely, the genetic substances. The genetic substances, each of which is "not subject to inevitable death," however, are practically joined in a particular combination in each germ, and thus several individuals can share a large number of hereditary factors. Nevertheless, because of the great number of elements combined, the overall combination is unlikely to be duplicated, except in the case of identical twins.[14]

Thus, from the "inside" the individual is completely determined by the hereditary factors and their combination. Humanity, then, is a variety of combinations of immortal genes; nothing essentially new can appear. What creates the illusion of newness are (always leaving aside environmental influences) new arrangements in the play of combinations. In this context the problem of genotype variation completely recedes into the background for Scheidt. Nor is Woltereck's line of thinking, which leads to the theory of the reaction norm, pursued. A series of vague expressions covers up the inevitable question of what exactly is transmitted from the parents to their offspring if the material, the germ substance, does not itself remain identical. Scheidt states that the hereditary factors can be "transmitted"; then they are "just as present" in the offspring as in the parents; therefore many people may have part of their hereditary factors "in common," and so forth.[15] All these expressions stop one step short of the one that led Woltereck to the separation of changing substance from the "inextensive variety" of the reaction norm. Scheidt thus develops the concept of characteristics to a level of clarity where he defines it unequivocally as an amount of substance with particular reactions, but not to a level that would unequivocally show that the genes of the parents and those of the descendants are identical in substance or in the inextensive variety or that they are evolving substances, that is, substances that became individualized and unrepeatably unique within a particular framework, the species.

The interplay of environmental influences and the characteristics as defined above produces the traits, which are the components of the human phenotype. Characteristics and traits are synonyms

14. Walter Scheidt, *Kulturbiologie: Vorlesungen für Studierende aller Wissensgebiete* (Jena, 1930), 12–13.
15. *Ibid.*, 12.

for idiotypical and phenotypical constituents. An unequivocal, reversible connection between characteristics and traits cannot be established because numerous traits—for example skin color, which is so important for race theory—are polymers, that is, they are brought about by a larger number of genes or characteristics. Hence, to be methodologically correct, race would have to be defined as a group of characteristics selected within the species.[16] The definition of a race according to a group of traits is not useful, Scheidt notes, since individuals varying widely in phenotype can nevertheless share the same genetic factors. It is therefore also methodologically incorrect to speak of hereditary traits of body or soul, for only characteristics can be inherited, and Scheidt chooses the more correct expression of traits of body and soul conditioned by heredity.[17]

Now while the study of physical traits in their determination through heredity is comparatively simple, since physical traits can for the most part be described more or less clearly—colors, proportions, skull measurements, and the like—"when it comes to the psychical traits, we are frequently in no position to define exactly what we are dealing with."[18] Very much like Lenz, Scheidt also begins his study by complaining about the intangibility of the object on which judgment is to be pronounced. But Scheidt probes more deeply into the reason for this difficulty than Lenz tried to do. Though the psychical traits themselves evade our grasp, their existence can be deduced from the behavior of the carrier of these traits. The trait of "reserve," for example, manifests itself in taciturn, withdrawn behavior, "endurance" in unflagging pursuit of goals, and so forth.[19] Folklore, ethnology, and history give us comprehensive descriptions of performance [*Leistungsbeschreibungen*], and from the performances we can deduce the capabilities that gave rise to them.[20] "*Performance as the measure of behavior* primarily represents the object immediately accessible to observation when dealing with the soul's traits. Concerning these traits, statistics on

16. Scheidt, *Rassenkunde*, 327–28.
17. See, for example, *Rassenkunde*, the chapter title on page 433. It is true that elsewhere (for example, page 435) Scheidt speaks of psychological characteristics and race characteristics.
18. *Ibid.*, 433.
19. *Ibid.*
20. *Ibid.*, 435.

heredity and statistics of populations tracking the accumulation of traits can capture 'traits' only to a small degree (traits are often not accessible to description, either in general or in detail) and to a greater degree those performances from which (with certain precautions) traits or 'capabilities' can be deduced."[21] In this context it is crucial to what extent performance and behavior allow us to draw any conclusions about traits, and, of such conclusions are permissible, whether those "certain precautions" are applied.

Scheidt does not deal with this question in great detail. He describes his fundamental position in somewhat vague terms. To allay the concerns that must arise when the subject of the study is not given, he points to the analogous situation in studying characteristics in relation to physical traits. Until now no one has "seen" the hereditary factors for skin color or even determined or estimated their amount, and yet it is certain that they exist, he argues. Analogously, until now no one has been able to describe the trait or traits that, in the form of "abilities," enable someone to express himself in music, and yet they must exist because there is no other explanation for the performances we can clearly see.[22] At first glance, there are many reasons why this analogy does not hold. In the theory of characteristics as the "inner" determinants of the life form at least the object of the investigation is clearly defined as far as its ontic sphere is concerned—it is a piece of matter of a particular construction—and fundamentally accessible to sensory perception. If the genes, as they are understood by most scientists of heredity, cannot actually be perceived directly, this is due to technical reasons. But what, in contrast, the "psychical" traits are supposed to be in a theory that aims at denying the existence of soul and spirit is incomprehensible. Furthermore, the theory of genes is by no means as unequivocal and definitive as Scheidt presents it. For example, Woltereck maintains, based on the finding that the majority of all mutations are pathological and some even lethal, that the sites on the chromosome strings that have been found in studies of *Drosophila* to be causally connected to mutations of traits can justifiably be interpreted as fault sites [*Störungsstellen*]. However, from the existence of such fault sites we can

21. *Ibid.,* 434–35.
22. *Ibid.,* 435.

locate, it does not follow that these same sites have a positive function in the appearance of the unchanged traits. This is an argument, I might add, that applies equally to all "localizations," including those on the brain, that are based on the pathology of life phenomena. And finally we must rigorously deny that psychical faculties must be assumed to exist "because there simply is no other explanation for our empirical observations."[23] The "explanation" given by race theoreticians typically consists of assuming a corresponding "faculty" for every cultural achievement. There are people who create works of music, and therefore there must be the faculty for music; since there are statesmen, there must be a talent for statesmanship; because there are poets, there is a talent for poetry; there are technical-practical achievements, therefore a predisposition toward intelligence and a talent for invention; and so on. It seems to me that explanations of this sort are due to the fact that race theoreticians do not base their statements about phenomena of the mind on humanistic inquiries into the fine arts, poetry, religious experiences, music, and the like and we, in fact, are not familiar with them at all. And I believe that if they were to try, with the help of these empirical investigations, to get a clear idea of what a painting, a figure, or a poem is, if they would for once confront the problem of why a Shakespearean sonnet is a poem while formally quite perfect verses by Wilhelm von Humboldt constitute a non-poem—then the problem of psychical faculties in race theory would at once look very different. The barbaric notion that Dante and Beethoven were pretty talented guys surely would disappear; perhaps race theoreticians would then even get an inkling that for man as a spiritual being spirit is an "environment" of the same reality the environment is for man as an animal.

It is only right to acknowledge that Scheidt indeed has an inkling of many things. The faculties that are inferred from performance—for example, musical or mathematical talents—do not seem to him a sufficient explanation even when they are broken down into their components. He notes that especially when it comes to the achievements of genius, qualities of "character" have to be included in the explanation. Of course, evaluating or describing character is incomparably more difficult than intellectual tal-

23. *Ibid.*

ents, for example, because the latter "still can be more or less un-equivocally measured in particular performances."[24] But even though this new object, the "character," is again defined on the same pattern as the other capabilities (except that it is more diffi-cult to deal with), even though it is considered to be merely one more additional ingredient in the total arrangement of dispositions, we nevertheless find the following very cheering sentence: "If we focus our observations on the will power and circumspection of a military commander of genius and on the so-called actual mathe-matical aptitude of a mathematical genius, this is a one-sided over-estimation of these special dispositions insofar as by themselves they may perhaps have been sufficient to produce a competent of-ficer or a skilled mathematics professor, but certainly not to form-ing the hereditary basis of a genius."[25]

To conclude this section on psychical characteristics, let me add a brief reference to the wealth of problems that is by no means concealed here but is revealed in its full extent. The question of "characteristics" is of practical concern primarily to graphology. I will give a few citations from a chapter entitled "About Character-istics that Are Not Characteristics," in Ludwig Klages' work.[26]

Even some professional psychologists have not yet freed themselves from the fundamental error of believing in the existence of *the* talent of military command, *the* artistic talent, *the* poetic talent, *the* politi-cal talent, *the* acting talent, and so on although there is not and cannot be any such thing. Hannibal, Frederick the Great, and Napoleon were three battle commanders who were incomparably above average: they may have been so because they shared several or at least one faculty, but they may just as well have been so as the result of entirely differ-ent gifts. Everyone sees that in the case of several armies, one might be destined to be victorious because of the strength of its power of resistance, another because of the swiftness of its movements, a third because of the thrust of its attacks, a fourth because of cunning as-saults, the fifth by superior skill in the use of arms. Consequently, there must be a much larger number of mental dispositions, each of which would offer a more than usual guarantee of strategic successes! Not even the great chess masters are what they are *necessarily* be-cause of the same talent. Some among them win almost exclusively

24. *Ibid.*, 447.
25. *Ibid.*, 49.
26. Ludwig Klages, ed., *Graphologisches Lesebuch: Hundert Gutachten aus der Praxis unter Mitwirkung von Fachgenossen* (Leipzig, 1930).

thanks to their wealth of brilliant insights, and then again some triumph just as exclusively by their ability to anticipate combinations. How much more will we have to consider the possibility of completely different reasons for a talent in such undertakings with infinitely more associations, such as building, painting, waging war, and the like![27]

The same analysis applied to the faculties here cited, which are assumed to exist because certain achievements cannot be "explained" otherwise, holds true also for those classifications that aim at categorizing types of behavior, such as reliability, trustworthiness, loyalty, righteousness, gratitude, devotion, honesty, adaptability. Let us add Klages' analysis of this last type:

> Let us say that someone is very adaptable. If we investigate more closely, we find that he is cautious, ambitious, skillful and has smooth manners. One *consequence* of all these is his talent of adapting. Let us say that another man is equally adaptable. Our investigation shows that he *lacks* ambition and is very good-natured. A consequence of *these* can also be a capacity for adapting. Here we have the same result in both cases even though the two characters not only are dissimilar but are even more or less opposites.
>
> With this, however, our considerations are by no means concluded. The *gift* for adapting is one thing, the *will* to adapt another. Both can be present in equal measure, and that is perhaps the more frequent case. But it is also possible that only the will to adapt is present, without an equal amount of the gift for it, *and* finally, we can find the gift for adaptation in the absence of an equivalent will to adapt. For example, if we combined a *very* strong drive for independence with a lack of ambition and great good-naturedness, the will to adaptation would be smaller than the gift to adapt; on the other hand, if we combined good-naturedness and lack of ambition with considerable awkwardness and shy reserve, then the gift for adaptation would lag behind the will to adapt.[28]

In general we recommend that those who have so much to say about spirit and soul read, among other things, some works by Klages—not in order to adopt his theories but simply to learn what they are actually dealing with.

27. *Ibid.*, 40.
28. *Ibid.*, 39.

§4. The Psychical Type of a Race (Lenz, Günther)

The crowning achievement of a good race theory is the listing of the psychical types of the major races. The procedural difficulties of this undertaking are sufficiently clear from the analyses presented above. Scheidt's carefully constructed theory makes it clear that in the scientific study of race the concept of characteristics must be strictly confined to genetic structure, and what are usually called soul-characteristics would be better designated as traits—even though Scheidt himself, as some of the passages cited above show, did not abide strictly by the terminology and usage he introduced, and instead of speaking of psychical traits conditioned by heredity, he simply calls them soul-characteristics. We have no wish to be more Catholic than the Pope nor to insist as lowly scholars of the humanities on a degree of precision in terminology that the solid scientists consider unnecessary. We will therefore below also speak of soul-characteristics in the sense of traits as defined by Scheidt, and will use the less ambiguous technical terms *gene* and *genetic structure* for the characteristics or hereditary predispositions.

Let us now ask ourselves under which of these categories we are to subsume the "characteristics" enumerated in the theory of racial types. Neither Lenz nor Günther—whose type-formations we will adopt, as they are the most comprehensive and basic—intend to supply an analysis of genetic structure in its causative role in the development of the soul-characteristics of a race. The study of human genetic structure and its effect on physical traits has not achieved any results that can even remotely be compared to the localization in *Drosophila* chromosomes, and about soul-characteristics we know absolutely nothing. The next possibility would be to formulate the characteristics themselves in terms of type concepts—but this effort will not be undertaken either because it would require that we know what a characteristic of the human soul is in the first place. To know this, however, we would need a fully developed characterology and psychology of mind, and, as is well known, both these sciences are still in their infancy. I have referred to Klages in order to remind the reader that in response to the requirements of graphology, a theory of character has developed that has produced considerable findings but is still very

83

far from offering completely satisfactory results. The passages cited above were meant merely to call attention to some problems that open up anew with every term used to designate a characteristic; without working through them thoroughly a characterological type theory [*Typenlehre*] of man is impossible. Perhaps I may be permitted in this context to refer to my inquiry into the form of the American mind. As far as I know, that was the first attempt to create a precise instrument for dealing with mental types.[29] In that work I chose the dialectical structure of speculation on time as the basis of type formation; and the national mental types were distinguished according to the arrangement of the philosophical problems in this dialectical field. Without saying more about the outcome here, already the restriction to such a narrow field as the basis for type formation shows *what* there is to be examined and worked through in order to acquire the equipment for a theory of types! Of this entire class of problems pertaining to mental styles that prove themselves in the shaping of a mental field—and which must be made the subject of a far-reaching empirical science—the race theory of psychical types has as little to say as of its types' character structure based on a characterology. Indeed, it cannot have anything to say about these things because the sciences required for establishing race types simply do not yet exist in a form that would permit their simple application to such diverse and complex areas as the soul of a race [*Rassenseele*]. Types of characteristics in any conceivable sense grounded in a theory of science are likewise not defined. And so we must ask the further question: What takes the place of scientific inquiry in the theory of psychological types within race theory?

In the work of Lenz and Günther the so-called psychological types are made up of two principal classes of data: (1) the data of the intellectual history of nations collected through a more or less thorough general education and incompletely understood; in these data the physical types of the races are clearly recognizable; and (2) data from so-called social-anthropological studies. These are statistical studies of the "talents" of people of a particular physical racial type and are based on school reports and intelligence tests.

29. Eric Voegelin, *Über die Form des amerikanischen Geistes* (Tübingen, 1928). [Published in English under the title *On the Form of the American Mind* (Baton Rouge, 1995).]

In each case the point of departure of the inquiry is the race's physical type; as a real-ontological a priori, it is assumed that every physical type has a corresponding psychological type, and the data mentioned above are then rhapsodically assigned to this physical type. We do not need to go into more detail; otherwise our critique would turn into an exhausting repetition of applications of the premises we developed above. We will therefore limit ourselves to a few forays into the Nordic types established by Lenz and Günther, since these are presented with the most care and devotion with the greatest wealth of illustrative material. First a few examples of the type established by Lenz.

"The Nordic race has created the Indogermanic (Aryan) languages and cultures."[30] As evidence he lists: India, Persia, the teachings of Zoroaster, ancient Hellenic culture, the Roman Empire, the Germanic empires, the German Empire of the Middle Ages, the Renaissance brought about by the Lombards, the Spanish Golden Age and the empire of Charles V created by the Visigoths, the maritime superiority of the Dutch, Sweden under Gustav Adolf and Charles XII, the British Empire, and the colonization of North America. In the Byzantine Empire, however, "which was overrun not by Nordic tribes but by the Mongolian Turks, no Renaissance came to flower."[31] The name of Reibmayr and his theory that the flowering of a culture can occur only through a mixture of races to which *both* of the mixing races contribute is never mentioned.

Some "characteristics" are granted to the Nordic race without further ado: creative mental powers, high intelligence, outstanding character traits, steadiness of will and caring foresight, self-control, pursuit of objective goals over the long term as well as a talent for technology and mastering of nature, love for the sea (which the race shares with tribes of related races, such as the closely related Phoenicians and Polynesians), a gift for the fine arts, architecture, and profound research, "northern boldness," the "pathos of distance," aristocratic reserve, honesty, sincerity, cleanliness, the rare appearance of lice (because of its cleanliness, for example, "Sweden probably has the world's highest level of culture"), love of nature. The Nordic type is inclined to Protestantism and to speculations,

30. Lenz, "Erblichkeit," in Baur, Fischer, and Lenz, *Menschliche Erblichkeitslehre*, 540.
31. *Ibid.*, 541.

albeit only reasonable ones, while "that 'German Idealism' that indulges in magical words and vague phrases" is not an expression of the Nordic mind.[32]

The minor drawbacks—inadequate musical talent (which Günther, however, grants in his description of Nordic man), inferior capacity to empathize with other people, dry-heartedness, and so on—we can pass over, and rush to the conclusion: "I do not believe it is an exaggeration to say that when it comes to mental gifts the Nordic race marches at the head of humanity."[33]

In concluding our discussion of this topic, we want to reassure the reader once more that we have not the least doubt that there are connections between body, soul, and mind; we are fully convinced that blood inheritance is of paramount importance to man's total spiritual nature; but we are equally convinced that this significance can be discovered only by the most thorough inquiry into the mental structure itself and not by joining bits and pieces from a smattering of knowledge into a pseudoscientific edifice.[34]

The situation is not much better when it comes to the data furnished by statistics based on school report cards and tests, and indeed for the same reason why the rhapsodic type formations fail. There is certainly something being tested that is labeled "intelligence" or "talent," and no doubt it is of great significance for the person being tested as far as making his way in modern urban civi-

---

32. *Ibid.*, 552.
33. *Ibid.*, 547.
34. We will deal with the content of Günther's typological concept of psychological characteristics of the Nordic race in Part II of this book. Here it is enough to note that Günther posits "core characteristics" [*Kerneigenschaften*]: discernment, truthfulness, initiative; others are grouped around these in a plausible arrangement. Discernment, for example, is the center from which emanate the sense of justice, a tendency to fragmentation [*Zersplitterung*], objectivity, imperviousness to hackneyed expressions, skepticism, a toughminded sense of reality, mistrust of strangers, a not very conciliatory nature, and so forth. This process makes it amply clear that any effort to prove heredity has been abandoned—it is a matter of loosely sketching a type of traits of character, soul, ethics, and so forth; these traits can be vaguely grouped around very generally defined basic traits. However, the connection between the traits is not always logical, for example, discernment supposedly leads to lack of human warmth. The two characteristics, one pertaining to the intellect and the other to the soul, are completely unrelated. Here the lack of a theory of mind and character makes itself felt. The same is true for the statement, "Given his disposition [for discernment], he easily grasps the concept of duty." Why? Could he not just as easily grasp his advantage and turn into a cunning scoundrel? Overall, however, Günther's typology is better thought out than Lenz's. Günther, *Rassenkunde des deutschen Volkes* (15th ed.; Munich, 1930).

lization is concerned. But what these actually are, defined in the terms of a characterology or a well-grounded psychology of the mind, cannot be ascertained. I will select two cases in an effort to choose the most convincing ones, the ones seemingly least contestable; I will not discuss those whose shortcomings are all too obvious.

The first is the case of a set of identical twins, two girls, separated at the age of two weeks because their mother died giving birth. The children were raised in different families (the case occurred in America). Thus we have the ideal case of two human beings with the same genetic blueprint raised in different environments. If in spite of the different environments and their very different paths in life the "talents" of the two are "the same" when they are adults, there is a great probability that the similarity is due to the same hereditary factors and that their surroundings and their development as determined by external factors are less significant by comparison. The expected result was actually observed—given the Alpha Test used by the American army, one twin scored 156, the other 153 points. The more precise Otis Test resulted in 64 points for one, 62 for the other. "The probability of two persons coincidentally performing so similarly in aptitude tests is less than 1:2,500."[35]

However, if this case were constructed with methodological rigor, it would have to include the following analyses: (1) The composition of the two environments would have to be meticulously described with regard to the question whether their impact on the same predispositions—and indeed on specifically which predispositions—would be likely to foster widely differing characteristics. And (2) it would have to be shown in detail that the design of the two tests makes them suited to capture the differences in the matured predisposition that have potentially developed in these two environments or whether the tests are not in fact designed to filter out the differences like a sieve and capture only those characteristics that were developed by possible similarities in the two environments. A very close examination of the relationship between the test design and the structure of the environment is clearly needed.

35. *Ibid.*, 493.

After everything we have heard so far, it almost goes without saying that these basic questions of methodology have not even been addressed. Of one of the environments in this case it is reported that the adoptive parents are members of the working class, that the girl raised in this milieu went to school for four years, then worked as a shop clerk and secretary, that because of her work she traveled a great deal, even abroad. The other girl was raised on a farm, went through secondary school and college, became a teacher, married, and had a child. The relevant differences are considered to be: the working-class family versus the farm and the differences in schooling and work experience. These facts (they are all Lenz has to say on the subject; perhaps the original documents on which he bases his discussion contain more) are, in my opinion, completely irrelevant. An American worker is not necessarily a proletarian in our sense, a farmer is not a peasant; the environments of a working-class family and a farming family can be entirely alike in their effect on the formation of intellectual and emotional traits. The same magazines can be read in the one and in the other, in both milieus people may listen to the same radio programs, the Sunday sermons may have the same depth and content; community life may be organized along the same lines; attitudes toward intellectual and political questions may be identical; manners and customs of eating and dress may be similarly standardized; speech habits may be the same. The development and polishing of predispositions that one twin experienced thanks to a higher level of schooling may be more than made up for by the other's professional activities and travels abroad; in short, nothing supports the conclusion that the different environments in fact differed in any way relevant to the development of predispositions. Finally, that the relationship of the test design to the structure of the environment could be a problem does not follow from this case cited by Lenz.

Let me repeat once more that with this analysis I do not mean to deny that similarity of the genotype is of immeasurable importance for psychological and mental development. I do not need evidence to be firmly convinced that environmental influences cannot make a genius out of a fool and that they cannot turn a great mind into a fool though they may stunt his development. I merely want to point out the naivete of these studies masquerading as science.

The other case concerns the aptitude tests given to American recruits during the First World War. These tests were meant to show that Negroes are less gifted than whites and that among the white draftees of European descent, those from northern and western Europe attain considerably higher scores than those from eastern and southern nations. I do not wish to go into too much detail. The white soldiers born in America had average scores of 58.9, the Negroes from the southern states, 12.4. To understand these scores that so brilliantly reveal the superiority of the white race, I will only note that per capita education expenditures in the southern states are many times higher for white students, sometimes as much as seven times higher, than for colored students. We *may* be able to deduce how strong environmental influences are in this case from the fact that though the southern Negroes scored only an average of 12.4, those from the northern states, where education is better, scored as high as 38.6.[36]

The aptitude figures for recruits born in Europe show overwhelming superiority among the English, Scottish, Dutch, and Germans. Russians, Italians, and Poles come away with the worst scores. Here, though, even Lenz had second thoughts since the "Russians" and "Poles" are mostly Jews, and given all other proof we have of their abilities, it is hardly conceivable that just these men would be the most stupid. In addition to the disadvantaged social situation of this segment of the population, therefore, we must also take into account, as Lenz puts it, "that the Beta Tests, which are tailored to concrete aptitudes, are little suited to the Jews' abstract talents."[37] Here at least the problem of the relationship between test design and the structure of traits tested is touched on; at the same time this sentence casts a glaring light on the value of tests tailored to particular types of aptitudes as a result of which all other skills appear as non-aptitudes.[38]

---

36. On attempts to prove that the results obtained so far are faulty because of the testing methods themselves, see the summarizing speech by Franz Boas in *Rasse und Kultur* (Jena, 1932) and the literature cited therein.

37. Lenz, "Erblichkeit," 546.

38. In order to understand the importance of these procedural questions, we must recall the social reality underlying them. For example, one time I visited a chemistry class in a school in New York where instruction was given by having the children do experiments at small work stations; one boy fiddled around helplessly and desperately although according to the teacher he was the hardest-working and brightest student in the class in languages and abstract subjects. If this boy were given an aptitude test measuring skill in the handling of objects, he would fail completely

The pointlessness of this procedure has been expressed very clearly by Ludwig Clauss in the following sentences:

Aptitudes are "measured" in part by mechanical procedures, in part by school reports, and the average for every race is statistically calculated or estimated, whereupon each race is then given a kind of report card. The races are compared with each other according to their average amount of aptitudes and—since, it goes without saying, the learned censor himself does not belong to any race but floats above all races—arranged in a system of merit, in a hierarchy according to which one race is ranked as more gifted than another. If we were to ask *for what* a race is gifted—after all, it will hardly be gifted per se but must have a gift for this or that—the answer is that it has a gift for "culture." Should it really have escaped even the brighter minds that there exists not simply *one* culture but many, fundamentally different from each other because each is the result of a different type of soul and is thoroughly governed by the law of style pertaining to this type [*artliches Stilgesetz*] (or a combination of several laws of style)? The suspicion suggests itself that those scholars weighing and measuring the aptitudes of the various races do so using *one particular* culture as their touchstone. This culture is given preeminence over all other cultures and is equated with culture as such; it is made the norm of culture and becomes a standard for all types. Thus, those people have mental aptitudes who have aptitudes for *this* culture. If we take a closer look at what this culture is like, lo and behold, we find that what is meant is . . . the culture that derives from the Nordic soul. Consequently the result of aptitude tests must be that the Nordic race is the most gifted of all; the others are more or less gifted— or rather, have no aptitude at all for this (Nordic) culture. That the Nordic race has the greatest aptitude for its own culture is surely as self-evident as is the truth that every human being knows his native language better than all other languages. To come to this realization did not require so many experiments, so much statistical data, and so much scholarly perspicacity as a number of scholars have expended.[39]

§5. Race as Form Idea [*Gestalt-Idee*] (Clauss)

The reason why the doctrine of psychical race types as espoused by Lenz and Günther is inadequate is its lack of insight into the nature

---

and perhaps be classified as a hereditary cretin. (This is, consciously or unconsciously, the purpose of applying aptitude tests to Negroes, who according to their psychical type cannot respond positively to such tests.)

39. Ludwig Ferdinand Clauss, *Von Seele und Antlitz der Rassen und Völker: Eine Einführung in die vergleichende Ausdrucksforschung.* (Munich, 1919), 95–96.

of the object under investigation. No matter how interesting the material is that is compiled, it has no scientific value because the goal of the investigation remains vague. The works of Ludwig Clauss, to which we now turn, differ from all other contemporary race studies in that the author is very clear about the object under discussion. All Clauss's writings are informed by his fundamental knowledge that "soul-characteristics" cannot be things that somehow float independently of each other in an indescribable sphere; rather, the unity of the soul and its kind is the framework necessary so that something like characteristics of the soul can become visible in the first place. "Unless his language is confused by scientific terminology, anyone who speaks of race does not refer to a collection of characteristics but to something that *pervades* the *entire being* of a living creature and that therefore naturally manifests itself in every artificially isolated detail—in other words, an inner law."[40] No matter how important the individual characteristics may be, this inner law must be understood.

The ontological nature of the substance whose inner law is to be investigated is described by Clauss with almost, but not quite, complete clarity. The kinds of souls in question, he claims, are types— that is, form ideas manifest themselves in individual people, become evident in them as the law of style pervading their souls. In Clauss's works the "ideas" are not a pallid synonym for thoughts but ideas in the Platonic sense. "The capacity of seeing ideas—ideas in the Platonic sense, as primordial images of beings—constitutes the best part of the human capacity for knowledge." People who are permeated by the same kind of soul, the same form idea, constitute a race in the empirical sense.[41] Within this realm of ideas, however, the ideas are arranged in a variety of ways whose internal order Clauss does not present consistently. He exemplifies the nature of the form idea first with the idea, the primordial image of the human individual. In this sense the idea is, "so to speak, the plan according to which this individual person is formed and which he now (perhaps imperfectly) embodies." The idea here is identical with the singular person of the individual, as it unfolds more or less completely in the concrete course of a person's life.[42] But a philoso-

40. *Ibid.*, x.
41. *Ibid.*, 59.

phy of the individual person cannot serve as the basis for a race theory that deals with collectives of persons of the same kind. The concept of the form idea must therefore take on the further meaning of an idea that is individuated in several persons, permeating their personal habitus. This concept of idea is developed, not entirely correctly, by way of the universality of the idea although Clauss himself does not use that expression. He supports the nature of the idea with the example of the mathematical idea of the triangle whose lawfulness is not found by analyzing a great many drawings of triangles for their common properties but by seeing the triangle "idea" in the individual empirical triangle. And now Clauss continues with a "correspondingly": "Correspondingly, for our terminological investigation our object of study is not the individual person we have before us here and now but the form idea, the primordial image that person embodies."[43] From this follows directly that other individual persons can also embody the same primordial image. That universality of the idea, the opposite [Gegenbegriff] of which is embodiment in the concrete human being, in this conclusion blends in with the universality an idea can have insofar as it is embodied in many individuals. The problem of a hierarchy of ideas is thereby obscured; no differentiation is made between ideas whose nature it is to create concrete being only once—for example, the ideas that are singular persons—and those other ideas that are articulated in many concrete cases. The transition to the universality of the idea is made all the easier for Clauss because he also deals with the types of social relationships under his heading of form ideas. The individual under investigation has various relationships to the social community; for example, he is husband, mayor, farmer or craftsman, and so forth. There is something in these relationships that transcends human individuality: "a type, and this, too, is a form idea."

These inconsistencies in methodology prevent Clauss from laying a comprehensive foundation for his theory and in particular keep him from clearly formulating the relationship between the singular person and the community. Nevertheless, Clauss consistently pursues his ideas within a typology of the soul, of its char-

42. *Ibid.*
43. *Ibid.*, 61.

acter. The terms *form idea* and *primordial image* do not imply that this idea refers only to something concerning the body as the visible form [*Gestalt*]; rather, the term *form* refers to the "person as a whole."[44] It refers to man as a whole, to the unified form that is maintained as unity through the mind—and precisely for this reason the term does not refer to the mind as an isolated element but to the mind as the law of human unity. In this respect the body is also included, and in a methodologically careful race theory it can therefore not be the same as the body representing our animal nature—which is the subject of biology—but is the mind-permeated [*geistdurchwohnt*] body of the human being. "Thus the body is here seen 'from the inside' and is understood as something whose form is conditioned by the form of the soul."[45]

The inquiry into the characters of souls, which focuses on the total human being, must begin with the study of the lawfulness of the soul and include the phenomenon of the body insofar as the latter appears within the soul sphere [*Seelenraum*]. Here we cannot recapitulate Clauss's complete discussion of this topic and we must confine ourselves to two or three of the fundamental concepts he develops that shed light on his procedure. The first of these concepts is the "behavioral law of the ego." According to this law the ego can respond in various ways to all the experiences of a person. The ego can behave in various ways toward the experiences that flow through the soul. "In this behavioral law of its ego lies the source of all the characters of a soul."[46] The attitude the ego takes to its experiences is based on this behavioral law: "Whether it decisively or searchingly reaches out into its experience, or rejects an experience with the appropriate inner gesture, or whether it simply abandons itself to the chosen experience (not reaching out toward the experience but being pulled into it), and, with the appropriate inner gesture, does not actively reject the experience not chosen but flees from it." The character of soul here indicated is an ultimate reality that can be intuited directly or be deduced from the gestures of a soul but that cannot be further explained by other premises. This character cannot be formulated in terms that are

44. *Ibid.*
45. *Ibid.*
46. Ludwig Ferdinand Clauss, *Die nordische Seele: Artung, Prägung, Ausdruck* (1923), 41.

93

generally understandable but is disclosed only in description. It can be seen completely only by those who share in it. Seen from the inside, this soul character is a "destiny" for the soul of the person; it is a power that gives the soul direction, a power not subject to conscious control by the person.[47]

This character, Clauss continues, is the most profound, though not the only, element of all that can be called the fate of a soul. Character determines the choice and acceptance of experiences and attitudes toward them—that is to say, the pattern and gesture of the soul—but it does not determine the "characteristics" or "dispositions" a soul possesses. The soul contains a wealth of "germs," an entire "stock of germs." "In each of the germs, however, is embedded one and only one single goal pattern [*Zielgestalt*] into which it can develop."[48] Clauss does not conceive the characteristics or germs in biological terms in the sense of genes or genetic structure; rather, he defines them as developmental possibilities inherent in the soul, which, once again seen from inside the soul, are an ultimate reality, a "destiny"—indeed, an inner destiny like the character. Now whether the germs are developed or not, or in which sequence they are developed, whether one germ developing perhaps in more advanced age has to struggle for a place in the soul landscape in which other germs have already developed, and the like, depends on the environment, on nurture, on educators, and so on. Thus, seen from the standpoint of the soul, this also is "destiny," but this time an "external" one. "Two souls with the same stock of germs develop differently if each is summoned by a different occasion. This situation of *if* and *so*, of external and internal destiny . . . prescribes the manner and the mode of the unfolding of all life, and thus is constrained in a twofold way."[49]

Clauss's theory, as noted above, goes beyond the per se of the soul and considers the human totality. The body as the field of expression of the soul is not the animal body but is itself a unity of the soul's modes of expression. Human bodies are formed differently, but a form idea can be discerned in them as well, and it is an important question for each person's life whether the forming law of his body is the same as the forming law of his soul, whether the

47. *Ibid.*, 91.
48. *Ibid.*, 93.
49. *Ibid.*, 94–95.

body is the adequate field of expression for the soul's form within him. In those instances where the soul has the field of expression appropriate to it, Clauss speaks of "pure blood." "It is this pure unity of the soul with its body that the term 'pure blood' is intended to signify."[50] So we are not to understand "blood" to mean the body in the biological sense either, but the "soul character in its connection [*artliche Verbundenheit*] with its field of expression, the body."[51] If blood in this sense is not pure, the result can be a warping of the soul character [*Missartung*] because it has been blocked in its expression. This can happen if a soul does not find the paths of expression it needs in the field of expression of the body given to it, and so forth.

Concerning the means to describe the form idea, Clauss developed no system but finds the descriptive terms in connection with the material he is dealing with. Thus many things turn out well, others go amiss because a schema thought out in advance is missing. One felicitous instance, for example, is the attempt to construct a soul type, the Nordic soul, around the concrete movement of the ego toward the world of objects, the "reaching out" [*Ausgriff*]. The nature of this "reaching out" can be made clear with the help of its opposite, the passive taking things as they come [*Auf-sich-zukommen-lassen*]. We have cited above Clauss's description of the opposites of reaching out and abandoning the ego to the experience. He concludes this characterization with the statement: "Only the ego that meets experiences by reaching out can rightfully say of itself: 'I am experiencing.' But the one that does not reach out, that meets experiences in such a way that they draw the ego in, such an ego should properly say of itself only, 'Experience is happening within me.'"[52] This distinction of soul types—and here we are not concerned whether it is correct as a description of the "Nordic" type—is immediately clear because fundamental possibilities of soul attitude [*Seelenhaltung*], of approaching things and letting them approach, are used in the characterization.

Continuing this train of thought becomes more difficult when it moves away from these very simple movements and undertakes to explain how such movements function in the various situations

50. *Ibid.*, 121.
51. *Ibid.*, 147.
52. *Ibid.*, 41.

and concrete fields of action [*Bewegungsfelder*] the soul encounters. Among the qualities of the reaching-out type Clauss lists "exuberance," "self-squandering" [*Selbstverschwendung*], the climax of life in the moment of downfall. Here (1) several problems converge that would be better separated; and (2) something else might play a part that lies too deep to be illuminated by the more superficial relationship to the world of concrete, tangible objects. Clauss gives the following description: "Reaching out to victory, then, is the highest moment for the Nordic fighter—not the moment of victory itself nor the enjoyment of victory, which comes 'after' the victory. . . . Enjoyment, the feeling of the here and now, is of little value to the Norseman as compared to the moment that still carries distance within it."[53]

This "moment that still carries distance within it" comes much closer to the center of excitation [*Erregungsmitte*] of total human existence than the simply active attitude toward the environment, the "reaching out." If one of these can be elucidated through the other, it is not the deep excitement of the moment rich with distance through the "reaching out" behavior, but rather the reaching out into the world of objects as habitus of everyday conduct through the distance content of the moment that excites existence. With this we approach the point from which a theory of soul characters must start, namely, human existence in relation to its course in time. *Every one* of life's moments contains "distance" to the extent that human existence is directed toward its future. Future is ever in the sights of my existence as I live in the present; I live toward the future and its contents. Now I can, but I do not have to, experience my activity as exciting to the extent that it holds upcoming events in its reach, or to the extent that I stretch beyond the limits of the present toward something that is not yet present, not yet fully realized. The excitement of my present existence for its future is the exciting basic experience by which all other habitual behaviors are colored.

And if we now ask further why this directedness toward the future, essential for all existence, contains such an element of excitement, we are led to the ultimate ground, which Clauss also saw. "That is why the Nordic soul—and perhaps it alone—knows the

53. *Ibid.*, 191.

high point [*Hochgezeit*] in *downfall;* it is able to squander its body on this highest moment that shines 'shortly before the victory' and that receives its brightest radiance only through such squandering, through the squandering of the body that excludes the enjoyment of victory."[54] The reason for the excitement is that all existence is a ripening toward death. The "reaching out" not toward things but toward the future of one's own existence can be full of excitement because every such anticipatory reach [*Vorgreifen*] is pregnant with the final reaching out toward death. Living toward the future is so exciting because it is lethal.

So we should really turn the method applied by Clauss around and begin with the question of how an existence experiences its dying. It is from the viewpoint of *this* basic attitude that behaviors in the various fields of action should then be interpreted. In our case, for example, the experience of the "moment" would consist precisely in the enjoyment of the tension toward the goal. The statement: "Enjoyment, the feeling the here and now, is of little value to the Norseman" as description would then be wrong because the "moment" of reaching out in suspense is surely also a "here and now" that is "enjoyed" profoundly, that is, savored in its lethal excitement. The juxtaposition of an unsavored [*ungenossen*] moment with the enjoyment of victory clearly seems derogatory, precisely because a different kind of "enjoyment" is not recognized in its naturalness—indeed, it cannot be so recognized because it is sought in a field, "battle," that is not adequate to this other kind of "enjoyment."

The comparison with western European activity and battle, which comes off very unfavorably in comparison with the Nordic type, is therefore rather unfortunate. Based on the premises of Clauss's theory, it is methodologically inadmissible to compare gestures of soul in related fields because every soul character has its own arrangement and preferential hierarchy of concrete fields. Just because one soul character may express itself most completely in "battle" does not mean that it has to be the same for the other character. To juxtapose the figure of Cyrano de Bergerac to the heroism presented in Old Norse literature would seem to us a sign of deliberate malice if Clauss's work did not otherwise bear the stamp

54. *Ibid.*

of sincere effort. If I were to find in French literature "western European" phenomena comparable to the attitude of soul, called "Nordic" by Clauss, that savors most fully the moment of tension between present and future, I would choose Baudelaire's *Fleurs du mal* or analyze Valéry's *Charmes* or his dialogues, or I would trace the threads that lead from Louise Labé's *temps retrouvé* to Marcel Proust's *temps retrouvé*. Quite a different image of the "western European soul" would emerge than the one presented by Clauss. Perhaps we could then see that the excitement of existence running its course is not felt in the anticipating reach of the ego toward its future but rather in the distancing of the ego from life's passing, in a certain paralysis at the sight of this inexorable course (surely one of the roots of the unwaning interest throughout French intellectual history in the problem of lassitude, *paresse*) or in polishing and perfecting an intellectual product whose hard and smooth polish is to save it forever from the dissolving stream of life.

I hope that in spite of having selected only a few of the great wealth of possible, more easily presentable examples, the basic considerations regarding procedure at stake here have become clear. The theory of soul characters envisaged by Clauss must be firmly grounded in the field of those possible attitudes of the ego toward the whole of its existence, the attitudes that, in real terms, determine all other gestures of the ego and elucidate them for the interpreting observer. An examination of the structure of existence and the position of the ego in it would have to precede such a theory; furthermore, there would have to be a typology of the various fields in which the fundamental attitude is to manifest itself. This, as it were, would create a system of translation on the basis of which alone comparisons become possible. Though Clauss is still far from this goal, his working method nevertheless moves in that direction.

I hardly need to note that the criticism offered here is immanent and that the suggestions I have made merely pursue the lines first sketched out by Clauss and therefore do not represent my opinion about the best method to accomplish the task.

Clauss's later work, *Seele und Antlitz der Rassen und Völker*, testifies to the enormity of the research field opened up here. Though his procedure is the same as the one employed in his analysis of the Nordic soul, the mere wealth of illustrative material addresses the inherent problems and peels away their layers. As an example let me point to the "type of calling" [*Berufungstypus*] described in this work. As in the study of the Nordic soul, a characteristic gesture serves as point of departure; just as in the earlier work the "reaching out" seemed the most accessible characteristic point of attack, here it is the "close listening" [*hinhorchen*].

> This close listening of the soul harbors two elements. It is, as we said, the basic attitude of this type, and thus the element that remains unchanged in all its experiences. But it is close listening to the coming moment, which arises from within, and to what it will bring: that is to say, to what changes in experience and does not remain the same. And it is also part of this close listening that the soul surrenders to its changing moments with trusting composure, abandons itself to their whims as to a miracle flowing from the hand of a higher being. Herein lies the danger—the "weakness," if you will—of this kind of soul and also its greatness, the wellspring of its characteristic creative power. Because when a creative spark lives in a soul of this style, close listening becomes attentive listening [*lauschen*] for a divine *call*, and the most perfect life of such a person will be that of someone sent by God [*Gottgesandter*]. He is someone who feels called into the world—into this world, the only world—on a mission from God vouchsafed to him from moment to moment through revelation.[55]

With this we enter on an entirely new field of the soul realm. The polar opposites of active and passive—or, in terms of the body, away from the body versus toward the body—have become irrelevant next to this non-sensory close listening to a higher power that can affect or call a person. Once again we must demand that not the gesture as such, namely, the "close listening" that may have empirically given us access to this type, should be made the focus of the characterization. Instead, the investigation must penetrate to the fundamental structure of the soul in which this gesture as well as others are embedded as predispositions and from which the various gestures, especially bodily gestures, become understandable. Because—and this is the main theme of this work by Clauss—the soul style "permeates and rules [*durchwalten*] the soul and its expression: it rules the characteristics of the soul (for example, its talents) and its experiences as well as their expression and the theater—that is, the body—in which they express themselves."[56] Each type of style has a corresponding body type

55. Clauss, *Von Seele und Antlitz*, 27.
56. *Ibid.*, 93–94.

belonging to it in whose channels of expression [*Ausdrucksbahnen*] its typical modes of experiencing can best be active. Using a wealth of illustrative material, Clauss lists a number of such types that are quite convincing. Though many of them still need improvement, the procedure he uses to arrive at his results is what is important here. In contrast to anthropometric race theory, which focuses on individual physical traits, Clauss sees the body, and particularly the face, as a whole, ruled by a style of expression. What matters here is not the body at rest but the field of expression in motion, in proving itself as the vehicle of the soul and its order of experience [*Erlebnissablauf*]. Physiognomic interpretations therefore should not be based on single photographs of a face but in principle only on what Clauss calls "mimetic series" that, if possible, should provide a series of images capturing the entire course of an experience. These series of pictures, as extensive as possible, are important because empirically faces are frequently a mixture of styles, and it is difficult if not impossible to determine the stylistic type from a single photograph. Clauss offers outstanding examples to show that in profile one head may be "Nordic" but a frontal view will show it to be "Oriental"; in another profile "Mediterranean" traits predominate while "Turanian" ones are revealed in full face, and so on. The findings of this part of his work are so indisputably correct that I will place his summary of this principle of his procedure here. It pronounces judgment on the kind of race classification preferred, for example, by Günther. Clauss's findings have invalidated Günther's voluminous illustrations and their apodictic captions, which assign the people depicted to a particular race type. Writing about them, Clauss notes:

> An isolated illustration that is not part of a mimetic series or that the researcher cannot verify from his own knowledge of the person depicted is worthless for the determination of racial style or racial styles of which the person portrayed partakes. Faces in which the styles are slightly mixed can easily be portrayed by a somewhat skilled photographer so that now this and now that stylistic element is so highlighted as to render the same face a pure representative now of this and now of that race. In the same way, with appropriate lighting and choice of perspective and expression, a face with a strong mixture of styles can be artfully portrayed as stylistically pure. And what a skilled photographer can do intentionally, an amateur may accomplish out of ignorance, namely, to falsify a portrait [*umphotographi-*

eren] through an unintentional but decisive shift in the style accent, thus making it representative of its opposite—not to mention the possibility of skilled or bungling "retouching." The fundamental truth is: never trust any picture you have not taken yourself or can check through your knowledge of the subject. We must leave it to anthropometric race research, to decide whether the isolated pictures, taken by others, it generally works with are actually adequate by themselves. In any case, comparative expression research and all its branches as well as the psychology of races can draw only on the illustrative material it has produced itself and the production of which it thus has monitored.[57]

We have considered the investigations by Clauss in more detail because in our opinion they have followed the path by which race theory can develop as a science. For Clauss, "races" are the representatives of his stylistic types in the factual world.[58] The stylistic type is an idea that permeates man as a total being; it is not the soul in the sense of an isolating construction, but the unity of the human form as a body permeated by the mind. The undeniable phenomenon of races as varieties of body-soul types within humanity becomes accessible to science at the very moment that the study of this phenomenon is heavily compromised by the carelessness and, above all, ignorance in philosophical-anthropological questions on the part of those conducting the study. The achievement of Clauss cannot be overrated, and that is why we may be permitted to overlook the shortcomings his procedure still shows.[59]

57. *Ibid.*, 72.
58. *Ibid.*, 56.
59. Here I could only touch on the most important points of the task Clauss set himself. For example, I have not mentioned the application of his style types to animals and landscapes. The results are so far only modest and tentative. But the scope of the idea is so far-reaching that we find nothing comparable unless we go back to Herder's *Ideen,* which connected the living world and the form of the earth. Except for Clauss's work, therefore, we want to refer the reader to Prince Friedrich Wilhelm zur Lippe's *Vom Rassenstil zur Staatsgestalt* (1928), which except for its pictures, is a rather insignificant book.

5

The Race Theory of Othmar Spann

In our time the only major philosophical attempt to get to the heart of the race problem was undertaken by Othmar Spann. We must come to terms with this study and see where we agree and where we disagree with Spann. To establish a basis for comparison, we will first contrast the procedural principles of the two approaches.

Our procedure can be described as following:

1. We must set forth the fundamental experiences that occasion all thinking about this subject; relevant here are experiences of the parts of the total human existence—of matter, of plant and animal existence and of the mind—and the experience of total human nature, of the total human form as one permeated by the mind.

2. We developed the dialectical forms our thinking on fundamental experiences employs. We spoke of the differential concepts formed by juxtaposing fundamental experiences within the course of our existence [*Daseinsablauf*] and in comparing the classes of being [*Seinsklassen*]. Every mode of being can be seen as a concrete whole, unified, or as a structure of lower levels of being governed by and assimilated into a higher level of being. An organism can be seen as a living whole or, with the help of differential concepts, as ensouled matter. The total human being can be a unified whole or a spirit-imbued animal.

3. From this simple analysis we next distinguished several construction types in which real-ontological speculation deems it necessary to join this contradictory material of experience into a unity. Among these constructions were those that identified the whole of existence with one of its parts—as in the case of identifying the human being with the mind—as well as the theses about the interdependence of the levels of being on each other and also the construction of intermediary links in order to unite the parts.

Thus, we distinguish between the classes of being as open to direct experience, the thought problems arising from such experiences, and their solutions. In our opinion, pointing out these experiences and the conflicting ways of thinking [*Denksituationen*] they lead us to is the only true task of science. Speculations concerning the interdependencies among the realms of being go beyond this, and judgments of this sort are, strictly speaking, irrelevant because the matter on which they speak—namely, the relationships between realms of being—is not a matter of experience for us. Indeed, to the extent such matters are implicitly asserted in such statements and the relationships between realms of being are presented in a satisfactory systematic way, that is, to the extent that the thought problems are resolved, such statements are wrong. For it is in the nature of these realms of being that they exist together [*Miteinander*] in a way that though undeniable is not accessible to human experience. Here we deliberately avoid the word *unity*, which would already anticipate a construction in the sense explained above.

Now if we relate the principles of Spann's attempt to our arrangement of the problem area, the following picture emerges:

Spann agrees with us on the premise of the fundamental experiences, but he limits the number of these fundamental experiences to two: that of mind and that of matter. All intermediary levels of being, which we also consider original experiences—the worlds of plants and animals of all ranks—are not, on his view, original realms of form but unions of matter and mind or—to use his expression—pairings of a higher order [*Gezweiungen höherer Ordnung*] (hereafter we will omit the words "higher order," which Spann uses to distinguish between pairings of minds). Thus (1) the fundamental experiences are fewer in number than in our premises, but (2) the resulting thought problems are not considered separately, and (3) the step to constructions follows directly that, in our opinion, to some extent distort the problem though they do not completely obscure it by any means.

We can summarize this provisional characterization as follows: while we try primarily to clarify experiences and avoid, as much as possible, any constructions, Spann starts with the premise of a narrower base of experiences and finds himself faced with the necessity of using more extensive constructions.

When it comes to details, Spann's procedure is very similar to ours, at times even being congruent with it, and offers more for the boundaries of the problem field than we do. For we limited ourselves above all to the center of the body-soul-mind relationship but Spann, in line with his more comprehensive philosophical aims, is concerned especially with the upper and lower boundaries. For us, matter was an ultimate reality the structure of which we did not need to deal with. Spann goes further and applies to matter the same analytical procedure we applied to the higher levels of being. Matter, too, can be seen, on the one hand, in the totality of its appearance and, on the other, in the analysis of its components, analogous to the body, which can be seen as matter and as ensouling principle. In regard to matter, too, we can distinguish its formative principles (laws of motion, laws of reaction, and the like) from the substance *in which* they appear—a pre-material substance. Aristotle already carried out this separation under the names of *materia prima* and *materia secunda*, with the second matter being the one that has form and the first the something without form that lies at the basis of all matter appearing formed. Spann designates these moments he has isolated as matter or substance (the one that has form) and pre-spatial or immaterial roots or pre-material or super-material beginnings (*archai*, ἀρχαί) for the something underlying all formed substance.

Just as spatial matter has its pre-spatial or pre-material roots, so the mind unfolding in time has its pre-temporal roots in the timeless realm of ideas. The rationale for the juxtaposition is analytically the same as that for splitting matter into its components. In the temporal course of ensouled or inspired forms (plants, animals, human beings) in the succession of generations, something unchanging is preserved amidst all the changes. This self-identical, unchanging something, unity or whole—for example, the unified whole of an animal species—articulates itself always anew in and around the succession of individuals; the crucial point is "that in the change brought about by ever new articulations, something that remains or endures unchanged, namely, what is not articulated in the articulating whole (the ego in thinking, life in life's actions, genus in creatures)—in other words, the self-identical whole is juxtaposed to the constantly changing stages of articulation. Thus a self-identical and a changing element face each other. . . . This self-identical something, which does not disappear in the re-articulation, points to the timeless element in time."[1]

To some extent we have carried out these analyses in similar ways or would have to carry them out in the same way if this task were assigned to us. Matter would have to separate into its form and that which is formed in it; we, too, would have to distinguish between the chemical composition and reactivity of a substance, or its resistance to pressure, or the form of its crystallization, or its three states, and the underlying substratum or *hypokeimenon* in which all these form qualities appear. Similarly, we distinguish between the unified whole of the person as a timeless substance and its temporal unfolding in the course of a person's life, and so forth. However, these experiences and the thought problems they pose for us will not lead us to any other conclusions than, simply, that according to experience, the classes of being have each their own proper lawfulness and that they are able to enter into connections with each other whose inner nature remains a mystery to us. Spann, however, considers it necessary to bring this variety of phenomena under one roof through his theory of the original pairing between mind and matter, thus letting the upper and lower boundaries of the ontic field touch. The variety of connections between classes of being is said to arise from pairing between the pre-spatial roots of matter and the pre-temporal roots of the mind, the ideas. Mind and matter cannot be in direct contact with each other or mingle; this possibility is precluded by the autonomous self-enclosedness [*Geschlossenheit*] of the natural and mental world. Spann also acknowledges this self-enclosedness as independent fundamental experiences, in deliberate contradistinction to the emanatistic [*emanatistischen*] theories of the derivation of the levels of being from each other. The mind cannot simply make use of formed matter, as though it were a tool, for its "embodiment" ["*Verleiblichung*"]; it cannot imprint itself to matter. Instead, to connect itself with matter the mind must pair itself with the protomatter, the immaterial roots of matter. We respect this attempt at a construction to the extent that it reflects the experience of the completed union of mind and matter. We consider it questionable insofar as the term *pairing* and the listing of the substances forming pairings could

1. Othmar Spann, *Der Schöpfungsgang des Geistes* (Pt. 1; Jena, 1928), 377.

convey the impression that thanks to this construction we know anything more than we already knew without it, namely, that there are classes of being that can be described analytically as unions (or pairings) of isolated moments.

The detailed reasons for our reservations are as follows:

In the analysis of the levels we meet in the isolating construction the mind in itself of being at the top, that is, we encounter the mind that has not entered into union with a body—in other words, the idea in the sense of Spann's usage.[2] At the lower end of our break-down, we encounter the *prima materia,* or what Spann calls the immaterial roots of matter, as an ultimate reality that acquires form and can no longer be broken down into a forming and a formed moment. It is now tempting to bring the first forming moment, the idea, and the last formed moment, the pre-material roots of matter together, as Spann did, and to let the two elements meet in a common root, whether that shared point is a source of the split, or whether, as Spann claims, it is a point of pairing, of becoming through each other, as a possibility of becoming real [*Wirklichkeit-werden*] through each other, whereby reality refers to the experienced classes of being in which the two pair into autonomous forms. I can see no argument to prefer either the moment of separation or the one of union; both are equally elements of our direct experience of the unified whole of the classes of being and of our experiences of parts of this whole in isolation from each other. Therefore, we fully accept the concept of an original pairing only if it is meant as containing within itself these two moments without one being subordinated to the other. However, on the basis of

2. Our analysis of the problem will here be restricted to the stages of being that are built on top of each other; our observations will not include the problem of time or, generally, the problem of becoming although Spann takes his illustrations of what he means by idea precisely from the processes of being and the unified wholes being articulated within them. If we followed suit, we would only complicate our presentation without gaining anything for our cause. For this reason I also omitted this half of the problem in my first chapter. The relevance of the problems of being and becoming may, in this context, be most clearly recalled by a reference to Scheler's theory of time: According to Scheler, the condition of internal time [*In-nerzeitlichkeit*] of the human mind must be attributed to the relationship of the mind, in itself timeless, to the body. Temporal succession is the result of a unification of mind and body. The mind's nature as idea can thus be made visible both in the multi-leveled structure of being, in which the mind can be isolated from the body it inhabits, and also in the course of the mind in time, which can be isolated from the unity that is consistently maintained amidst processes of change.

Spann's explications, we cannot dare to claim this with any certainty as his intended meaning.

Furthermore, we can accept this concept only if it serves to designate pairing on the levels of being that is experienced as real. We cannot accept the concept if it is meant to say—and we believe that Spann means it to say—that idea and proto-matter actually are in contact in some form of pre-existence. "The contact," Spann writes, "occurs in pre-existence; it is a contact between the pre-sensory roots of both, of mind and matter, in the shared higher center between them. . . . This shared center can no longer be found here below."[3] We disagree with this idea because it hypostasizes the moments of proto-matter and idea, which were isolated in analysis, into independent beings [*Wesenheiten*]. We do not believe that it is meaningful to speak of a realm of independently existing ideas, since ideas—whose reality we do not otherwise doubt—are given to us only as unified with other being, that is, concretely united to matter, and nothing in our total sphere of experience indicates that the assumption that ideas exist independently, outside of such unions—or, as Spann puts it outside the process of articulation—is permissible. By the same token, we cannot experience anything pre-material that is not yet formed in matter. The "pre-sensory roots" of matter and mind are dialectical concepts of boundaries [*Grenzbegriffe*], gained *within* our experience of being; they do not designate a sphere of being *beyond* our experience. "Pre-existence" as a zone in which the two boundaries make contact with each other is likewise merely a concept that can be understood from the experience of these boundaries. This term also cannot be used to designate a class of being that really lies beyond our experience. Therefore, we must call virtually as wrong the statement that "In this earthly world we see only the untouchable quality of the two planes or orders of being."[4] For although we perceive the realms of inorganic nature and mind as autonomous and not requiring a mutual explanation, we are also aware of the contacts and "pairings" of these levels in the whole beings, such as plants, animals, and people, we find on all levels of being. If we did not know of these pairings from our direct experience, especially

3. Spann, *Schöpfungsgang*, 199.
4. *Ibid.*

the experience of our own human existence, there would be nothing to make the idea of such a contact in a realm of pre-existence conceivable for us in the first place. We know only that being separates into the variety of its forms; these forms can be arranged hierarchically so that they extend from the lowest, that which unites what is formless and cannot be experienced into forms, to the highest, which receives its form from a formative element that cannot be experienced. And finally we can go so far as to say that two opposing streams of determination—from bottom to top and from top to bottom—unite with each other into forms or pairings in the various forms of being.

This first inconsistency in Spann's reasoning, which starts from the experience of the pairing of matter and mind in being and ends by denying this pairing and displacing it into a realm of pre-existence, leads to others in particular aspects, one of which we will have to consider because of its relevance to our topic, namely, the question of the body. In contrast to the result the preceding line of reasoning led to—namely, that in the world here below the two orders of being, matter and mind, cannot be in contact—Spann starts in his thinking about the body with the correct insight that the two are in contact on this earthly world. "The obvious process whereby we experience both externally and internally the pairing of a higher order with matter is the human body. How does it come about?"[5] His analysis of this correctly formulated thought problem is not entirely successful because the breakdown of total being, which Spann executes so masterfully for the boundary form of inorganic matter and mind, is missing for the intermediate levels. Because the same term is used for designating both, no distinction is made between the soul as an embodied element, in Fichte's sense—which is identical with the pneumatic body—and the soul apart from its embodiment. Further on, therefore, no distinction is made between the completely different questions of the relation between the soul in itself and the pre-material roots of matter, between the embodied soul and the pre-material roots of matter, and finally between embodied soul or pneumatic body and formed substance [gestalthabender Stoff]. Therefore Spann comes up with the following statements: "Physical life is the capacity of the mind to

5. Ibid., 501.

enter into a pairing with the immaterial center of articulation [*Ausgliederungsmitte*] of matter. We call this capacity the growth or vegetative capacity of the soul."[6] Here we can agree with his equating mind and soul since it does not matter for the question most important to us at the moment what the "uppermost" element isolated is called. However, for reasons explained earlier, we must object against talk of a pairing of the pre-material centers inaccessible to human experience; the pairing between the two hypothetically autonomous substances of the soul and pre-material centers is nothing more than an image signifying the enigma posed by the fact that we are facing the primordial phenomenon of living form, which can disintegrate into pure matter, and, obviously, another element we call soul. The fact that behind the immediately experienced primordial phenomenon of life lies a problem called pairing is visible only in the processes of metabolism and death, that is, in processes where living being enters into relationship with other classes of being. We therefore believe that Spann's statement provides an explanation for something that does not actually need to be explained but is puzzling only because of this relationship to another being different from its own kind. Inherently, life in its unity and the organic form as a whole being is a primal mode of being.

The same difficulties attend the following statements: "What is told of magicians and saints—that they are able to send the centers of nature into ecstasies, that they walk on water, conjure up clouds, affect events at a distance—all this, whether one believes it or not, would be an example of how the human soul could attain *direct* rapport with the centers of nature."[7] If I understand this statement correctly, the question considered here is whether the embodied soul, the pneumatic body—that is to say, the soul shaping matter, which is bound by the conditions of its shaping—and nature—that is to say, formed nature, not pre-material nature—burst the chains of their formation and, in spite of their connection can make contact beyond this connection and its laws. This rapport is "direct" insofar as the contact between formed being normally can only be mediated—through the relevant lawfulness of its form. Further: "If

6. *Ibid.*, 501–502.
7. *Ibid.*, 502.

this rapport is *mediated* by the body, then this is a pairing of a higher order, namely, a pairing of the soul with the immaterial centers of the material world."[8] In my opinion (aside from the reservations we must repeat here concerning pairing in general), if any rapport can be called direct, it is this so-called "mediated rapport," because in it the unmediated contact of soul and matter, through which a formed being is created in the first place, is completed. Subsequently, this formed being, once it has a structure or shape [*Gestaltlichkeit*] can enter only into mediate relations to other classes of being, that is, relations mediated by its form. This line of reasoning is completely unclear unless we know that here and even more clearly later a shift of concepts takes place. As a result of this shift, the immaterial center of the material world is no longer to be understood as the boundary concept of *materia prima*, but the organic germ substance. For the body, the mediator of the rapport, is "that already bound matter in which the pairing of a higher order proceeds in a specific and relatively continuous way. If the unmediated pairing of a higher order—without body, without seed, without already given organic matter—were at all possible, it would be only as 'ecstasy.'"[9]

Here the body is quite clearly no longer the result of the pairing; it is no longer for us the enigmatic primordial phenomenon of living form but is now the mediator of a pairing between matter and soul, and the "supra-material root of nature" is equated with "given organic matter." Thus, we have moved away from what occasioned the whole inquiry, namely, the phenomenon of animated matter, in which matter is subjugated under a law that in itself is foreign to it, and the fact that soul and matter join in an unmediated way into a unity for we cannot explain based on our knowledge of the lawfulness proper to the two substances, that there is actually something like an ecstatic contact (if the expression may be permitted here) of being in its various forms—a contact that takes place constantly throughout the entire duration of each individual life. The starting point of this inquiry is so obscured by the web of the various lines of construction that Spann even begins to doubt this unmediated contact, this "ecstasy," so that the reality we ex-

8. *Ibid.*
9. *Ibid.*

perience directly in every animal or plant body and which was the argument's point of departure is revealed as a questionable reality in the end.

Based on these premises, Spann interprets the races as a special case of the pairing of matter and mind. The two substances meet in the unity of the living body; their encounter gives rise to "the sensibility or the system of vitality" as the embodiment of those contents of the soul that result from the life of the mind in the body; that is to say, mind and matter reciprocally acquire a form equipped with external sense organs and internal sensory powers, at once spiritual and material, the instincts. This schema of pairing is abstractly true for the sensory nature of organically living forms; wherever the abstract schema becomes particularized into a concrete variety appearing in a collective of living forms, the phenomenon of race arises. Originally, what is essential to race is its societal nature. "The form in which sensory nature assumes a definite position in society beyond the merely abstract presentation of the mind in the body that is race."[10] The societal character of race includes the following: (1) the constancy of the formal structure through generations or of the genetic material, and (2) the ability of this genetic material to become the basis for the unfolding of the mind.

The insight into the societal character of the phenomenon of race shapes Spann's further interpretation. The teachings of Gobineau and his successors up to the modern race theoreticians are declared wrong because they are based on the ontological principle that the mind depends on matter. Society is a world of the mind and manifests itself with the help of the racial-organic [*rassenmässig-organisch*] genetic material. Nevertheless, the same applies to this special case of the pairing of matter and mind as to the relationship of matter and mind in general: spirit does not indeed create matter for its purposes (for then there would be no race problem at all), but manifesting itself in matter, the mind must submit to the laws of matter although the mind is the dominating element in the pairing. "Therefore race is not solely determined by the Mendelian laws of heredity nor by the lawfulness of the genetic material (not even in

10. Othmar Spann, *Gesellschaftslehre* (3rd ed.; 1930), 359.

animals, which, however, we will not discuss here) but also by a mental element."[11]

The great advantage of Spann's theory lies in the fact that it is unlike other race theories. While other race theories take the biological fact of the existence of races as their point of departure and then have trouble to get to the inherently anthropological problem, if they get there at all, Spann's theory starts in the midst of a direct contemplation of the world of the mind and its law of social articulation [Ausgliederung]. From this vantage point it merely has to prove that it is compatible with the facts of animal existence. Because society is mind, every person not only descends from the parents who beget him but is also a member of humanity as a self-articulating idea. As such a member, related again to the genus idea, each person develops characteristics that are not found in his forebears and that cannot be explained by heredity in the biological sense. The biological laws of heredity, in particular the Mendelian laws in their more recent version, point to the constant recurrence of certain traits and the law of their recurrence, but they leave room for the unique characteristics of each human being. They give the law of the constancy of certain traits, but they have nothing to say about variation—neither individual variation nor the origin of species and races.

Following the doctrine of the primacy of the mind, even the concepts usually understood as biological—such as the "purity" of a race—must be reinterpreted. Pure races in the biological sense of an unmixed line of descent do not exist among humans. "What distinguishes race is not racial purity of the genetic material but something else, something we call *stylistic purity of the phenotype*. 'Stylistic purity' [Stilreinheit], however, is already a mental concept; it is the unity of mental expression; it is general likeness of image."[12] In this concept Spann's theory comes very close to that of Clauss. For Clauss, too, race is a stylistic law of mental gesture and expression, which thoroughly governs mind, soul, and body. For Clauss, pure blood is the harmony of all parts of the whole being under *one* stylistic law; for Spann, racial purity means nothing less than this general unity of a style.

11. *Ibid.*, 360.
12. *Ibid.*, 363.

And finally, the theory of the societal mind as the prevailing and style-forming element leads to a theory of the emergence of races in which Spann joins Schelling. The idea as the unity among the variety of members of the same race marks the place where mind erupts into the material world. Races come into being and change not according to biological laws, but according to those of the mind. "The formation and change of a race is a fundamental fact of the mind and not one subject to the inherent lawfulness of the genetic material."[13] This principle must not be misunderstood as implying that an individual's mind could change his race by an effort of will. Rather, it must be understood in terms of the societal nature of the mind, that is, in reference to a social, historical event that shook humanity most profoundly. New socially-formative ideas spring up or are articulated out of others and acquire the physical image appropriate to them in the organic genotype. "Race history must not be pursued merely as a natural science; it must also—even primarily—be carried out as intellectual history. The great founders of religions, sages, and rulers who filled their peoples with new religious life and a new, profoundly exciting [uraufregend] warlike spirit of heroism, who deeply stir their feeling of being alive—it is they who also give new impetus to race formation, and thus have the potential to change man's hereditary species image [Artbild]. The intellectual history of primeval man is, however, primarily religious history. Schelling has already attempted to explain the formation of races from this standpoint."[14]

We will stop here. Spann's race theory shows us once again—even where we had to be critical of it—the depth of the philosophical foundation needed to interpret this phenomenon. Supporting our own position, Spann's theory indicates for us the level on which this subject must be dealt with. Furthermore, it refers correctly to the societal character of the mind, within which the physical basis for the manifestation of the mind is a subsidiary problem.

13. *Ibid.*
14. *Ibid.*, 365.

PART II

THE RACE IDEA AND THE STRUCTURE OF COMMUNITY

1

Idea and Community

The question concerning the race idea and its function in structuring the community in general and its effectiveness in the governmental organization of the community in particular confronts us with a confusing abundance—not of the material, but of the organization of the idea problem. The term *idea* is to be understood as the real unity of the plant, animal, and human individual and collective wholes that are articulated in spatial and temporal variety. The person is idea in relation to the course of his personal life; humanity is idea in relation to the human variety; animal or plant species is idea in contrast to the individual animal or plant belonging to the species. Thus by *idea* we mean not a concept but the real substance that appears as the *one* in the *many*. According to the structure of the speculative field, as we analyzed it in Chapter 1 of Part I, the idea of a manifoldness of phenomena can be seen either in a part of its being or in the totality. Thus, in accordance with man's high degree of complexity, the idea of man can be seen in the mind but it is also possible to grasp the idea of man as animal, and finally, the idea can be found in the human totality. Examples for each of these possibilities abound in the history of ideas about community. Herder and Kant saw the idea of man in his reason and formed the idea of community of a humanity to which each man belongs as a specimen of the rational species. The races of the more recent political race theory of a Günther or a Lenz are primarily animalistic ideas, and only secondarily intellectual ideas; each of the partial beings is examined separately, but in such a way that the intellectual community of a race depends on its community on the animal level. In Spann's race theory and in the studies of Clauss we find race as the idea of a total being: for these two scholars racial purity or blood purity is not a property of the genetic material in the biological sense, but rather the stylistic purity of the human form in all its parts, the possession of a mental stamp recognizably the same in its physical and psychological expression. According to our interpretation of the relationships between body, soul, and mind, it is not possible to reconcile these two concepts of idea, one of which refers to parts of man, the other to the being as a whole. One cannot say that the one is formed correctly and the other erroneously, since both follow the dialectical structure of theory formation on this theme. We have to acknowledge as the first premise of our present investigation the twofold meaning of the idea concept imbedded in the construction of the theories.

The ideas can be ranked according to each of the two idea concepts. The ideas that unite a limited variety of people into a community are characterized through their position *between* the highest idea, humanity, and ideas of individual persons. They unite groups of persons and in the process also isolate them from other individuals and communities. Each limited community idea contains a hierarchy of three ideas: (1) the idea of humanity, in whose framework (2) the idea of the limited community is articulated, and (3) the ideas of individual persons, which are articulated in the framework of the community. This hierarchy is not limited to only three levels; it can easily be augmented by additional intermediate stages, and in fact this occurs in history, when, for example, empirical sociology attempts to grasp the wealth of gradations of the idea of humanity that has developed throughout history. Humanity can, for example, be divided into cultural groups, permeated and shaped uniformly by a culture soul; within these groups humanity may organize into nations, and these, in turn, can form superordinate units of more closely "related" nations. Within nations, the subdivision continues further with tribes, leading, for example, to attempts to explore the intellectual and literary history of tribes; smaller units, such as "movements," "trends," or "schools," also develop in great variety. The hierarchical nature of this variety of ideas allows the ascent from the lowest ideas to the highest and links the lowest—that of the individual person—through all the others with the highest, that of humanity. On the other hand in descending, it circumscribes ever smaller circles, isolating them from each other. Thanks to these two movements of "up" and "down" a corresponding variety of experiences is possible, allowing us to respond either more to the connecting or to the isolating moment of the idea hierarchy, depending on each person's basic meta-physical attitude, historical circumstances, and the imponderable elements of the personal soul. Each idea is related to every other idea through their shared connection in the idea of humanity, of which they all are individual articulations [*Ausgliederung*]. But each one is also isolated from all the others by virtue of being a particular individual and historical step of articulation. The individual person *can* lead his conscious life in any level of ideas—in that of humanity, and thus in relation with every other contemporaneous, past, or future one—or in a narrower level, which nurtures and guides the sensory perception, customs, institutions, beliefs and tools of individual existence to such an extent that the view of others and connection with them is blocked off.

Contemporary theories on society differ basically in which of these ideas they consider the "destiny" of the individual, on which he feels dependent in the ground of his existence and which he believes to be at work in him and in which he finds the particular meaning of his life. We distinguish the great classes of international and national ideas. For example, the ideas of humanity in the Christian sense, the doctrine of humanity as the total person in which all men are united in solidarity typically belong to the international class. Furthermore, ideas such as Spengler's of cultural souls as the fateful wholes within which individuals must lead their lives, closely circumscribed by the respective developmental phase of the cultural soul, also belong to the transnational class. Among national and subnational ideas we find ideas of nations and their missions and, in part, the race ideas aiming at a destined unity within the nation. Thus, as our second premise we must accept the hierarchy of ideas with all its ramifications. Combined with the first premise this gives us two series of ideas, depending on whether we focus on the idea in the sense of the differential concept or on the idea as the law of being as a whole.

In discussing the hierarchy of ideas, we have already alluded to the related question of the objective and subjective status of the idea. We wish to discard as meaningless the concept of idea according to which this word means the independent existence of substances accessible to some form of human perception but without having any reality in the historical development over time. Whether we speak of the idea of the part of the being or of that of the whole being, in either case we refer to the idea as an evolving reality that can be directly perceived in its development in time. Thus the idea of a community cannot be found anywhere except in the mind of the people belonging to the community and in their intellectual creations. There this idea can be experienced directly in the common structure of the intellectual worlds and persons created by the community in question—national types of mind are not illusions but objects of experience. However, the idea is real not only for the outside observer, but first and foremost for those living within it and creating it. It is in the nature of the mind—as per our discussions and definitions in Part I—that it is a self-conscious center of acts, that it possesses the faculty of discursive thinking, and that in reflection it generates intellectual worlds. Among these worlds is the community, of which we have so far spoken as an objective reality for the observer, independently of the minds living in it. Yet not only does the community encompass its members, but they also possess it in their knowledge of customs and rules of law, their mythic consciousness, the craftsmanship of their daily lives with regulations and prohibitions, and so forth. The idea as historically real is in the process of becoming in the transition points of personal mind; the individual mind is the point where the idea as objective reality penetrates as and, at the same time, where the idea as subjective reality is being created. The idea does not just *exist* as an object does, it also *becomes* in the minds of those who have it.

Here we have arrived at the point where we can justifiably speak of the effect of an idea on the building of a community. Viewed objectively, the community *is* real as the realization of the idea; subjectively, its reality is a constant becoming through the process of idea generation in the minds of people who, precisely through the work of the common creation of an idea, build the community we subsequently see from the standpoint of the observer as the idea-imbued one in the many. The personal mind of man is the locus where an idea is perceived as objectively existing while at the same time being created, that is, made real, in this act of perception.

This is not the place to explore the theory of ideas in detail; we will do so elsewhere in connection with a doctrine of the idea of the state. For our present purposes it is enough to acknowledge with some clarity the individual mind as the point the objective and the subjective idea meet and to know what *idea* means when we speak of its contribution to the building of a community. The idea we mean here is created and created ever anew; in terms of its content it can comprise the whole hierarchy of ideas or of some of its parts, as we earlier analyzed them, and this both in the sense of a speculation isolating a part of the whole being and in the sense of a speculation focusing on the whole being. Thus the content of the idea is determined (1) by the position of the idea in the hierarchy of ideas or, to put it another way, by the position of the community created with it among all the historically real communities; (2) by the position of the idea in the dialectical structure of speculation (isolating construction or being as a whole); (3) by the specific part (if the total being is not chosen) that is integrated into the idea as essential to the building of the community. This specific part is determined by the structure described in the ontology of man, philosophical anthropology. The idea of a community can be realized in objective contents [*Sachgehalte*] of an intellectual, psychological, technical-practical or physical kind or in any combination of these partial contents, or with all of them at once, or with some predominating over others. The idea of a family is permeated with physical, spiritual, and economic-practical content; in the idea of religious community, on the other hand, matters of soul and spirit may predominate although those pertaining to the body and the neighbor are not completely absent either. The various attempts to define the nature of the "nation" give us an idea of the wealth of contents that are woven into an idea in various layers and with varying degrees of importance: geographical, ethnic, linguistic connections, common political destinies, cultural contents, and the like. One of the different ideas, in its objective and subjective meaning, that can enter into a multitude of connections with others is the idea of bodily community, which can be based on various facts of the bodily sphere.

2

The Body Idea

As we examine the problem of the body idea more closely, we will primarily have to draw the logical conclusions from the premises presented in the preceding chapter. These conclusions, however, are quite complicated because of the number of premises and possible combinations. We will not go through the entire range of combinations but simply emphasize some of the empirical possibilities that are important generally as well as specifically for race theory.

1. We will begin our survey with the idea of the body as part of the human being. Man belongs to a part of the realm of the living, he is an animal, with all the characteristics of an animal. Man is not a self-enclosed individual, but is part of the chain of generations. He belongs to a bloodline extending backwards beyond his parents through an infinite number of ancestors and stretching forward beyond him to children, grandchildren, and on into infinity. Man belongs to other groups of bodily kinship, the so-called races, and finally, he is a member of the largest group, the human species as a whole. In the hierarchy of ideas, we descend from the idea of species through the smaller groups to the bloodlines and finally to the individual. The whole hierarchy is objective animal reality in that it is humanity branching out and propagating in the variety of its bodily forms. In this type we accept the premises of the idea of the animal part, the hierarchy of ideas, and the objectivity of the idea. The individual has an objective position in all these ideas, but this position does not necessarily have to be reflected in the realm of the mind. Objectively the individual is part of the chain of ancestors and descendants, objectively he belongs to a race, and objectively he belongs to the human species. On the lowest level the individual exists objectively as this particular animal in the overall context of the idea of humankind. This situation does not yet in itself involve anything specifically human—the same observation

also applies to any other animal species. The idea on this level brings to bear its unique effect on the building of a community only when we add a further premise, namely the reflection of this in the subjective idea of the mind.

2. The human being as animal is at the same time the human being as a unified whole and thus able to experience this animality not only directly but also in the sphere of the mind as well. The idea of humanity as an animal species loses none of its objectivity in this translation into mind and can be experienced as "fate" in all the objective levels of its hierarchy. Individual animality (which concerns us less here) emerges again, for example as the individual structure of the instinctual nature in the character, as personal possibility of quick or slow association of thoughts, as personal capacity of vital memory, as personal structure and personal intensity of the emotional life, and the like. The species-wide animality specific to human beings appears as the general human connection between the mind and the sensory nature in which the mind must live its life. This is, for example, Kant's position on the problem of man; from this follows the idea of the humanity as a community in which non-sensory mind articulates itself in animal-sensory variety. This mind now has to awaken to itself and to overcome the animal tarnish of its purity—in spite of its animal tie to the genetic history of its kind. This animal species character can be experienced as human fate and can become the basis for an idea of community in which *all* people, as belonging to the same species and therefore incurring a shared fate, are faced with the same ethical community obligation of overcoming animality and purifying the mind. The transposition of the objective animal idea into a subjective idea of community can occur on any level of the hierarchy. Dynasties and clan relationships [*Geschlechterverbände*] are two such transpositions, of which the former is based on the narrowest bloodline of ascendance and descendance and the latter on the broader line and the spreading branchings of a clan line. The narrower and broader generational relations can become intertwined, so that within the total clan the principal line of eldest sons, going back directly to the earliest ancestor, for example, stands out in terms of rights to estates and titles. Furthermore, the connection can be seen bilaterally—that is, including both paternal and maternal ancestors and their offspring—or unilaterally, either as pa-

triarchy or as matriarchy, with all the subsidiary constructions of familial rights, such as exogamy, levirate, and sororate, with their concomitant linguistic formations [*Durchbildungen*] for nomenclature of kinship relationships, such as the so-called Dakota type, etc. In one sense of the term, races are also objective animal ideas transposed into ideas of the subjective mind. As animals, individual human beings belong to one or another or to several of, presumably "pure," races; membership in a race, just as membership in humanity or a family, can be experienced as belonging to a community sharing a common "fate," that is, as a community of soul with other people of the same animal type. Of course, we have no illusions here that this level in the hierarchy of ideas, namely, that of humanity as animal species, has any greater or lesser fateful impact than any other. In addition to their systematic content, which pertains to their scientific, factual orientation, scientific race theories, such as those put forth by Lenz or Günther also represent a theory of ideas that contributes to the building of a community by elevating an objective animal idea into the realm of the mind. Clauss's race theory also belongs to this type insofar as the congruence between physical style and soul character—or lack of such congruence—is understood as "fate." When ideas of this type dovetail with other ideas of community, they can serve to support very different political attitudes. By its nature, Kant's idea of humanity is democratic; a race idea can be democratic as well if it encompasses empirically the same group of people as other contemporaneous community ideas—when, that is, a national community, also constructed on the basis of different ideas, is at the same time also a community of race. However, the race idea will have an aristocratic effect if it singles out one community within another more comprehensive one, as happens in the case of the "Nordic" idea. Basically, a body idea, like any community idea starting with a level below that of the human species, is democratic on the inside and aristocratic on the outside. In practical terms, the one or the other of these possibilities usually predominates, depending on whether the community so constituted is comparatively isolated or is integrated into communities built upon ideas of a different content. In what follows we will gain greater familiarity with the democratic and aristocratic formations of the race idea.

3. Another series of types is constructed if we do not derive the

body idea from a partial sphere of man as animal but begin with the idea of the human being as a whole, in which the body is included, but in this case the body as permeated and governed by the mind. In principle, in this type the transformation of the animal idea into one of the subjective mind can be omitted, for the idea of the human being as a whole is, objectively speaking, already rooted in the mind. Thus it is only the objective element of the one idea that, on its subjective side, is seen in the mind of those it encompasses as a thought image [*Denkbild*] in the strict sense of the word. In the historical development of humankind this type will hardly ever occur separately from the type discussed under number 2 above, just as that type will hardly ever be found except in close connection with the idea of the human being as a whole. Though we can give the pure schema, as we did above, we must cite some of the same examples as we did for the previous type. We find the idea of the human being as a whole wherever the context of the mind is understood wholly in terms of the idea of the intellectual community, down to the body as its bearer. Thus, when, for example, in the ideas of the Greek phylae, phratries, demes, and poleis the community is constructed primarily as a mythical and cultic context, and this cultic context also shapes the details of the communal order in the form of a bodily connection, such as in the reverence for a common ancestor of the cult members. This type is especially clearly seen when (as in the case to be discussed in greater detail below) a cult community organized on the basis of gens is broken up and replaced by a new cult community for the purpose of destroying the aristocracy of the old community and then a new order based on gens and a new aristocracy develop in the new community before too long. However, the idea of the human being as a whole reveals itself not only in such models but quite simply in all formation of community because this, being human, is *always also* connected to the *mind*. All human beings have ancestors in the biological sense, but only where the bloodline is also a community of intellectually important people, where the individual has "noble ancestors," only there do we have "eupatridae" as a result of this intellectual distinction. The idea of the human being as a whole cannot be fully eradicated even in the deliberately scientific race theories; the "racial types of soul" are in fact not proven to be transmitted by heredity but are created as ideas from the raw material of history, and their connection to body types remains a merely external one. The fundamental impossibility of really separating the various ideas (ideas of being as a whole or in part) from each other has become evident in the studies concerning race as an anthropological unit. Neither Walter Scheidt nor Eugen Fischer was able to clearly define the concept of this unit because the structure of the body-soul problem makes a unification of the biological unit with that of the human being as a whole impossible; juxtaposed, the two are not linked methodologically and cannot be linked. Thus, physical anthropology as a science that is based on units of communities of human beings as unified wholes will never arrive at methodologically clear results.

4. The idea of the human being as a whole in its objective and subjective significance and the transformed animal idea can be combined into various empirical-historical configurations. A relatively pure community of human beings as unified wholes typically arises when a group that is relatively closed in terms of interbreeding with outsiders lives under a clear idea of the human being as a unified whole, has a clear mental image of the desirable character traits, religious and social conduct, economic behavior, etc., and consciously or without explicit intention carries out social selection (in the choice of marriage partners, in the judgment of public opinion, in choosing a leader, and so on) guided by mental image. The notion of such a process underlies theories that, in a racially mixed community, for example, a nation, promote a maximum of mixing under the guidance of an intellectual idea; this process is to lead to the creation of an intellectually and physically homogeneous group, of a community in which the intellectual idea has found its appropriate bodily foundation. The case of the newly established cult community that returns to a structure based on gens is very different. Different also is the case of the gens-based cult community that admits people from outside the blood lineage [geschlechtsfremde Mitglieder] into the cult and thus also incorporates them into the lineage [Geschlecht] (a typical example is the granting of citizenship in ancient Greece). In such a case the legal expert would speak of a "fiction"; in this view, the clan community is not real but merely fictitious. These formations of the mind, however, have nothing whatever to do with fictions in the scientific sense. Instead, it is in these formations that a religious idea of

community, namely, the cult community, and an idea of community that can envision community only in the mental image of a unity of the human being as a whole that penetrates even down into the body, and, finally, a transformed animal idea on a low and therefore easily understandable level in the hierarchy of animal ideas, namely, that of narrow blood kinship, meet. (Here I wish to remark only parenthetically that a material theory of legal fictions must begin with *this* question of idea concretion.) Regarding modern citizenship rights, blood relationships continue to be important to the extent that citizenship can be inherited; but generally they are increasingly pushed back to the extent that granting citizenship is no longer linked to the "fiction" of admission into a blood relationship. Recent race theories, however, develop the concept of "ethnic citizenship" [*Volksbürgerschaft*] in contradistinction to political citizenship and with that they revert to the idea of that citizenship fiction.

3

Two Major Cases of Body Ideas:
The Classical Tribal State and
the Kingdom of Christ

We now want to present two major historical examples to support our contention that body ideas in principle can always contribute to community building and indeed have contributed significantly to the formation of our Western communities. We are concerned with taking from the emergence of the race idea in our time the character of the extraordinary it so easily takes on in the eyes of people who have come to consider the political ideas since the seventeenth century with their anti-body [*leibfremd*] rationalism the natural and only conceivable kind of political theory. The modern race idea is one body idea among others; in Western political history it stands alongside the body ideas of the classical political communities and the Christian empire. Just as the gens-based body ideas of antiquity, which were based on close blood kinship, were replaced by the idea of humankind proper to the body of Christ, so, too, the latter idea and its echoes were replaced by new body ideas suited to help build the structure, consisting of masses and elites, of the modern political community. If we are to understand the contribution of body ideas, we must keep in mind that the body idea itself can never be the central idea of the community but is always only a co-constitutive idea in a more or less complex structure of ideas the model for which exists in the mind. In looking at a human community, we are never dealing with an objective animal idea but always at least with an intellectually transformed idea or with an idea of the human being as a whole that reaches right down to the body. The body that, as an idea, contributes to constructing the community, is not the body of biology; it is not an animal body but always a body of the mind. The idea of this body may be pictured in objective animal ideas, but it can never coincide with them and may stray very far indeed from this image. The gens-based idea is relatively close to the objective animal idea of the bloodline, but the two are not congruent, as I indicated in referring to the *"eupatridae."* The thread linking the idea of the body of Christ to an objective animal idea is very thin indeed. Nor is the relationship between the race idea and the "real" races very strong, as some of our analyses in Part I have already shown and as our further investigations, especially of the Nordic idea, will show. The meaning of the category of *corpus mysticum,* which was formed particularly for Christianity as the body of Christ, basically must be expanded to include other cases of body ideas. The classical phratry or gens is also a mystical body and so is race; in any case a biological-real connection never constitutes the essence of the body unity among the members of such a *corpus.*

Let us first glance at the classical cult communities already cited as examples. In his work *La Cité antique,* Fustel de Coulanges tried to elucidate the history of Greek and Roman institutions from the central point of their beliefs about the soul and the dead and their ancestor worship. Many of Fustel de Coulanges' claims, especially those pertaining to the earlier periods, were based more on intuition than on historical knowledge. Even Erwin Rohde, in his work, *Psyche,* has already refused to trace the whole complex of Greek religious phenomena to original ancestor worship. Nevertheless, that idea, though exaggerated in its construction, finds strong support in the institutions familiar to us from the historical period. In fact, in spite of all transformations, these institutions again and again reveal their tendency to a gens-based organization of political units. "While we are fully justified in saying that Cleisthenes perfected democracy by using a legal fiction to make all Athenians members of the aristocracy, the process had begun in the time before the known history of Athens. But even after Cleisthenes, the gens-based legal fiction was never abandoned; it always remained valid for the concept of citizenship."[1] Thus by the historical period known to us, the gens-based organization of the polis had become a mere "fiction," and we can only guess at the great power exerted by the body idea over the souls in the earliest period on the basis of its persistent influence in later days. If we arrange communities under the body idea according to how real the blood kinship is, the result is a series that extends from the alliances of close blood rela-

1. Ulrich von Wilamowitz-Moellendorf, *Aristoteles und Athen* 2 (1893), II, 51.

tives through the families and phratries to the gens-based phylae. In Attic law, the alliance of blood relations was called *anchisteia* and encompassed relatives down to the children of siblings' children and the grandchildren of the uncle. These close blood relations "formed a legal family [*familienrechtlich*] and sacral community with closer entitlement to inheritance, with the obligation of burial, the death cult, blood guilt [*Blutklage*], and expiation. Its exclusion of other lines of relatives was rooted in natural conditions, for the family alliance tended to collapse beyond the children of cousins."[2] The formation of families depends on external circumstances—residency, inherited wealth, social standing. Under such favorable conditions, a family tradition and the worship of a common ancestor can develop. These larger clan groups led to the development of the aristocracy and its legal separation from the rest of the people. The bond unifying a family was the descent from a common ancestor, whose name the family usually bore, as well as his cult. Clearly separated aristocratic clans did not develop until the later Greek middle ages when "the long-established big landowners gained economic, political, and military supremacy."[3] Along with various cults shared by all, each Athenian clan had its own ancestor cult. "Besides their temples and priests, they owned at least an assembly hall and a joint money fund. The family was headed by an *archon*, who was probably appointed by lot for the term of one year."[4] The phratries were more inclusive associations, comprising blood relatives, clans, and communal cult groups, and according to their idea of being a brotherhood they shared a common ancestor. Aside from various special cults, all Athenian phratries practiced the cults of Zeus Phratrios and Athena Phratria. "Each phratry had its own cult space with the shrines where its festivals and official family ceremonies took place. Thus, each phratry had its local center within a community."[5] The old tribal phylae were on the next higher level above the phratries; they were gens-based associations, but by historical times, especially in Athens after the reforms of Cleisthenes, they essentially had only sacral

2. Georg Busolt, *Griechische Staatskunde* (3rd newly revised ed. of *Griechische Staats- und Rechtsaltertümer*, 1920), I, 248.
3. *Ibid.*, 249.
4. *Ibid.*, II, 957.
5. *Ibid.*, 958.

functions and had ceased to be fundamentally important for the organization of the polis.

Most important for our question of the body idea in the structure of the community is the peculiar reinterpretation of the subdivision of the state into administrative districts, a subdivision that was part of Cleisthenes' reforms. To break the predominance of the aristocracy in the clan associations and phratries, Cleisthenes replaced the old constitution with a new democratic one, based on a territorial subdivision of the state. The area of the state was divided into ten phylae, and each of these into ten demes. From then on, citizenship was based on membership in one of these communities or demes. The new demes and phylae took their place alongside the old associations; like the latter, the demes as cult communities had an *eponymos*, its cult, and the land necessary to practice the cult. The new districts did indeed drive the old associations into the background, but they did so by virtue of an effect the reformer had not intended. Membership in the deme was the basis of citizenship rights, and every citizen therefore added to his name the *demotikon* as the designation of domicile, and the new title replaced the clan. The significance of the aristocracy diminished and was restricted to the right to the priesthood. "Conversely, quite against the intention of the lawgiver and as a result of the Greeks' way of thinking completely in terms of gentility, right of citizenship in the community developed along those lines and became hereditary, just as aristocratic titles had been. Thus, the local principle was destroyed."[6] Membership in the community did not change when the resident moved to another deme. "Therefore, alongside the genealogy of the aristocracy, a genealogy of communal citizenship developed that did not trace descent back to heroes but rather to those ancestors that had attained domicile when the deme was established. As clans practiced the cult of their ancestor, so the citizens of the demes worshiped their local deities. They, too, formed a sacral community."[7] Considering that the old gens-based communities also subdivided the state along local lines—after all, their members had settled in one undivided area—the difference be-

6. Ulrich von Wilamowitz-Moellendorf, "Staat und Gesellschaft der Griechen," in *Kultur der Gegenwart: Staat und Gesellschaft der Griechen und Römer* (2nd ed.; 1923), 103–104.
7. Busolt, I, 264.

tween the old and the new subdivision lies less in the social *reality* than in the *intention* of the reformer; the new arrangement was *intended* to be a territorial organization in contrast to the old, personal one.

As the second example of body ideas in the community structure we will outline—once again in a schematic sketch, without going into the wealth of historical details—the idea of the kingdom and body of Christ as it was articulated by Paul and his circle and expanded in the course of Christian history into the idea of the spiritual-worldly empire.[8] The idea of the *corpus mysticum* did not spring entirely new from the ideas of Paul; the ground had been prepared by the Hellenistic idea of the heavenly person and his embodiment in the cosmos, and especially by the doctrine of the second Adam. Christ as the second Adam is presented, in analogy to the first Adam, as the ancestor of a clan, not in the physical but in the spiritual sense; thus the tribal idea echoes through the doctrine of the body of Christ and facilitates the transition to Paul's mystical idea of the inclusion of all Christians in the body of Christ.[9] If we disregard historical preconditions and consider the Pauline teachings in themselves with regard to our schema of the body-soul-mind problem, we must increase the number of fundamental experiences by *one* to understand the problem—we must add Paul's religious experience of the body of Christ as He appeared to him on the road to Damascus: as a light phenomenon that nevertheless bore the physical traits of the historical Jesus. The specu-

8. For what follows, see the excellent monograph by Traugott Schmidt, *Der Leib Christi (Σῶμα Χριστοῦ). Eine Untersuchung zum urchristlichen Gemeindegedanken* (1919), upon which we depend for everything substantive. See further the new monograph by Georges Staffelbach, *Die Vereinigung mit Christus als Prinzip der Moral bei Paulus* (Freiburger Theologische Studien, fascicle 34, 1932). Pages 117–18 contain a very good bibliography covering our problem, under the title "Die Christusverbundenheit nach dem heiligen Paulus (Die mystischen Elemente in den Schriften Pauli)."

9. For the question of derivation from clan-state ideas and cults, the Last Supper is of special significance: "Paul himself here provides us with the *analogies drawn from religious history*. In the sacramental meals of antiquity a principal means of union with the divinity is eating and drinking. A wealth of examples is found in primitive religion, which lived on vigorously even in the Hellenistic mysteries. Indeed, the affinity between Christian and pagan ideas is so close that Justin the Martyr (in *Apology* I, 54, 66) branded the feast of the followers of Mithras as an imitation of the Last Supper anticipated by the devil. Could Paul, under the influence of the notions of the sacraments predominant in his pagan surroundings, not have revived the ancient belief in unification with the divinity through eating and drinking?" ("Abendmahl," in *Die Religion in Geschichte und Gegenwart.*)

lative questions concerning Paul's teachings follow from this visionary experience, combined with the experiences on which worldly anthropology is based.

Man consists of body and soul, of *soma* and *pneuma;*[10] *sarx*, the flesh, is available as an alternate to *soma*, so that man can also consist of flesh and soul.[11] *Soma* and *sarx*, however, are not only synonyms, but *sarx* can also stand for the matter out of which earthly *soma* is formed.[12] Thus the concept of *soma* acquires the meaning of a form into which various substances, not *sarx* alone, may enter. Moreover, the meaning of *soma* can be expanded to include not just the body in contrast to *pneuma*, but also the human person as a whole.[13] And finally, *soma* can be the opposite of *pneuma*, not in terms of a contrast between outside and inside of the earthly person, but as a contrast between being an earthly and an otherworldly being—*pneuma* is a technical term for demon or angel.[14] This opens a new series of conceptual meanings in a teaching about nonearthly beings, in contrast to an earthly anthropology.

The *pneumata*, demons or angels, are not spirits in the sense of a differential concept in contradistinction to the earthly body; they are completely spiritual-bodily [*geistleiblich*] beings of a class of being different from the earthly ones. A *pneuma* is not a nonmaterial spirit but a material being with a *soma;* this *soma* consists not of *sarx*, the flesh, but of the *pneuma* itself, a substance of an airlike or breathlike quality. In the pneumatic being, and especially in regard to Christ, we further distinguish between bodily matter and spirit. Christ as He appeared in the vision on the road to Damascus, had a body of light, a body that consisted of a lightsome material, the *doxa* (or glory). And his *pneuma* is not that of just any demon but the divine *pneuma*, the *pneuma* of sanctity—*doxa* and holy *pneuma* correspond to the earthly *soma* and *pneuma*.[15]

10. See, for example, 1 Corinthians 5:3, where Paul says of himself, ἐγὼ μὲν γὰρ, ἀπὼν τῷ σώματι, παρὼν δὲ τῷ πνεύματι . . . [For I verily, as absent in body, but present in spirit . . .].

11. For example, Romans 7:25: Ἄρα οὖν αὐτὸς ἐγὼ τῷ μὲν νοΐ δουλεύω νόμῳ θεοῦ, τῇ δὲ σαρκὶ νόμῳ ἁμαρτίας. [So then with the mind I myself serve the law of God; but with the flesh the law of sin].

12. Colossians 2:11 and 1:22 mention σῶμα τῆς σαρκός [the body of the flesh].

13. For example, 1 Corinthians 6:15: οὐκ οἴδατε ὅτι τὰ σώματα ὑμῶν μέλη Χριστοῦ ἐστιν. [Know ye not that your bodies are the members of Christ?].

14. See Schmidt, *Der Leib Christi*, 11ff.

15. See *ibid.*, l.c., 20 ff. We are dealing here with complexities and subtleties of

The two sets of premises of earthly anthropology on the one hand and divine ontology on the other lead us to the fundamental questions of the Christian doctrine of community we will outline below. The earthly Jesus was already a God-man, in the experience of the community, that is, the divine spirit dwelled already in him. In addition to the earthly *pneuma*, which he had by virtue of being human, he also possessed the *pneuma* of holiness. And just as in the earthly *anthropos*, the divine *pneuma* also dwells in the members of the community who share in Christ; they, too, have a *pneuma* of holiness in addition to the earthly one. It is this *pneuma* that establishes their communion with Christ and that will lay aside the earthly body and rise again one day in imperishable form.

---

meaning that even Schmidt failed to grasp in all the details of their reciprocal dialectical interdependence because he lacked the investigative schema at our disposal. Because the German translations do not do justice to these complexities, I will note here some of the most important passages to show that Paul, as no other thinker, presented the fullness of potential meanings because he was not trying to bring them under a rational system. 1 Corinthians 15:44: εἰ ἔστιν σῶμα ψυχικόυ, ἔστιν καὶ πνεῦματικόν. [There is a psychical body, and there is also a spiritual body (*soma*)]. The contrast of the psychical and the pneumatic *soma* can refer to the *soma* that serves as vessel to every psyche, or *pneuma*, as well as to *soma* in the sense of a person named after its essential part, and it may also refer to the body according to its substance. (The Latin translation has *corpus animale* and *spirituale*; Luther translates these as "natural" and "spiritual body.") For the relationship of *pneuma* to *doxa* we must compare 1 Corinthians 15:44: σπείρεται σῶμα ψυχικόν ἐγείρεται σῶμα πνευματικόν, [It is sown a psychical body; it is raised a spiritual body], where psychical and pneumatic body are contrasted such that animal procreation is the origin of the psychical body and the resurrection that act of the pneumatic body, as in verse 43: σπείρεται ἐν ἀτιμίᾳ, ἐγείρεται ἐν δόξῃ, [it is sown in dishonour; it is raised in glory], where *atimia* and *doxa* indicate the two realms in which the originating act produces either a psychical or a pneumatic *soma*. *Doxa* identifies the general status of a pneumatic body: the glory, the majesty, or the brilliance of the kingdom of God. The body of Christ, which has entered into this glory, can therefore be a σῶμα τῆς δόξης [glorious body], as Philippians 3:21 calls it. When *doxa* identifies the kingdom of God in general, the Latin translation speaks of *gloria*; when it refers more specifically to the body, the Latin translation uses *claritas corporis*. The double meaning of *doxa*—as a realm of being and also an individual being within this realm— allows, in conjunction with *doxa*, the further multiplicity of meaning of *soma*, a body consisting of *doxa* and therefore serving as a vessel for *pneuma*, and *soma* in the sense of a person who has his status in the realm of the *doxa*. To the extent that the *doxa* designates the bodily substance, it is the vessel of the *pneuma*, not of the earthly *pneuma*—which all people possess—but of the *pneuma* of holiness. At the beginning of the Epistle to the Romans, Paul says that he has been called: περὶ τοῦ υἱοῦ αὐτοῦ τοῦ γενομένου ἐκ σπέρματος Δανὶδ κατὰ σάρκα τοῦ ὁρισθέντος υἱοῦ θεοῦ ἐν δυνέμει κατὰ πνεῦμα ἁγιωσύνης ἐξ ἀναστάσεως νεκρῶν. [Concerning His Son who was descended from David according to the flesh and designated Son of God in power according to the Spirit of holiness by his resurrection from the dead]. The *pneuma* of holiness here is opposed to *sarx*; the two concepts designate the crucial parts of the earthly and otherworldly whole being.

Here a large field of possible constructions is marked out for the relationship of the individual and the whole community to Christ, a field Paul paced off in every direction. The closest intermediary between the community and Christ is the *pneuma*. Each individual and the whole community live "in Christ," and Christ lives "in them." With their *pneuma* they are immersed in that of Christ, and Christ's *pneuma* lives in each individual and in the whole community.[16] Here we find one of the crucial differences between Paul's doctrine of Christ and the general demonology of his day. One demon or one *pneuma* could dwell in an individual, or several *pneumata* could take hold of him, but what distinguishes the divine *pneuma* of Christ is its *pleroma*—the fullness by virtue of which it is spread into a multitude of people and becomes the unifying bond of the community.[17]

In addition to the idea of the community being joined in the *pneuma* of Christ, there is the one referring to a bond through the *soma*. While in the doctrine of *pneuma* the personality threatens to disappear into an impersonal spirit, real only in the earthly individual persons of the community members, the doctrine of the *soma* more uniformly emphasizes the *pneuma* of Christ as a personal one in contrast to the community, which is the *soma* of the raised Christ, the heavenly person. Christ as the resurrected one is simultaneously present on earth and has an earthly body, namely, the community as the vessel of His divine *pneuma*, just as the *pneuma* of holiness already dwelled in the earthly Christ. Thus we must distinguish among three concepts of the body of Christ: the *soma* of the crucified one, the *doxa* of the resurrected one, and the mystical *soma*, the community in which the resurrected one has earthly, historical reality.[18] While in this idea Christ's *pneuma* is distanced from His body, the community, resulting in the fundamental possibility of ordering the earthly realm under the image of the body, in the Letters to the Ephesians and to the Colossians the concept of the body is seen somewhat differently. To prevent the personality of Christ as the source of grace from disappearing into the community, Christ is called the "head" of the community, that is, He is seen as one of the components of the *soma*. At the same

16. See the detailed exposition in Schmidt, *Der Leib Christi,* 72ff., 147ff.
17. *Ibid.,* 95; on *pleroma* in particular see pp. 180ff.
18. *Ibid.,* especially pp. 206ff.

time, however, in these Letters the head as the ruling element is distanced from the body, and *soma* merely refers to the body *without* the head—as in Colossians 1:18, "And he is the head of the body, namely, the church." The concept of the body contained in this is explained in greater detail in verse 24 of the same chapter: "Now I rejoice in my sufferings for your sake, and in my flesh complete what is lacking in the afflictions of Christ for the sake of his body, that is, the church." The distancing of the head from the body becomes fully clear in 2:19, where Paul speaks of the head "from whom the whole body is nourished and knit together through its joints and ligaments, grows with a growth that is from God." The head is an image for the guiding spirit that holds everything together; it symbolizes the unity of the connecting power more clearly than does the concept of *pneuma*, which we cannot perceive with our senses. The independence of Christ and community is more strongly emphasized in the one group of ideas than in the other, in which the identity of the two comes to the fore.[19]

If I, as a nonspecialist, may be allowed an opinion on these philological and objectively uncommonly difficult questions: it is completely pointless to search—as some theologians are doing—for a doctrine "free of contradictions" in the web of speculations presented by a man as astute as Paul, who realized, or at least touched upon, practically all speculative possibilities following from his premises. In principle, we can find in Paul's thinking all the contradictions inherent in the structure of the speculative field (and we have by no means touched on all of them here). The only meaningful approach is to draw from the web of speculations a core that proves to be uniquely Pauline, perhaps in comparison with the theological-speculative stance of the Letter to the Hebrews. This is what Alois Dempf has done:[20] the will and the orientation to an idea of an articulated kingdom that, in its further development, could incorporate into itself the whole historical richness of the empire.

The definition of the body of Christ as taught by Paul is well

---

19. On the question of the image of Christ as the *Kephale* of the body, see *ibid.*, pp. 168ff., and the literature cited there. On the question of the identification of Christ with the community and their simultaneous distancing, see *ibid.*, passim, especially p. 147.

20. Alois Dempf, *Sacrum Imperium: Geschichts- und Staatsphilosophie des Mittelalters und der politischen Renaissance* (1929), 72ff.

known. I will point out only Ephesians 4:11–12, "And his gifts were that some should be apostles, some prophets, and some evangelists, some pastors and teachers, to equip the saints for the work of the ministry, for building up the body of Christ." The building of the body of Christ is the work assigned to the saints, the members of the community, and it is carried out by each person exercising the office assigned to him by virtue of the particular gift bestowed by Christ. The ranking is more explicit and specific in 1 Corinthians 12:27–28: "Now you are the body of Christ and individually members of it. And God has appointed in the church, first apostles, second prophets, third teachers, then workers of miracles, then healers, helpers, administrators, speakers of various kinds of tongues." And the same chapter carries the idea of unity in multiplicity through all the body-soul and spiritual bonds of the community: "Now there are varieties of gifts, but the same Spirit" speaks of the unity of the *pneuma*, which is divided into the charismata (verse 4); "And there are varieties of services, but the same Lord" speaks of the division of the ministries, of the offices under one Lord, the structure of work performed (verse 5). Verse 6 names forces with varying effects, the *energemata*, all of which are nothing less than the operative power of God. And finally, verse 12: "For just as the body is one and has many members, and all the members of the body, though many, are one body, so it is with Christ." Charisma, service, living force, bodily membership [*Gliedhaftigkeit*], are the ways the One Whole, the person of Christ, is individuated. This articulation is carried through in such detail that it can adapt to new historical situations and assimilate new charismata and offices. Out of the thousandfold fullness of this process of expanding the Pauline community to the unity of Christendom, in which church and state are only two offices under Christ the priest-king, we will only mention the profoundly important likening of Christian *fides* to the allegiance of retainers and fiefs and the likening of the priestly office to the worldly ministry.[21] The office of king is categorized as one more charisma, no different from the others. "Hincmar of Reims used the model of the Old Testament to categorize the special royal charisma in a series of anointings: *sacerdotes, reges, prophetae et martyres.*"[22] In the benediction at the

21. *Ibid.,* 136.
22. *Ibid.,* 148.

coronation of Charles II in 869, Hincmar called upon God to "place the ruler among the charismatically distinguished members of the *corpus mysticum*, priests and kings, prophets and martyrs, who were victorious through *fides*, through loyalty and faith, and have attained righteousness and the promises."[23] The categorization of the charismata follows a principle similar to that applied by Paul, except that the category is augmented with new elements as necessitated by history.

The analysis has clearly shown that there is more to the Christian community than merely a body idea, just as was the case with the clan state [*Stammstaat*] of antiquity. In both cases the body idea is one idea contributing to the total structure of the community. In the Greek ideas of clans and phratries, the community idea is based directly on the more or less strictly defined animal ideas of the succession and branching out of generations and separates it from this substratum to such an extent that the characteristic "fictions" develop—that is, outgrowths of community ideas in which the body idea is not abandoned although their basis in reality no longer exists. The idea of the *corpus mysticum* also does not entirely relinquish its grounding in the animal world—without the resonating image of a second Adam, of a second man as the ancestor of a new humanity, it would hardly have attained as strong a response. However, its principal content is drawn from other sources of experience, namely, from the experiences, both contradictory and yet reconciled in the immediate religious experience, of the dual nature of the historical Jesus as an earthly and yet otherworldly man, of a man consisting both of earthly *soma* and earthly *pneuma* and at the same time of *doxa* and the spirit of holiness. The idea of the mystical body is therefore worlds apart from any biological or organic doctrines of community of our time; at the same time, it is not simply a metaphor, not merely a symbol, but a real idea. Since it is not based on objective conditions of animal existence, it cannot sink to the "fictional" character of the idea of the clan state, but it can be constantly threatened by body ideas of that type and find its force weakened to the point of dissolution. Throughout its entire period of its activity this idea has been struggling with the idea of rights based on bloodlines. Charisma and the

23. *Ibid.*, 150.

ministry in the *corpus mysticum* are basically independent of inheritance through bloodlines; however, the hereditary nature of an office, especially of kingship, is of the greatest political significance for the position of the ruler and the preservation of his independence from the persons on whom the bestowal of charisma and approval for office depends. Dempf's major work deals exhaustively with this aspect of the struggles surrounding heredity and election.

To speak of the "causes" of the destruction of the *corpus mysticum* is a questionable undertaking, since it is impossible to be sure whether new ideas of community and their growth were causes for the displacement of the old ones or whether exhaustion of the older ideas created the space for new ones, which might otherwise have been incorporated, to flourish independently. We can only state that in fact the unity of Christendom has grown ever weaker—a process that continues to this day—and has retreated before the new national states, which have become more and more sharply defined. In Jean Bodin's time, in spite of the idea of the sovereignty of the princes of the nation-states, the unity of the empire was still preserved in the honorary prerogative that ranked Pope and Emperor ahead of the French king. Louis XIV's idea of his kingdom already shows a clearly developed hierarchy within the nation with all offices converging upon the king at the apex of pyramidal order and with the king deriving his office from God. By the end of the eighteenth century, the concept of the natural organism was developed to the extent that it could be applied to the state. Accordingly, the state was seen as bearing its formative principle within itself just like a living being, and thus the state was completely detached from the unity of the *corpus mysticum*.[24] The process of classifying and defining the community should be carried out for all stages of social construction and at all levels of the *anthropos*. We have just pointed to the differentiation of the office of ruler from the Christian Empire, which culminated in Frederick the Great's idea of the king as the servant of his state. The development of the proletariat and of the idea of a working class are already outside of this context since it took place almost entirely after the flowering of the idea of the body of Christ (even though

24. I have given a more detailed account of the development of the concept of the organism in the eighteenth century and its consequences for theory of the state in my studies on the intellectual history of the race idea cited in the introduction.

the Christian idea survives in the democratic content of this development and in its belief in the dying of the state and the coming of a millennium). In his monograph, Bernhard Groethuysen has described the process of dissolution and confrontation with the social doctrine of Christianity as it applies to the bourgeoisie (in France): the Christian worldview, with its hierarchy of charismas and of human types, the rich and mighty and the poor, in its ranking of offices and the people, did not make any provisions for the bourgeoisie.

> The man who lives in splendor and wealth and the man who spends his life in poverty and need are both personalities of Christian legend; both belong equally to the world of the Catholic faith. . . . Whether poor or rich, sinner or saint, somehow he has a place in the drama of the Christian idea and fulfills his calling in a world of tensions and struggles. . . . But if there is an entire class of people who are neither poor nor rich, and who do not embody any of the great opposites characteristic of human life on earth, how can its meaning and significance in the universe be determined? . . . The problem of the relationship of the modern middle class in France to the social world of the Catholic Church might be expressed in that vein by someone who starts with the views of a Bossuet and on that basis attempts to determine the meaning and significance of bourgeois life in society as a whole.[25]

The bourgeoisie stands in a different relationship to the idea of the Christian community than do the social powers that had been "incorporated" into the all-encompassing unity in earlier centuries. Unlike those, the bourgeoisie could not readily welcome such an incorporation as integration into the community of the Western mind because it was already living in the secular atmosphere of the sciences and social ethics. The bourgeoisie has grown up in the new nation-state as one of its most important economic supports, and it developed its own self-sufficient life form, often consciously feeling itself equal or superior to the old powers as regards economics. The intellectual and economic prestige of the traditional main members of the *corpus mysticum*, of clergy and aristocracy, is no longer so predominant as to be able to absorb and transform the

25. Bernard Groethuysen, *Die Entstehung der bürgerlichen Welt- und Lebensanschauung in Frankreich.* Vol. II: *Die Soziallehren der katholischen Kirche und das Bürgertum* (Halle, 1930), 9ff.

new self-generated [*eigenwüchsig*] life form.[26] Instead, the reverse process occurs, and the idea of solidarity among the members of the Christian community becomes an idea *within* the secular context of the nation. What remains of the *corpus mysticum* is the imperial claim of a community of united members, but the community itself in its motivating forces is not a humanity-wide but a national one. The possibility opens up for new body ideas to take the place of the old one of the *corpus mysticum* in the life of the community, and this they do, depending on internal politics, the expansion of the concept of history, and the understanding of racial differences and their impact on history and depending on the relationship to the national idea, to which they may possibly be in opposition. The introduction has already mentioned the basics and also supplied the justification for focusing mostly on the German phenomena in our discussion below of the effect of the race idea on community building.

26. The best illustration of the new middle-class-bourgeois life form, of its conviction of being an independent middle class, distanced equally from poverty and worldly greatness, seems to me to be in the opening pages of Daniel Defoe's *Robinson Crusoe*, with its paean to the middle class. Here we find in one passage, rounded off into the picture of a type, what Groethuysen claims on the basis of his rich material to be true for France. Defoe's description agrees down to the choice of words, with Groethuysen's analyses even for example when Robinson's father is speaking to his son:

> It was men of desperate fortunes on one hand, or of aspiring superior fortunes on the other, and who went abroad upon adventures, to rise by enterprise, and make themselves famous in undertakings of a nature out of the common road; that these things were all either too far above me, or too far below me; that mine was the middle state, or what might be called the upper station of Low Life, which he had found, by long experience, was the best state in the world, the most suited to human happiness not exposed to the miseries and hardships, the labour and sufferings of the mechanic part of mankind, and not embarrassed with the pride, luxury, ambition, and envy, of the upper part of mankind. He told me, I might judge of the happiness of this state, by this one thing; viz. that this was the state of life which all other people envied; that kings have frequently lamented the miserable consequences of being born to great things, and wished they had been placed in the middle of the two extremes, between the mean and the great; that the wise man gave his testimony to this, as the just standard of true felicity, when he prayed to have neither poverty nor riches.

The description continues for another page. We should also look at the little-known third volume of *Robinson Crusoe*, a moral-philosophical treatise, that sums up the ethical maxims the two volumes of adventure are designed to illustrate through concrete situations; especially Chapter 2, "An Essay Upon Honesty."

4

The Idea of the Particularist Community

The sphere of ideas in which, after the dissolution of the *pneuma* and *soma* of Christ, the new body ideas can unfold is the spiritual unity of the people, and the people seen as political unity, the nation. At the close of the previous chapter I suggested that in the transition from one complex of ideas to another the new one does not simply take the place of the old, obliterating it completely and leaving no trace of it. Rather, essential idea contents of the earlier period survive and combine with the new idea of the *Volk* [*Volksidee*]. We begin our discussion of this process of dissolution and reintegration with the point where the idea of the all-encompassing empire [*Reich*] enters into sharpest conflict with the idea made finite of the community and threatens to burst apart the unity of the social-political system despite the powerful constructive force of its creator—that is, we will start with Fichte's thinking.

In Fichte's thinking, fundamental experiences, the historical data he chooses to incorporate into his system, and the ideas at whose turning point he finds himself, all clash so fiercely that the miracle of their reconciliation strikes us as overwhelming each time we reread Fichte. Fichte retains the Kantian idea for a history with a cosmopolitan purpose as a general framework. Humanity is a whole that continues to develop ad infinitum; the human race is endlessly perfectible and can develop its spirit to ever higher levels. These premises lead to a number of questions that were already raised by Kant and elaborated and partly answered by Schiller in his letters on the aesthetic education of man.[1] If humanity as a whole progresses and reaches perfection only in its final stage, what is the meaning of the individual life, which must of necessity remain so

1. For a detailed discussion, I must refer the reader once more to my studies in intellectual history.

imperfect? Fichte provides us with several answers to the question, each somewhat independent of the others. To begin with, Fichte does not insist as rigorously as Kant on the idea of infinite progress, of the infinite perfectibility of human reason [*Gattungsvernunft*], to which the individual willy-nilly must contribute. Instead, in his discussion of the problem of the individual the notion of an infinite becoming of humanity repeatedly (unintentionally?) takes the place of progress, and this process of becoming does *not* have a *goal*. The individual is the vessel of the divine will and a member of God's kingdom in that he leads his life out of God's spirit in freedom; he is not used, and perhaps misused, as a tool but has his place in the divine plan for the world, a place that is assigned uniquely to him and cannot be filled by anyone else. His contribution to the eternal becoming of the whole is irreplaceable and carries its own meaning. Thus the speculative field becomes intelligible in all its breadth. For when the place of the individual becomes unique, irreplaceable in the construction of the whole, the whole is no less an overriding, more meaningful reality in which this individual is significant only together with others. How can it satisfy him to contribute to this realm he himself cannot experience fully?

Fichte thus cannot do without the other speculative line that leads to personal immortality. The human race is to build up God's kingdom, and this construction is the meaning of the eternal "making of oneself" ["*Sichmachen*"] which never stops because of birth and death. But the goal for the individual and for the whole is a higher life, in which there is no longer any becoming and where everything exists in a state of timeless being. However, this is still not enough to secure the meaning of the individual life. The individual life is not only against devaluation through the higher life of the person and the entire kingdom; but, quite independent of the idea of contribution—whether made to an infinite becoming or to an infinitely self-perfecting realm—the individual existence is endowed with meaning in this world. For Schiller the person of Goethe was the great figure that, in a fragmented time and in the Kantian speculative situation, assured him of the possibility of a self-enclosed, meaningful, contemporary existence independent of the future development of humankind.[2] The person of Jesus serves

2. See the previous note.

Fichte as an equally meaningful "figure." He has become the "founder" of the Kingdom of God by becoming its first "citizen." The Kingdom of God is built by surrendering all human freedom to God, thus creating the world in which God alone is the principle of all activity. In contrast to the principle—predominant in the "Old World"—of a God governing people's social relations with absolute arbitrariness, the direct relationship to God had to be realized in a historical person, so that he could found the heavenly Kingdom through his example. A first messenger from God [*Gottgesandter*] was needed to create the image "of this calling of self-sacrifice and self-surrender," the model by which other men could guide their lives. By surrendering their freedom in becoming followers of Christ, people become human out of God and thus attain the meaning of their existence.

We will cite some further steps in the transitions, in which the life of the individual becomes increasingly self-enclosed and finite in its orientation. (1) "Humanity is nothing but this freedom that should conform to the divine will."[3] All men are equal as far as their freedom is concerned; Christianity is the gospel of freedom and equality in the metaphysical sense as well as of freedom in its political meaning. Since each person is called in the same way to realize God's will through freedom, all without exception depend upon the deity in the same way; none is excluded from the same grace, none is sinful and condemned. (2) In spite of this fundamental metaphysical equality, people are not all equal in the kingdom of God as it unfolds in history. For it is one of the tasks of humanity to subjugate nature to the "concept," and not all men are equally equipped for such work with the gifts of intellect. This inequality will lead to a categorization of humanity into rulers and subjects; the uniqueness of the individual in the Kingdom of God is not meant as a metaphysical uniqueness but as a functional one in the order of work. According to a "law of nature," endowments differ, and the law of nature must be regarded by all participants as a dispensation from God. Thus, rulers, when they command, do so as God's subjects, and the subjects in obeying follow not their ruler

3. Fichte, *Staatslehre* (1813), in *Johann Gottlieb Fichte: Werke. Auswahl in sechs Bänden,* ed. Fritz Medicus, Die Philosophische Bibliothek edition (Leipzig, 1910–12), IV, 523 (page numbering according to the edition of the *Werke* supervised by I. H. Fichte; quotations from the edition of the Philosophische Bibliothek).

but the will of God that speaks through him. If we remove the belief in divine dispensation from this inequality of people as given by natural law and replace it with the body as the natural cause, the result is the schema of race theory. (3) Fichte himself already took a big step in this direction by reversing the shared subject status [*Mituntertanschaft*] of those rich in intellectual terms and their contribution to the building of the heavenly Kingdom into the idea that these people are the goals for which the world and the rest of humanity exist. A brutal Romanticism of the great man occasionally breaks through in Fichte and is roughly the same as Nietzsche's view of the state at the time of *The Birth of Tragedy*.[4] But while Nietzsche's view arose from a detached, almost aesthetically cool attitude toward a violent and even terrifying drama, Fichte's idea grew out of the malice and arrogance of the intellectually active man.

> There are some individuals in history who are worth more than millions of others. In a very few of them the divinity expresses itself directly; these are the ones in whom and for whom the world actually exists. The masses are here to serve as tools for the few, and even this segment includes only the smaller part of the masses; the great majority of people exist only to put the others to the test, to scare them, and to hinder them in every way so as to allow their full powers to develop. In the general order of things, the masses are merely the antithesis and the negating and obstructing forces, so that in the struggle with them the affirming and progressive powers will come to light.[5]

Here the relationship between the kingdom and the service given to it is, as noted, inverted; the world exists for the sake of the few men sent by God, and the rest must be their tools. More than that: the overwhelming majority of people does not even hold this subservient position in the kingdom but remains outside it as an enemy spurring the well-intentioned on to ever new efforts. The greatest part of humanity has a place in the world plan only as the antagonist of an elite of God-imbued men. They are not members of the kingdom but its opponents, only understandable from the viewpoint of a higher "order of things" as a counterkingdom to the Kingdom of God.

4. But see also *Wille zur Macht*, aphorism 997.
5. Fichte, "Berliner Vorlesungen über die Bestimmung des Gelehrten" (1811), in *Werke*, XI, 192.

Fichte then fills the schema of kingdom and counterkingdom, of the Kingdom of God and the Kingdom of Evil, with the stuff of contemporary history. The struggle between the Germans and the French is raised to the level of Christian philosophy of history and interpreted as the battle of the Kingdom of God against the Kingdom of Evil. Napoleon, with the enthusiasm of an absolute will to world domination, is the embodiment of evil, since his will originates not in freedom and concern for the building of the heavenly Kingdom, but in a "whim." In a battle for life and death, in a "True War," all the forces of the original people [*Urvolk*], the Germans, must take the field against him. The Germans are the original people [*Urvolk*] and therefore the bearers of the Kingdom of God because they, in contrast to the French and the English, are the only one of the Germanic tribes to have preserved their original language in their unbroken history, and with that language they have access to the deepest sources of the spirit in God. As a people they alone are able, by means of their language, to have full intellectual understanding and personality. Therefore, the kingdom of freedom begins with them. "Only from the Germans, who have been here for this great purpose for thousands of years and slowly growing toward it;—there is no other element for this development in humanity."[6]

Devotion to God means penetrating to the sources of freedom and at the same time the intellectually clearsighted comprehension of the divine will—the spirit of God operates in man as conceptually clear [*begriffsklar*] knowledge of right action. Fichte therefore preferred to base his interpretation of the Kingdom of God on the Gospel of John rather than relying on the Letters of Paul. Fichte translated the *logos* that was in the beginning, that was with God, and that itself was God, as wisdom, reason, or consciousness or concept. According to Fichte, John 1:3 means that the concept alone was the creator of the world and, through the subdivisions implicit in its nature, it was the creator of the many things in the world. "Just as primordial as God's inner being is His existence, and the latter is inseparable from the former, and is itself exactly like the first: and of necessity is itself in its own substance knowledge; and in this knowledge alone does a world and all things that

6. Fichte, *Staatslehre*, 423ff.

occur in the world become real."[7] With these sentences Fichte wants to render in his own language the meaning of the first verse of the Gospel of John. The life of God, the concept, becomes light, "conscious reflection," in real people; in every man who vitally understands his unity with God and leads his life based on this insight, the word has become flesh. Spreading Christianity and promoting the Kingdom of God is therefore first of all a matter of an effort on the part of the intellect, of making transparent the teachings of Christianity, the relationship between man and God, for everyone to reflect upon. "First and foremost, recognition of the heavenly Kingdom must be made independent of historic faith and the special affinity of mind some individuals have for it, and must adopt the form that is compelling for anyone endowed with human intellect."[8] This task—to loosen Christianity from its historical ground and to form it into a doctrine that can be forced upon every intellect—is performed by Fichte's philosophy, especially the *Wissenschaftslehre.*[9] As Fichte admitted, it still has to fight for understanding and acceptance, and might have to wage this fight for a long time, but it can never perish because it was "an absolute requirement of the generation by God and from God,"[10] made by the Word of God become flesh, Johann Gottlieb Fichte. The divine idea lives and works directly in the scholar who posed this requirement and so collaborates in building the heavenly Kingdom. His whole life was permeated "by the unshakable awareness that it was one with the divine life, that God's work was being brought about on him and in him, and that His will would be done; he therefore looks on it with inexpressible love and with the indestructible conviction that it is right and good."[11]

Let us sum up more clearly the idea we have gained from this analysis. The new idea of community combines the remnants of the idea of a Christian kingdom encompassing all humanity, with the idea developed through history, of the nation, a part of humanity. To put it differently: In the type of Fichte's idea of community, we are facing the possibility of granting any partial human

7. Fichte, *Die Anweisung zum seligen Leben* (1806), in *Werke,* IV, 481.
8. Fichte, *Staatslehre,* 589.
9. *Ibid.*
10. *Ibid.*
11. Fichte, *Über das Wesen des Gelehrten und seine Erscheinungen im Gebiete der Freiheit* (1806), in *Werke,* VI, 418.

community—whether it be a people, a tribe, a race, a class, or a party—the imperial claim of the Kingdom of God. In particular, this imperial claim means (1) that the community in question is chosen by God for a particular mission, that all other communities have to adjust to its specific nature and bow to its domination; (2) that anyone who fails to adapt, who offers resistance or even attacks, is not simply an ordinary enemy against whom the community must defend itself, but the "evil" enemy, a satanic evil spirit. This enemy does not offer resistance out of a desire to prevail based upon its conviction of its worth, but it is an embodiment of hostility toward God; (3) that therefore the battle against the other is a true and just war, and the community may dedicate itself to this war with full force, in the awareness of its divine mission, filled with deep, well-founded hatred for the devilish principle that opposes it; (4) that the community chosen by God does not act in blind faith but is wide awake, in possession of scientific insights into its relationship to God, its relationship to its enemies, and its mission in the world; and (5) since this insight has a scientific character, it can be imposed on anyone possessed of intellect; those who refuse to be persuaded are dim-witted or diabolical people or criminals.

I do not need to cite many examples to prove that this schema of ideas is followed by a great number of modern communities. All of post-Christian community development has increasingly followed it; there is a growing number of ever more sharply defined partial communities claiming to be the Kingdom of Christ. Each modern great nation has the conviction that it is the chosen one, selected before all others to bring happiness to humanity—this is true for the French and Americans as well as for the Germans. I refer here only in passing to the extreme expression of this conviction in "war psychosis." Even great political movements have also followed this type. Common to all is the idea of mission, all share a readiness to hate in case of conflict, all are persuaded of the absolute "scientific" correctness of their political demands, all are ready to suppress opposing views as "wrong" and therefore evil.

Fichte is not the originator of this movement; the formation of the nation-states as the principal types of the new particularist communities with a claim to the Kingdom began many centuries before him but in his philosophy, located at the turning point of ideas, the thought image of the new type is most clearly visible.

And, to be sure, Fichte presents his idea still unreflected; he lives in it, through his philosophizing he brings it into German consciousness at the crisis hour of the struggle against the Satan Napoleon. Fichte is not yet detached from it and cannot yet account for what has happened here in him and through him; he is only aware of having accomplished God's work and "looks upon it" with satisfaction—he looks upon it but does not look at it with a critical eye. Several decades later, Friedrich von Schelling looks critically at the work of the creation of nations out of the unity of humanity. Schelling examined this process not by looking at post-Christian pagan development but by focusing on the mythical tribal states of pre-Christian pagan history. Schelling deals with the problem of the descent of humanity into particularist communities in his investigation of the origin of myths: How does a myth emerge among a people? Schelling provides the answer that is crucially important to the real construction of the community and the method of investigation: Myths did not emerge within or under a people; rather, the reverse holds true, a people emerges from its myth. A people's or nation's ground of being [Seinsgrund] and its unity is its myth. Simply living together in an area does not unite individuals into a people; nor do they become a people by virtue of their shared pursuit of agriculture and trade or by a common legal order. What makes a people and sets it apart is "community of consciousness," "a common world perspective," a shared "mythology." A people or nation is not given its mythology in the course of its history; instead, its mythology determines its history. In fact, for Schelling the verb "to determine" still implies too great a distance between history and mythology, and therefore he formulates the statement that mythology *is* history itself; it is the destiny of the people, "just as the individual's character is his destiny, the fate cast for him from the outset."[12] Mythology is a people's consciousness, and with the rise of mythology peoples come to be, set apart from the context of humanity.

The impulse for the emergence of a people or a nation does not come from outside. The propagation and spread of man can create

12. Friedrich von Schelling, *Einleitung in die Philosophie der Mythologie. Book One: Historisch-kritische Einleitung in die Philosophie der Mythologie* (*Schellings Werke,* based on the original edition in a new arrangement, ed. Manfred Schröter; Vol. VI, Munich, 1928), XI, 65 (page numbering of the original edition).

new groups and tribes but not new peoples or nations. A "spiritual crisis" is needed to shake the consciousness of unity and drive men apart into nations. The unity was effected by a spiritual power, and separation into many is caused by new spiritual powers springing up. The principle binding people into unity was *one* God; the means of separating them is polytheism. The readiness to separate is already inherent in the primordial consciousness as a tragedy that can befall man. In the mythological process he deals not with things; "it is by powers rising within consciousness itself that he is moved."[13] The theogonic process, the process of creating gods, the process in which the myths and with them the peoples come into being is subjective in that it proceeds within consciousness and is evinced by generating images, but the causes and objects of these ideas "are the real in themselves theogonic powers." "The content of the processes are not simply *imagined* potencies but the *potencies* themselves."[14] In the doctrine of potency [*Potenz*] power is defined as the same being we have discussed above in the chapter on ideas in its two aspects of objective and subjective idea. The community reveals itself as idea, as thought construct in the minds of the people sharing in it, and precisely by appearing in the subjective idea the community also became objective reality. The mind of the concrete person proved to be the place where the objective mind entered and, at the same time, it was also the place where the idea was subjectively generated. Objective and subjective aspects of the reality of the mind [*Geistwirklichkeit*] that is called community are conditioned by the structure of self-awareness of the human mind. If the being in which the two aspects appear is seen as a unified, powerful, active, and self-presenting element, the meaningful content [*Bedeutungsgehalt*] Schelling calls potency comes into being. The potencies, the active powers, present themselves to the observer, who stands outside their processes: they are, on the one hand, the products of a community in the broadest sense, including characters as well as legal orders, works of art, economic systems, and doctrines of faith; and, on the other, the subjective ideas, the mental images, in which the community is created ever anew by its members. Schelling's doctrine of myth as

13. *Ibid.*, 207.
14. *Ibid.*

the ground of being of all peoples or nations seems to us the first profound insight into the religious nature, in the broadest sense, of all community formation. Fichte constructed his idea of community with a naive attitude, as one of the players of his time; Schelling maintains a distance from his subject and views the formation of community objectively as a theogonic process. Though he develops his doctrine by using pre-Christian myths, its methodological principles are equally valid for the contemporary community building and shed a bright light on its basically mythical feature, from which the individual characteristics noted above flow.

Moreover, Schelling made the first contribution to the psychology of particularist communities separating themselves from humanity. He speaks of the barb of internal unrest, the feeling of being no longer all of mankind but only a part of it, of no longer belonging to the absolute One but to have fallen prey to a particular god; he speaks of fear, of the horror at the loss of all consciousness of unity that spurs on those who are still united to set themselves apart even more sharply from the others and to forge an even closer bond among themselves so as to keep at least the partial unity of the people secure even though the all-encompassing unity of humanity has been lost. "This fear of the total disappearance of unity and with it of all truly human consciousness gave them not only the first institutions of a religious sort but even the first civic institutions whose purpose was none other than to secure what they had salvaged from their insight and to preserve it against further destruction."[15] We must strip these thoughts of their calculatedly rational [zweckrational] finish and must not misunderstand the "fear" as a concern for maintaining the unity. Rather, we must understand it in its existential meaning it has for Schelling as an arousal in which the total existence is experienced as fatally threatened, not indeed by an attack from a specific external direction but internally, by a metaphysical annihilation of existence; it is a horror not only of earthly death but of total annihilation. Schelling thus describes the inner situation people find themselves in when they temporarily or permanently lose their connection to the world on one or another or all levels of their being. The disparagement of the cosmic-vital connection between man and nature that charac-

15. *Ibid.,* 115.

terizes Christian history (if we leave aside exceptions such as Francis of Assisi) generates a readiness, higher than in other cultures and at other times, to yield to experiences of isolation, forlornness, desolation. These possibilities are kept in check for as long as the strong idea of a spiritual connectedness unites humanity as a whole and gives each individual a sense of security in this community and the meaning of his existence within it. Life in humanity, the orientation of the soul toward the human context, is an essential social experience in Scheler's sense, and the experience of a void clamoring to be filled does not disappear when the unitary idea is displaced by particularist ideas. Particularity inevitably contains the experiences of a loss of world, the experience of forlornness, the fear in the face of losing one's standing in the world, the horror at possible expulsion from the world, at total extinction. Schelling quite drastically interprets the dispersal of peoples across the globe as the result of fear and horror. Each people sees its particularity reflected in other particular communities, and it flees from this sight "until each saw itself all alone and separated from all that was alien."[16] The fear of metaphysical forlornness can be allayed by isolation in space, which prevents seeing other unities.

In Schelling's theory spatial distancing thus is the expression of the fear of loss of world. We need only translate the image of spatial distance into the mental sphere to rediscover the basic characteristics of Fichte's idea of community. Today the fear can no longer be allayed by actually removing the "other" from sight, and leaving the community as "the only one" (not the isolated one), but only by spiritual distancing through belief in one's own chosenness and in the diabolical nature of the other. An imperial claim is needed that sets up one's own nature as the only normative one, equally valid for all the other people. The particularist community overcomes its fear of its forlornness by claiming for itself the status of "world" and regarding all others as "non-world," as forlorn. We recognize fear as the deepest root of the new idea of community in its individual features. Out of fear arises the hatred for the counter-worlds, which, by their mere existence, can at any moment cast me back into the experience of fear. Out of fear arises Fichte's radical separation between the Kingdom of God and the Kingdom of

16. *Ibid.*, 111.

Evil as it is applied to actual societies. In our time this separation has been revived by Fichte's follower Othmar Spann, in his philosophy of history, in the doctrine of the evil demon, the monstrous. Out of fear arises generally the resentment in Nietzsche's sense as the vital envy [*Lebensneid*] (Klages) the weak feels for the strong life and even the readiness of the strong life to hate the other strong life because it awakens awareness of its own limits and touches more or less strongly the sensitive spot from which the panic of abandonment springs.[17]

Thus we have furnished the basic outline of a doctrine of the modern post-Christian community. We will now examine in detail how this schema, which can include all subsidiary contents of the entire *anthropos,* is filled in by body ideas.

17. The significance of Schelling's philosophy of mythology for the theory of community is gradually becoming clear. See Ernst Cassirer, *Philosophie der symbolischen Formen,* Pt. 2: *Das mythische Denken* (1925), 218ff. Further, see Gerbrand Dekker, *Die Rückwendung zum Mythos: Schellings letzte Wandlung* (1930).

5

The Expansion of the Horizon
Through History

Before describing how the race idea penetrates the post-Christian particularist communities, we must first recall that body ideas are not independent constructs but appear as part of a complex of ideas whose model is located in the mind. The body idea *contributes* to the building of the community, it is not an independent building principle. The transition from the body idea of the Christian kingdom to post-Christian race ideas takes place in conjunction with the change from the idea of the Christian community as encompassing all humanity to the particularist ideas of limited communal realities. Humanity is divided into individuals of the community who are no longer members of the kingdom but lead their lives based on sources of their own potencies. Many powers co-exist, all equal and each an ultimate power and not subsumed under a superordinate unity. (I am sketching here the ideal type of the new plurality of community; this is not to deny that the idea of humanity also continues to survive in historical reality.) With the collapse of the *res publica Christiana*, the particularistic communities become the units of history, and the picture of history changes completely, since non-Christian and pre-Christian history attains the same historical dignity as does Christian history. The organization of history, which heretofore had been firmly fixed, dissolves into an infinite field of flourishing and decaying units, all of which lack the ultimate aim of the redemption of mankind. The Christian order is replaced by historical anarchy, caused by the enormously expanded horizon of our historical knowledge at the end of the eighteenth and the beginning of the nineteenth centuries, and this expansion in turn caused and increased this expansion of the field of vision. The expansion of the historical horizon has been accompanied by an equally powerful loss of meaning in history, which very soon found expression in the pessimistic tone of the philosophy of history. For Wilhelm von Humboldt, historical individuals emerge from inscrutable depths as unique beings, perhaps complementing each other according to some unknown law to form a totality, but in any case destroying for the observer the meaning of the totality of events through their structural sameness. He counters the conviction already widespread in his day of the outstanding achievements of contemporary culture and civilization with the skeptical question of whether this high level means that "simultaneously the inner appearance of human nature, such as we see it for example, in some epochs of antiquity, has also returned with equal frequency and power or perhaps even to a heightened degree."[1] As the historical horizon expands, the observer's readiness to regard peoples and cultures as autonomous and to study them in terms of their uniqueness comes together with the experience, continuously nourished by more research, of lack of meaningful connection between the individual historical figures.

We can present only a rough idea of the enormous mass of material compiled out of the will to history since the late eighteenth century and strengthening the willingness to see uniqueness by briefly listing the principal events in the process of historicizing. In particular the old, well-known sources appear in a new light, the works of Homer, Herodotus, and Thucydides for Greek history and Livy for Roman history. August Böckh's work on the Athenian national budget appeared in 1817; it was followed by Otfried Müller's works on the interpretation of myths: in 1825, *Prolegomena zu einer wissenschaftlichen Mythologie;* in 1824, *Geschichten hellenischer Stämme und Städte.* In 1836 the two volumes of Johann Gustav Droysen's *Geschichte des Hellenismus* were published; George Grote's twelve-volume *History of Greece* began to appear in 1846. Edward Gibbon's *History of the Decline and Fall of the Roman Empire* was a fundamental work on the history of Imperial Rome; Barthold Niebuhr, in his Roman history, the first volumes of which were published in 1811–1812, concerned himself with the early period and had planned to continue his work and end at the point where Gibbon begins his account. In 1816 A. W. von Schlegel's review of Niebuhr's work was published. The first volume of

1. Wilhelm von Humboldt, *Über die Verschiedenheit des menschlichen Sprachbaues und ihren Einfluss auf die geistige Entwicklung des Menschengeschlechtes* (Berlin, 1836), 21.

Joseph Rubino's study of the Roman constitution and history appeared in 1839; 1834–1844 saw the publication of Wilhelm Karl August Drumann's history of Rome in its transition from a republican to a monarchic constitution; Niebuhr's lectures on Roman history appeared in 1847–1848. More detail about Egyptian history became known after Napoleon Bonaparte's expedition of 1798 and its result, *La Description de l'Egypte*. Thanks to Thomas Young's and Jean-François Champollion's efforts, the hieroglyphics were deciphered in 1821, and so the basic characteristics of Egyptian religion and the history of the dynasties could be outlined. The French-Tuscan expedition of 1827 under Champollion and Rosellini followed. Sir John Gardner Wilkinson's 1837 work, *The Manners and Customs of the Ancient Egyptians*, popularized what was known about Egypt among English-language readers. And finally, there were the successful Prussian expedition under Karl Richard Lepsius in 1842 and the publications resulting from it. Sources on Persian history began to become accessible at the end of the eighteenth century, starting with the first still-unreliable works of Abraham-Hyacinthe Anquetil-Duperron, whose translation of the *Zend-Avesta* appeared in 1771. Indian history began to become known with Henry Thomas Colebrooke's studies on Indian literature, religion, philosophy, and science, followed by the works of Franz Bopp: in 1816, *Über das Konjugationssystem der Sanskritsprache*, which laid the groundwork for comparative linguistics, and in 1834, *Kritische Grammatik der Sanskritsprache*; etc. Chinese history became known in more detail as early as the eighteenth century through De Mailla's *Histoire générale de la Chine* (13 volumes, Paris, 1777–1785), a translation of a Chinese work on the history of China.

The new race idea must also be seen as part of this process of historicization. Race theory has existed since the middle of the eighteenth century—the first major classification of races was made by Buffon. He based his work on the extensive descriptive travel literature, which increased in the first half of the eighteenth century as much as historical works did in the first half of the nineteenth century. To characterize this period we may speak of an expansion of the spatial horizon of our knowledge of man comparable to the subsequent temporal-historical expansion. Buffon already knew about the principal races as they were dispersed over the earth, but his classification was based on territories [*flächen-haft*]; the races were arranged side by side on a plain, and their greater or lesser exotic character in comparison to the European norm was the ordering principle. The historicizing of race to the point of interpreting the historical achievements of individual nations as due to their descent or their race still met with bitter resistance for some considerable time. Herder refused to apply the "ignoble" word to human beings; Fichte firmly rejected the idea that the mission of the Germans was conditioned by their race, and he stated explicitly that descent was irrelevant compared to the possession of an original language, which offered access to freedom in the mind. Even Schelling, who had included bodily differences in his inquiries to the extent of attributing their origin to the same spiritual crisis that had given rise to the different nations—even he sees as races only the exotic peoples whom "we now see truly de-based into races," while "European humanity should not in fact be called a race."[2] Until the middle of the nineteenth century, when Carl Gustav Carus put the finishing touches on race theory, the concept of race remained part of the animal sphere. The historiciz-ing of race, interpreting it as a determinative factor in history, thus did not take place all at once nor, indeed, has it been complete. Next to the completely transformed race concept, there remain others that have only partially been transformed and partially re-mained stuck in their older meaning. And, finally, the purely ani-mal concept of race also still survives.

We can grasp the process of transformation at the point where all ramifications are still possible, that is, in Gustav Klemm's cul-tural history.[3] As in Fichte, the eighteenth-century idea of hu-manity still serves as the general framework for Klemm's concep-tion of history. He does not yet see humanity as disintegrating into a number of historical figures but considers it an individual on a large scale, the different members of which need each other in order to bring about the unified whole. The two members complement-ing each other are the two basic races of man, one active and one passive, in an analogy to the male and female character types. The whole of humanity is one nature like the individual person himself,

2. Schelling, *Philosophie der Mythologie*, 97.
3. Gustav Klemm, *Allgemeine Kulturgeschichte der Menschheit* (10 vols.; Leip-zig, 1843–52).

"divided into two halves that belong together, one active and one passive, a male and a female one."[4] These two originally separated types must now combine and blend to fulfill the purpose nature pursues in all the branches of its organic creation. "Only by the blending of both races, the active and the passive—I would like to call it the marriage of peoples—does mankind become complete, only in this way does it enter into life and bring forth the flowers of culture."[5] At the present time in Europe, he continues, the blending of active Teutons with the prior passive population, strengthened by the spiritual force of Christianity and the irresistible power of the doctrine of the equality of all men before God, has led to an almost perfect condition that promises a high cultural flowering. Hierarchy and aristocracy collapse as the doctrine of equality advances, and the peoples of Europe are organized politically in the form of a constitutional monarchy, "which affords the freest development of all life forms." "The rule of law and the equality of all before the law—that is what the Circassians and the Arabs strive for and what motivates the life of the peoples of the new Europe."[6]

Klemm's race theory is a pretty banal conglomerate of all the thoughts a diligent researcher could receive from that era. Precisely for that reason it becomes important for our purpose, since we can read in it the possibilities for the unfolding of later race theory. In Klemm's work races appear as crucial factors in history, but their effect does not yet have the character of Fichte's idea of community in his opposition of divine and diabolical communities. The contrast between active and passive is only an allusion to the future separation of the great culture-creating Nordic race from all other less talented races. Here the political opposition between races and its intensification to a world-historical battle between the principles of good and evil is already anticipated, albeit in a form much softened by the overall harmony of Klemm's worldview.

Before we go on to the continuation of this historicization by Gobineau, we must note additional ramifications of Klemm's position. He calls his work a "cultural history" of humanity, and with this term he places himself in deliberate opposition to historiciza-

4. *Ibid.*, I, 196.
5. *Ibid.*, 204.
6. *Ibid.*, 253.

tion along the lines of Fichte's idea. Klemm names Herder and Kant and their ideas of a philosophical history of humanity as the forerunners of his own view of history. In contrast to this view of history, he notes, a new form of writing history has developed since the emergence of nation-states, which has gained predominance after the American and French revolutions. This new "political orientation of history," which had already since the time of Charles V and Louis XIV expressed itself in specialized history [*Spezialgeschichte*], was now also taking over universal history. Like theology at an earlier time, so now politics had become the subject everything else must serve: religion, art, poetry, geography, commerce, and trade—all had to be considered from this perspective. "The wars that were formerly waged for the honor of God and the glorification of His servants from now on were waged for the honor of the nation, architecture and sculpture that formerly served only God, his saints, and his servants now were used for the honor of the peoples, the states—in monarchic Austria and Prussia just as much as in republican America and France."[7] As representatives of this new brand of historian he names Johannes von Müller, Ludwig Spittler, A. H. L. Heeren, Karl Pölitz, Heinrich Luden, Ludwig Woltmann, Karl Rotteck, and Heinrich Leo. Hegel's name is also mentioned in this context: his history of humanity, Klemm claims, is a history of humanity within the state. And, indeed, Klemm here touches on one of the moments of Hegel's philosophy of history. The individual phases of history, the kingdoms, are ranked side by side as historical-political figures, as individualities; they are held together by the idea of the step-by-step dialectical development of the world spirit, so that each is not only an individuality but also a member with a particular place in the progressive succession. This succession, however, does not extend to infinity but has reached its goal with the contemporary Christian polity—the present is thus the fullness of time, the truly perfected realm of the mind, and with this, the Fichtean idea of the mission of the German state is once more adopted. Klemm is unwilling to participate in this movement of political history—he takes as his aim "to investigate and demonstrate" a gradual development of mankind, "from the rawest and earliest beginning, bordering on weakest childhood,

7. *Ibid.*, 20.

even on animal nature, to its articulation into the organic body of a people or nation [*Volkskörper*] in all their orientations—that is, in relation to customs, knowledge, and skills, domestic and public life in peace and war, religion, knowledge, and art, under the conditions offered by climate and providence."[8] In this form, the idea of evolution from animal beginnings to the current condition of mankind is entirely Kantian. Moreover, its content outlines a program that will later be taken up by "cultural histories"[9] and be pursued by ethnography and ethnopsychology, and we now find it again in naturalistic sociology. Here we see anticipated the split of the history of mankind into a primary "political" history of the civilized peoples on the one hand and those various disciplines of ethnology, ethnopsychology, and scientific sociology on the other, all of which study the lives of "primitives" with whom the former kind of history could not really connect. This is the split that (aside from the many other factors at play here) is in part caused by the collapse of the *pneuma* and *soma* of Christ into particularistic communities and their "politics" based on Fichte's opposition between the divine and diabolical, or as it is formulated today by Carl Schmitt, on the existential friend-enemy opposition.

Gobineau develops race theory further in the direction of politicizing and historicizing. In his work it receives its decisive form the effects of which became manifest immediately and have not ceased to this day.[10] The general framework is still formed by the shallow ideas of progress of the Enlightenment. Gobineau's concept of civilization hardly differs from Klemm's in its placid banality,[11]

8. *Ibid.,* 21.

9. See, for example, concurrent with Klemm's *Culturgeschichte:* Hermann Burmeister, *Geschichte der Schöpfung: Eine Darstellung des Entwickelungsganges der Erde und ihrer Bewohner* (1843); further: Georg Friedrich Kolb, *Culturgeschichte der Menschheit, mit besonderer Berücksichtigung von Regierungsformen, Politik, Religion, Freiheits- und Wohlstandsentwicklung der Völker: Eine allgemeine Weltgeschichte nach den Bedürfnissen der Jetztzeit* (1869), I. Anthropology eventually separates itself from this thematic group. The connection with the idea of cultural history can still be seen clearly in Theodor Waitz, *Über die Einheit des Menschengeschlechtes und den Naturzustand des Menschen: Anthropologie der Naturvölker* (Pt. 1, 1st ed.; 1858).

10. What is new in Gobineau's work is the interpretation of historical facts. The facts themselves—the movements and overlappings of races—are in part already summed up much earlier; for example, in Auguste Desmoulins, *Histoire naturelle des races humaines* (Paris, 1826).

11. Arthur Comte de Gobineau, *Versuch über die Ungleichheit der Menschenrassen,* trans. Schemann (4th ed.; 1927), I, 118.

but within this general framework, historicizing takes effect fully. Gobineau is *thoroughly* aware that his work on race is based on the wealth of historical material described above. In the dedication of his *Versuch* to George V of Hanover, he writes:

> The thick fog, the deep darkness, that has since time immemorial concealed from us the beginnings of the civilizations different from ours—today it is lifted, dissolves in the sunlight of science. A wonderful clarification of analytic methods discovers and explains to us, after having presented to us from Niebuhr's hands a Rome never known to Titus Livius, even the truths that are mixed in with the sagas about the childhood of the ancient Greeks. In another region of the world the Teutons, long underestimated, are revealed to us as just as great and majestic as they had seemed barbaric in the works of the writers of the eastern Roman Empire. Egypt opens its tombs, interprets its hieroglyphics, confesses the age of its pyramids. Assyria uncovers its palaces with all their inscriptions without end, palaces that not long ago were still lying impotent under their own ruins. The Iran of Zoroaster could conceal nothing from Burnouf's formidable researches, and in the Vedas ancient India tells us things that are very close to the day after the Creation. The totality of these attainments, each of which is already very significant by itself, leads also to a more precise and more splendid understanding of Herodotus, Homer, and especially of the first chapter of the Holy Scriptures, this treasure trove of statements whose richness and truth cannot be admired enough if only we approach them with a sufficiently enlightened mind.[12]

The grand panorama of the history of humanity, in which the major cultural figures appear one after the other without any visible connection and disappear again is the first source of Gobineau's pessimism. In spite of the current high level of civilization, the careful observer is overcome by a somber mood. According to Gobineau, there is nothing to justify the naive belief in man's infinite perfectibility; on the contrary, history teaches us that the same thing repeats itself over and over, though not into infinity, but with an outcome we can already glimpse, namely, the spiritual death of mankind, which will be followed by bodily death. The belief in human progress may be supported by the discoveries of natural science and the achievements of technology, but Gobineau asks what value the knowledge of natural laws and technological achievements can have for insight into the great mysteries of life and death,

12. *Ibid.*, xiii.

the creation of life forms, and the origins of being. Today, Gobineau argues, we do not know anything more than what the ancients already knew. "We have, it seems to me, changed the methods used in earlier times to encircle the mystery, but we have not taken even one step to penetrate its darkness."[13] The conquest of the physical world brings us no closer to the essential truths. The arts, morality, and political forms of the great cultures of the past were not only equal in value to those of the present but also similar in their structure. As proof, Gobineau cites comparisons of classical and modern political phenomena that, as far as content and intention are concerned, already clearly foreshadow what Oswald Spengler in his *Untergang des Abendlandes* has turned into a richly illustrated system: the parallelism of the great cultural forms. In his comparison of forms, Gobineau finds in the Tusculan Letters the thinking of progressive conservatives; Pompey and Cicero were liberals compared to Sulla; under the principate, Pliny the Younger was a moderate royalist, a supporter of peace at any price, an adherent of Trajan's skillful administration; there were those who out of fear of slave uprisings called for the rigorous use of force; and others who demanded and received constitutional guarantees; and through his claim that the rich and the poor were hereditary enemies the Gallic caesar, C. Junius become the acknowledged spokesman for socialist views; and finally, there had been the great mass of people "who, glad of order if it was present, tolerating disorder if it came as best they could, at all times admired the progress of the material enjoyments unknown to their fathers."[14] Cultures recur uniformly; what one has achieved is lost and must be newly attained by the next; the greatest intellectual attainments of our age do not surpass those of antiquity; humanity cannot transcend itself, and it "is therefore not infinitely perfectible."[15] The insight into the peculiar nature of man ever compelling him to strive beyond his reach and to conquer anew the world of body and mind while, on the larger view, always having him to move in circles leads to the skeptical reflection whether man's fate is in any way better than that of the animals. Animals lead their lives guided by instinct, whose wise prescience is the equivalent of an act of the intellect and which allows them

13. *Ibid.*, 209.
14. *Ibid.*, 213.
15. *Ibid.*, 224.

to find what they need for their lives, while man's greater intellectual scope and diminished connectedness to nature awakens needs in him that he cannot satisfy and condemns him to anxieties from which he cannot free himself.

The second source of pessimism is the overview of the movement of races, the mixture of races and its consequences. According to Gobineau, the cause of the decline of cultures and ultimately of mankind is the mixing of races. While Klemm assumed an active and a passive type, Gobineau assumes two basic kinds of races, the strong and the weak. Accordingly, a community capable of civilization is established when a victorious, racially strong tribe conquers a weak one and thus creates the preconditions for the flowering of a civilization. From the beginning such a structure contains the seeds of its own undoing, since the weak races increase in number within the society, pushing aside the strong ones, until finally the culture is deprived of its creative soul, the strong race, and the empty shell is inhabited only by the races incapable of civilization, driving it to its death—"a walking corpse."[16] Now, this rise and fall of cultures does continue into infinity. Humanity is a whole, a unique cosmic revelation, and when it has fulfilled its purpose, it will disappear again from the earth. This cosmic purpose is the ultimate conformity of all mankind as a whole to each other. The differences between races increasingly disappear as a result of constant mixing, and a level of uniformity appears that sinks the lower the more homogeneous it becomes because the strong, culturally creative elements are increasingly diluted and displaced. At the present time, Gobineau points out, there is no longer any place on earth that is not affected by mixtures, and with the spread of Western civilization over the globe, the homogenized end of humanity is coming into view. Increasingly, people become mediocre in terms of bodily strength, beauty, and intellectual gifts. "Soon everyone will possess the same share of this sad inheritance; there is no reason why one man should draw a richer lot than another."[17] In phrases reminiscent of Nietzsche, Gobineau describes the end:

The peoples—no, the human herds—will soon, overcome by gloomy narcolepsy, vegetate without feeling in their own nullity, like the buf-

16. *Ibid.,* 42.
17. *Ibid.,* 319ff.

163

falo chewing its cud in the stagnating puddles of the Pontine marshes. Perhaps they will think of themselves as the wisest, most erudite, and most capable beings that ever existed. . . . Our descendants, covered with shame, will have no difficulty finding some . . . reason by virtue of which they can bestow pity on us and to turn their barbarity into a badge of honor.[18]

Gobineau believes to have reason to estimate the full length of man's rule over the earth to its wretched end as 12,000–14,000 years, the greater part of which has already passed; only about 3,000–4,000 years remain from the present to the end. However: "The distressing event we have to look forward to is not death, it is the certainty that we will meet it in degradation; and perhaps we could become indifferent even to this indignity reserved for our descendants if only we did not feel with a secret shudder that the thieving hand of destiny already rests on us."[19]

Gobineau's pessimism is especially remarkable because the first major interpretation of contemporary history that is permeated by the mood of decline arose out of it. The beginnings of the decadence we customarily interpret as a fin-de-siècle phenomenon go further back; their roots are evident in Gobineau's work. Gobineau's statement that man, the conscious creature endowed with reason and striving to transcend himself, is less happy than the animal guided by its instincts offers profound insights. Cultural pessimism as such goes back a hundred years; Buffon already occasionally added sentimental observations to his reports on children raised among animals. They were, he wrote, "un spectacle curieux pour un philosophe, il pourrait en observant son sauvage, évaluer au juste la force des appétits de la Nature, il y verroit l'âme à découvert, il en distingueroit tous les mouvements naturels, et peut-être y reconnoitroit-il plus de douceur, de tranquillité et de calme que dans la sienne, peut-être verroit-il clairement que la vertu appartient à l'homme sauvage plus qu'à l'homme civilisé, et que la vice n'a pris naissance que dans la société" [a fascinating sight for a philosopher, who on observing the savage would be able to assess the inherent strength of the drives of nature, perceive the soul exposed before him, distinguish all its natural movements and perchance recognize more gentleness, tranquility, and calmness than in his own;

18. *Ibid.*
19. *Ibid.*, IV, 323.

he would even see with clarity that virtue characterizes the savage rather than the civilized man and that vice has only come into existence as a result of society].[20] The praise of the savage, of natural man, equating him with prehistoric man, comes close to a general underestimation of the human being, in general, but Buffon would never have doubted the *noblesse,* the special nobility of the creature whom he regarded as *imago Dei.* His religious worldview allowed him to doubt the value of culture and to think of the savage as the better man, but for him the savage was still a human being. For him, the "natural" man was not animal but indeed human, albeit without the questionable additions of civilization. Even Jean-Jacques Rousseau's anti-civilizational outlook was nourished by the sentimental view of nature as a better condition of man. For Kant, on the other hand, and essentially because of him, the concepts of man, nature, and culture were more rigidly defined. His interpretation of the history of mankind, guided by Genesis, also acknowledges a paradisal condition before the fall into sin. However, it is only through the fall into sin that the creature, previously guided by God, becomes human, now ruled by his own intellect and his autonomous reason. Becoming human and entering to the course of civilization coincide. If we want to call conditions before the Fall a state of nature, it is also a prehuman state. The idea of the savage man as the better man and the concomitant sentimental contemplation of culture is no longer possible for Kant. The evils of culture, of which he also is very much aware, are evils inherent in man's nature as a finite being; they necessarily accompany him in fulfilling his great task of approaching the condition of a new rational perfection in the infinite future. Thus, Kant's idea of man is no longer different in structure from Gobineau's, but it has a completely different inspiration—the readiness to collaborate in the great, progressive, unending work of mankind's becoming fully rational [*Vernünftigung*]. Kant's progressive optimism occasionally comes close to being heroic, as when he demands the fulfillment of duty in full awareness that the individual himself will not share in the higher state he is helping to bring about.

The material available to Gobineau for his interpretation of human history was very different from what Kant had. The latter

20. Buffon, *Histoire naturelle, générale, et particulière* (1749), VI, 278.

based his interpretations on a minimal amount of material, with Frederick the Great's enlightened absolute rule and the rise of the Prussian state the most important. Gobineau, on the other hand, was faced with the not very tasteful picture of the bourgeoisie's political ascendancy, the incipient vulgarization of political manners, the lowering of the level of discourse through the daily press, and corruption as the necessary milieu of politics. Furthermore, he had to deal with the enormous amounts of material made available to him by the science of history of the first half of the nineteenth century—he experienced the widening of the historical horizon and with it the insight into the parallelism of cultures, into the recurrence of the same social structures, all of which rendered any idea of infinite progress naive and scientifically unjustifiable.

> Like everyone else, I, too, have felt the anxious thirst for knowledge the restlessness of modern times inspires in us. But by employing all the powers of my mind to understand the motive force of this thirst for knowledge, I have seen the enormous horizon of what astonished me grow even more. I abandoned—gradually, I confess—the study of contemporary times in favor of earlier periods, then of all of the past. I have compiled these various fragments into an enormous whole and, guided by analogy, have turned almost against my will to prognosticating the most distant future. It no longer seemed to me desirable merely to know the immediate causes of our allegedly reformational storms: I strove to uncover the deeper reasons for the essential unity of the social ills that even the most imperfect knowledge of the history books of all nations that ever were, of those that are in existence now, and, in all probability, of those that will someday come into being reveal with sufficient clarity.[21]

Here the idea of the analogy of cultures, based on the science of history becomes the guiding principle of the interpretation of history, taking the place of the belief in divine, providence oriented toward a specific goal. The systematic ordering of world events by an otherworldly power disappears, and man finds himself abandoned to an innerworldly ordering of being, a destiny that oppresses and paralyzes, a destruction of traditional values that spares no goal hitherto considered worthwhile. In Gobineau we find awareness of finality [*Endschaft*] in its initial wretched force, which is hardly softened by his somewhat rigid and external Christian faith—finality without the charm it takes on in the fin-de-siècle.

21. Gobineau, *Versuch*, I, xii.

6

Race and State

In the preceding chapter we have isolated, as far as possible, the experience of the expanding historical horizon and its possible consequences for the change in the concept of race, and we also had to allude to some of the contents of the new race idea that legitimately belong to the typical phenomena of later developments. We shall continue with the following series of statements outlining the principal type of the political race idea: (1) All great historical cultures are based on a symbiosis of races; (2) there are human racial types that are clearly differentiated, either active and passive (Klemm) or strong and weak ones (Gobineau); (3) all races, or at least the active or strong ones, migrate; (4) in the course of migration, conquests occur—the conquest of the weak by the strong; (5) conquest results in a symbiosis of races, which ends with the disappearance of the strong race either interbreeding or through quantitative displacement; (6) as a result of the disappearance of the strong race from the symbiosis, the tension of domination within the community disappears, and a uniform level is formed—and opinions differ radically on its value.

The basic outline of these six theses is filled in very different ways. We already briefly mentioned Klemm's and Gobineau's attempts. Klemm originated the concept of the marriage of peoples [*Völkerehe*], in which two human groups of polar opposite types—male and female, active and passive—join to form a unified cultural people [*Kulturvolk*]. Humanity consists of two parts: the active and the passive races, and according to Klemm, the active one is smaller in number but multiplies more vigorously. The physical type of the active race is that of the Caucasian man: tall, strong, with a rounded skull; dominant forehead; prominent nose; fine, often curly hair; heavy beard; delicate, white, translucent skin. The typical youth was represented by the Apollo of Belvedere, the adult male type in the Farnese Hercules. The psychical habitus of this race is characterized by predominant will; a striving for dominance, independence, and freedom; activity, restlessness, a yearning toward distant lands, a striving for progress in things spiritual, drives to research and testing, defiance and doubt. Historically, Persians, Arabs, Greeks, Romans, and Teutons belonged to this type. They were founders and overthrowers of nations, seafarers, researchers, and fighters for a liberal constitution.[1]

The passive races, in Klemm's view, are characterized by colored skin, the predominance of the back of the head; backward-sloping forehead; round, blunt nose; elongated, often slanted eyes; prominent cheekbones; receding chin. These types found their ideal representation in Egyptian and Indian works of art. Psychologically, these races, like women, develop rapidly but soon stagnate (as examples Klemm lists the numerous inventions of the Chinese that were not further developed and used). In these races writing was invented early but survived only in rigid forms; only the active races developed alphabets. Intellectually the passive races are indolent, avoiding research and thought; they have laws but no natural law; they are skilled in psychology but lack any philosophy; they know the human body and cures but have no medical science. Their forms of government merely repeat the structure of family life. They have all the advantages of women: they are charming, polite, preserve customs, are averse to violence. And they also have all the shortcomings of women; they are cunning, sly, focused narrowly on the present moment, and lack circumspection.

Klemm imagines both races radiating outward from centers located in Asia. According to his view, the passive race migrated first and populated the entire earth, covering it with a layer of "primal population." Then the active race set out from a point located somewhere near the Himalayas and subjugated this "primal population." Conquest and subjugation resulted in nations with a class structure, so that the passive race practiced agriculture and cattle breeding and the active race made up the warrior class and occupied itself during times of peace with hunting and other occupations worthy of free men. The governmental form that arises in the course of conquest is monarchy, and the decentralization of power

1. Klemm, *Culturgeschichte,* I, 192–93.

takes on the form of a feudal system in which the booty is distributed. "This is one of the fruits of every conquest, and we have seen
it recur in the age of Napoleon."[2]

Klemm was particularly concerned with the "migrations": he
supplied a detailed motivation for the wanderings of the active
races and a carefully elaborated system of the migrations that actually occurred in history.[3] The motivation for migrations, according to Klemm, is to be found in the desire for property, for fame, in
the longing for distant lands, the striving for independence and freedom that awakens under threat from forces more powerful than
we. The migrations proceeded south and north from a limited area
in Central Asia. The southern migrations extended westward to
Egypt (documented by the Caucasian-looking royal portraits in
Ippolito Rosellini's *Monumenti dell'Egitto e della Nubia*), eastward
to the South Sea Islands, where a "black indigenous population
with light-skinned rulers" is found. The northern migration went
as far east as Manchuria, as far west as the conquest of Europe.
Based on these waves of migration of the active race, we can distinguish a series of cultural periods in Europe. The first wave
brought the Iberians, Pelasgians, and Celts; they subjugated the passive indigenous population and established theocratic-aristocratic
forms of government in which the masses were oppressed and
treated despotically; cyclopian masonry and cliff dwellings are the
cultural remnants of this conquest. The second wave, the Hellenic
wave, saw "the Caucasian heroes attacking the old theocracies
with rough force." They succeeded in developing the forms they
found into freer ones, but the struggle with the traditional culture
sapped their strength, and their conquest ends with the Roman
monarchy and hierarchy. The third wave, the Teutonic wave, was
the strongest wave of immigration; supported by the spiritual
power of Christianity, it advanced relentlessly and reshaped the
political forms toward the ideal of constitutional monarchy—the

2. *Ibid.*, 200ff.
3. These studies are found in a section entitled "Die Verbreitung der aktiven
Menschenrasse über den Erdball" (The Spread of the Active Human Race over the
Globe) in Vol. IV of *Culturgeschichte*, inserted between the chapters on the Bedouins
and the South Sea Islanders (pp. 229–60). In terms of topic, this section belongs
among the discussions in the first volume; it is included in the fourth because it
was not written until after the earlier volumes were published. According to Schemann, this essay appeared in 1845 as a private publication (see Schemann, *Gobi-
neaus Rassenwerk* [1910], 296).

ultimate significance of which in Klemm's system we have already pointed out above.

Basically, Gobineau fills in the outline in the same way as Klemm, except that he explains one of his phases, that of the process of conquest and symbiosis, in more detail. An active people, in Gobineau's schema, must pass through a series of steps before it becomes a culture's ruling class and disappears in it. In the first step a tribe, "yielding to a crucial instinct of its vital force, imposes laws on itself and begins to play a role in this world."[4] Not all tribes are capable of reaching this first step; very many do not get beyond their primitive existence as a horde, and their entire statecraft consists of the victory of stronger individuals over weaker ones and the flight of the weaker from the stronger; the Australian blacks of Polynesia, the Samoyeds, and numerous African tribes persist in this primal state. Those tribes, on the other hand, that have attained self-awareness, grasp that "if they wish to increase their power and prosperity, it is absolutely necessary for them to compel their neighbors, by military or peaceful means, to enter into their own sphere of existence."[5] They reach the second step where as a result of successful wars against their neighbors, they integrate into their community as a social underclass, as slaves, and simple classes split off from each other. "Many are content with this system and atrophy in it."[6] But those who move on to the third stage find it more profitable to subjugate their neighbors permanently instead of plundering them now and then. They no longer take prisoners of war but seize the land together with its inhabitants. Between the conquerors and the vanquished there arises a community of work, of interests, and of life, and finally mixing of blood takes place, "and the people of both lines of descent no longer live separately in different tribes but more and more merge with each other."[7] The nation that thus comes into being will now itself fall prey to conquest and will eventually either merge with another nation or extend its territory by war and thus absorb ever more new blood elements. As interbreeding continues, the original rulers are gradually subsumed into the subjugated races. In addition, the rul-

4. Gobineau, *Versuch*, I, 33.
5. *Ibid.*, 35.
6. *Ibid.*
7. *Ibid.*, 36.

ers live in particularly precarious conditions; they are few in number and must recruit new members from the ranks of the subjugated groups to handle the increasing number of tasks resulting from the expansion. Moreover, the upper class has a lower birth rate, and finally, its kind of work diminishes its ranks further through death in battle and through ostracism or banishment as the result of dangerous positions in the state, and so forth. In this way is attained before too long the above-mentioned condition of cultural contents and social institutions continuing unchanged even though the composition of the blood of the people living in it has changed completely.[8]

The idea of the process we have delineated here in its main phases is based—implicitly in Klemm, explicitly in Gobineau—on the premise that the polar opposites of the race types, whose contacts serve as explanation of world events, remain constant throughout known history. For religious reasons, Gobineau has decided to assume monogenesis, the descent of the human species from an original couple, as taught in Genesis. Accordingly all racial differences could have come about only in the course of history, which gives rise to the question why the races are assumed not to change anymore, and passive races cannot suddenly become active, ruling ones. To explain this contemporary constancy in spite of prehistorical changes, Gobineau enlists Georges Cuvier's theory elaborated in *Révolutions du Globe*. There Cuvier assures us "that the current level of inorganic forces could by no means set in motion earthquakes, upheavals, and formations similar to those attested to by geology."[9] In comparison to those earlier epochs of earth's history, the omnipotence of nature has disappeared or at least is so diminished "that in a number of years, which are roughly equivalent to half the time that our species has spent on earth, [it] has brought forth no change of any significance, much less anything that can be compared to those fixed features that have permanently separated the various races."[10] According to Cuvier, the separation of the races must have taken place in the time period shortly after Creation, when powerful creative upheavals could still cause effects unimaginable today. After that primordial period, the types

8. *Ibid.*, 41–42.
9. *Ibid.*, 182.
10. *Ibid.*, 183.

did not undergo further changes. Here as elsewhere in the literature on this question, the favorite piece of evidence for the constancy of types is the reference to the Egyptian works of art showing people and animals with the physical habitus we still see in them today.

I have described Klemm's and Gobineau's method of filling in the outline in somewhat greater detail to present comprehensively the total range of the dogmatic content of culture-interpreting race theory; subsequent literature on race reveals hardly any important thought that is not prefigured in this scheme of dogmatism—even though the materials included in this outline vary enormously.

Although the huge amount of material allows a great number of possibilities for filling in the schema, in fact only a few have been used. The occasions for formulating race theories grow out of the two great sources of material, extensive knowledge of ethnology and of historical time. The existence of primitive peoples has been a source of uneasiness in anthropology and philosophy from the time they were first studied to the present day. Their significant deviation from the European human norm is indisputable, and scientific studies of them range all the way from devaluing them as "savages" to the contemplative stance of a Lucien Lévy-Bruhl, who is intent on showing the meaningful consistency of the primitive people's spiritual and intellectual world of forms. Even in this treatment eschewing value judgments does not eliminate the problem raised by the idea of man as a unified whole being [*Wesens-Einen*] but presents it even more clearly and more urgently. At this point explaining the different manifestations of the human being in its essence as caused by physical difference is always very tempting, and most especially so where our knowledge of the two types, the standard European and the primitive, is not limited to merely *seeing* them juxtaposed but where they enter into social relationships—a relationship of rule and obedience. The typical occasions for discussing race differences are the clashes between Europeans and people of color—in the colonialization of America and Australia, in India, and with the imported Negroes in America. Ideas about race differences were even carried to the point of metaphysical speculations that abolished the unity of the human being and assigned a unique ontic area to the colored races between man and animal.

In the tension of the relationship of domination to primitives, the moment of primitivity coincides with the factor of the differences in social power in a living community. The second factor taken by itself is a thread that runs through the entire history of national cultures as the unchanging motive for interpretations based on race theory. Wherever we find warlike tribes and peoples that, after conquest, become the ruling classes of the new social construct, the difference in power status can be explained and justified as arising from qualitative differences between the ruling and the ruled strata, differences that are in turn determined by physical differences. Since the history of national cultures in all periods is *also* a history of wars, of external and internal struggles, victories, and defeats, all its phases in principle can be interpreted in terms of race theory. Thucydides already found "migration" interesting because it was the preliminary phase of "conquest" and the founding of states; the "aboriginal people" is the boundary concept designating in each case the peoples about whose migrations and conquests we know nothing. As the study of history advances and new sources reveal that those peoples did also migrate, the "aboriginal people" are pushed back one step. The difficulties defining the boundary based on this view are perfectly obvious in all instances where it is applied honestly, as, for example, in Klemm's work. His active race migrates precisely because it is active, driven by a longing for glory and faraway places, a thirst for adventure and possession. But what about the passive races? They, too, migrated; and since they cannot have migrated for the same reasons as the active races (or else they too would have been active), their motives are shrouded in silence—unless we assume that in spite of their passivity, they migrated out of simple good nature, so that later the active race would find an aboriginal population for its conquests. The difficulty comes from the fact that, beyond the "migrations," the mystery of the origins of humanity arises. Since Klemm could not easily let the aboriginal population grow out of the soil everywhere as in the ancient myth, and since, on the other hand, he was uneasy, and rightly so, about the alternative to the myth, the "scientific" explanation of polygenesis, he stayed with a relatively biblical view, letting the races start out from "central" points to cover the earth in every direction.

The scope of the material that furnishes proof for a race theory coincides with world history; Klemm's system of migrations spans the entire globe insofar as each place possesses a cultural history, and subsequent race theories make use of newly discovered materials in the same sense. The South Sea Islanders have light-skinned rulers; Christ was a Nordic person; David had red hair; Dante was of Teutonic descent; the Chinese culture arose after the subjugation of the original inhabitants through a Nordic tribe; Central American cultures have their white gods, which indicate that . . . and so forth. The concrete motives for selecting and ordering the historical material in this manner are to be found in the political history of the period. The social upheavals in the history of England and, even more so, of France and the end of the European aristocracy as the ruling and privileged class draw attention to the losses and gains in power status and the "admixtures" of classes. The increasing general similarity of social levels through the equalizing of their overall lowering takes place in plain sight and guides our view to a future in which the process will have been completed and a new stable social order will have been established. This image of the future is judged differently, depending on the social class and political ideals of the historian making the judgment. Klemm's optimism grew out of his roots in the middle class, which saw in the development and consolidation of constitutional monarchy the political form appropriate to its style of being. Gobineau, on the other hand, regards the same phenomena pessimistically because he regrets especially the decline of his class, the aristocracy, and its way of life, and fears the coming rise of the *roture*, followed closely by that of the *crapule*. The fall of the aristocracy, the victory of the third estate, and the threat to the third by a growing fourth, are all crowded together in a half-century and accompanied by vehement agitation of social events so as to create such a strong impression of the uncertainty of all traditional forms that had been considered unshakable that the entire realm of national and class-based forms of thought and life becomes, as it were, transparent, making visible its solid underpinnings in rulership and its power base in all its nakedness. The second half of the century saw the reinterpretation of the political idea and the idea of law into an ideology by Marx, into Nietzsche's theory of power, and into the analysis of the "theory of power [*Gewaltstheorie*]" by Engels as well as the analysis of the power base of the constitution by Lasalle, whose influence can still be clearly seen in Max Weber's "massive" sociology.

Around the end of the last century, the motifs of race and power theory, the transformation of the community of warlike aristocrats into a peaceful middle-class society, the prospect of the future free association of working people in a community without classes were combined in various ways into doctrines on the nature of the state, and we must briefly look at their principal traits.

Ludwig Gumplowicz found caste distinctions in all states, and in his view, caste distinctions are racial differences: thus there is no state on earth without a multiplicity of races and without a clash between the races in its past. States arose because two races went to war against each other and the more advanced race was victorious and permanently subjugated the vanquished race. Here the active and passive races appear in the guise of more or less advanced races. Like other sciences, *Staatslehre* has also been affected by the theory of evolution, and what had earlier been accepted as simply given now was the product of development. According to Gumplowicz, the qualitative differences between races are the expression of their prehistorical or historical evolution: the prehistorical or cosmic age of a race depends on the time of its emergence—here mankind is presumed to have originated in many tribes at once, that is, polygenetically—its historical age depends on the time when the race formed a nation and thus entered into history. The cosmic differences determine the superiority in terms of the founding of a state; the historically developed race differences determine the relationships of superiority among the races within present-day nations. In the course of history a third class pushes its way between the first two, manifested socially as aristocracy and slaves; this third class, the middle class, did not develop out of the two others but immigrated as an alien race—Gumplowicz thus conceives of the typical social organization of his time entirely in terms of race theory. The various forms of the state—patrimonial state, feudal state, theocratic state—must be seen as phases in an evolution ending with the emergence of the modern nation-state, constitutional monarchy, and parliamentarianism. Gumplowicz's view of the content and goal of the process is very much like Gobineau's: the struggle of the races within the state "speeds up the course of culture and civilization by slowly softening the racial contrasts, clearing the way for cross-breeding and mixing of the races, and thus over time turns the former conglomerate of races into one people, one nation. Of course, with this the apex of the evolution of the state is reached, and nations cannot remain there for very long. For with the cessation of the race struggle, stagnation begins to set in within the life of the state, and this leads to the decline and collapse of the state, which now once again serves foreign conquering tribes as the arena for new activity and new nation building."[11]

Gumplowicz differs from Gobineau in the narrower scope of the temporal horizon he allows to influence the central tone of his view of history. Gobineau saw "the hand of destiny" already resting on his own time, and consequently his outlook is unmitigatedly gloomy. Gumplowicz foresees the same end but at a greater distance: he is more closely concerned with the prospect of an upward evolution toward an increasing mixing of the races in his native state, Austria-Hungary. The clash of nationalities in Austria served as a model and orientation for his theories of racial struggle in the state and its necessity. In Austria the disputes flourished so abundantly that he feared the decay of the nation through stagnation far less than its eventual collapse because of irreconcilable differences between the races. He also considered this possibility: if the races within a nation do not come together and reconcile, "then the nation perishes before its time because of the irreconcilability of its racial differences, that is, because of the impossibility of fulfilling its civilizing mission."[12] In the normal process, on the other hand, time mediates among the races: "Education and civilization fill the abyss that gapes between the various elements of the people; the original variety is raised to a unity; a focal point of patriotic and national feeling forms in the shared national consciousness, and the agglomerate of races turns into—the nation."[13] When comparing Austria to other nation-states that have already arrived at their goal of civilization, Gumplowicz consoles himself with the thought "that, even if we Austrians are not yet a single nation of brothers,

11. Ludwig Gumplowicz, *Der Rassenkampf: Soziologische Untersuchungen* (2nd ed.; 1909, 1st ed.; 1883), 397. The discussion in the text follows the treatise "Rasse und Staat" and the lecture "Über das Naturgesetz der Staatenbildung," both from 1875; they are reprinted in the appendix to *Rassenkampf*. The quoted section is from the lecture.

12. Gumplowicz, *Rassenkampf*, 391.

13. *Ibid.*, 392.

our race struggles are nevertheless historically justified and will surely help to fulfill a great historical mission in the future."[14]

After Gumplowicz, other motifs from ethnology were combined with the *Staatslehre*-based theories of race and power. Friedrich Ratzel developed a theory according to which the established organization of states and all higher civilization developed out of the encounter between two tribes, one of which had an agriculture-based economy while the other's was based on nomadic cattle breeding. The agriculturalist, according to Ratzel, is characterized by an inherent, natural weakness "which is easily explained through his unfamiliarity with the use of weapons and through his love of property and a settled life, which saps his courage and enterprise." On the other hand, political strength and the ability to form a state is found to a high degree in the hunter and herdsman, "especially among the latter, who combines the capacity to act on

14. *Ibid.*, 401. Gumplowicz' race theory is embedded in the doctrine of the implacability of natural laws as interpreted in Darwinian terms; the fate of the race and the process of founding and developing a nation are inexorable. This is the fatalism that typically must arise in every theory attempting to solve humanistic problems with the help of a materialist metaphysics.

Gobineau's pessimism is also inherent in his theory, in his assumption of race as an inevitable natural phenomenon, and all later materialist race theories include the same component of fatalism. Modern race theories give the impression of an aggressive optimism because, like technology, they are eager to put to use the lawful course of nature in order to arrive at a specific objective they consider desirable. With a fatalism no different from Gobineau's, they hold that the intellectual worth of a race and a person depends on a body of a particular sort, but they hope to rescue culture by eugenic [*volkshygienisch*] measures intended to increase the number of those members of the nation [*Volksmitglieder*] who are physically and therefore intellectually valuable. In Gumplowicz's work, too, we find an attitude of complacent and sometimes malicious pleasure in the inexorability of natural law, but it arises less from delight in inexorability or a tendency to fatalism than from the exalted feeling of the scholar, who experiences the naturalistic interpretation of history as his own and, relishing possession of the truth, triumphs over the spirit-forsaken [*geistverlassen*] creatures who hold an opinion different from his own. I cite here one passage on the science of history: "It praises the deeds of great men without noticing that they are merely puppets, pushed this way and that by the secret strings of an eternal law of nature— they admire these *puppets* instead of expressing astonishment at those secret mainsprings that, since time immemorial, noiselessly perform their unchanging movements in nature's workshop, making mankind always run along *the same tracks* by their iron leading strings—always the same circular path between death and life, between decline and rise, between destruction and rejuvenation, with the same eternal regularity and indifference with which the sun and the moon run their course, with which day and night and the seasons change. For this grandiose drama of nature . . . the 'science' of history has no feeling" (*Rassenkampf*, 160–61). For the genealogy of Gumplowicz's concept of nature, see details in G. Salomon's foreword to Gumplowicz's *Ausgewählte Werke*, Vol. I: *Geschichte der Staatstheorien* (Innsbruck, 1926).

a massive scale with mobility, discipline with strength." When a
herding people conquers an agricultural tribe, a firm structure develops "because the conquering and cohesive force of the nomads
here becomes wedded to the industry of the agricultural people,
who by themselves do not form states."[15]

Gustav Ratzenhofer integrated Ratzel's theory into Gumplowicz'
system by replacing the doctrine of the inequality of the warring
races because of their differing origins with that of an originally
uniform humanity that, on the basis of different types of economic
organization, separated into the aggressive, violent nomadic tribes
and the conservative, peace-loving, and settled agriculturists. Here
the above-mentioned active and passive races have finally become
tribal types whose character is determined not by physical differences but by differences in economic activity. That these types can
be interchanged is symptomatic of the close relationship between
the economic and the biological materialist view of man.[16]

An additional motif that blends with those already discussed
arises from Herbert Spencer's theory of the evolution of societies
from the warrior nation to the industrial-peaceful one. Gumplowicz already used this element to classify the ages of the races. He
distinguished between prenational existence, characterized by
hunting, fishing, cattle raising, and agriculture, and the two stages
of nations, the first of which is characterized by the rule of the
aristocracy and by war while the second brings forth the "arts of
peace," the sciences, diplomacy, industrial enterprises, and other
achievements of the "aging races."[17] Ratzenhofer echoes this idea
when he notes on one occasion, "This right of conquest, as the
consequence of superiority in violence, is at all times juxtaposed
to the right of work as the result of productive industry."[18]

Thus we have assembled all the motifs that make up Franz Oppenheimer's theory of the origin of the state [Landstaat]. Race
theory has disappeared entirely and is replaced with the cluster of
ideas surrounding the theory of power initiated by Karl Marx. "By
virtue of its origin the state is entirely, and by virtue of its nature
in the first stage of its existence it is almost entirely a social insti-

15. Friedrich Ratzel, *Völkerkunde* (1887), I, 18–19.
16. Gustav Ratzenhofer, *Soziologische Erkenntnis* (1898), 146–47.
17. Gumplowicz, *Rassenkampf*, 384.
18. Ratzenhofer, *Soziologische Erkenntnis*, 146.

tution forced on a vanquished human group by a victorious one for the sole purpose of regulating the rule of the latter over the former and safeguarding the rulers against internal uprisings and external attacks. And rule had no other ulterior motive than the economic exploitation of the vanquished by the victors."[19] Limiting this nature of the state to its first stage leaves room for Spencer's theory of warlike and peaceful conditions. According to this view, people can satisfy their needs in two ways, first, through peaceful economic exchange and, second, through the political means of violent seizure of foreign labor without payment. The state is the organization of political means and therefore could arise only where the economic means had already stockpiled a ready supply for the satisfaction of needs that was worth plundering. Therefore, the typical primitive beginning of the state, as Ratzel and Ratzenhofer have shown, was the attack by a tribe of herdsmen on an agricultural tribe and the subjugation and exploitation of the latter. When the conquest is achieved, the state gradually develops from its warlike-political condition to an economic status, with the ultimate goal of "free citizenship" ["*Freibürgerschaft*"]—a concept in which liberal ideas blend with the free association of the *Communist Manifesto*. Oppenheimer's inquiry ends with a harmonious vision:

> Philosophy of history, which has studied the trend of *state evolution*, and economics, which has studied the trend of *economic development*, have arrived at the same conclusion: the economic means have won out all along the line, the oldest and toughest form of the political means has disappeared from society: capitalism withers away with large-scale land-holdings [*Grossgrundeigentum*] and land rent [*Grundrente*].—That is humanity's suffering and redemption [*Leidens- und Erlösergang*], its Golgotha and its resurrection into the eternal Kingdom: from war to peace, from hostile fragmentation of the hordes to the peaceful unity of humanity, from animality to humanity, from the state of plunder to free citizenship.[20]

19. Franz Oppenheimer, *Der Staat* (1907), in *Die Gesellschaft*, Vols. XIV/XV, 8–9.
20. *Ibid.*, 168.

7

The Jews as Counteridea

Neither the type of the new particularist community in general nor its realization through body ideas occurs in its pure form in the early stages. The old ideas of an overarching human context are still clearly visible, and remain so, though to a lesser degree, to this day. Both Klemm and Gobineau conceived of humanity as a cosmic revelation, the one looking toward a happy ending and the other to an unhappy one. The Kantian idea of a final state of the perfect rationality of human beings is continued by Fichte in his theory of the extinction and withering away of the state, which recurs in identical terms in the Communist idea of the end of the state. The mood of redemption connected with the final state of blessedness still colors the National Socialist idea of the Third Reich. In the doctrine of Kant, Klemm, and Gobineau, the idea still embraces all of humanity; in Fichte a particular group appears as the bringer of salvation—the German nation; in communism, a class. In National Socialism, the field of redemption is confined to the nation, and its bringer is a particular community within the nation, presented as an elite. This narrowing is accompanied by the parallel dissolution of the traditional social structure, and "power"—of the sort described in the previous chapter—becomes increasingly evident as the connecting link between various particularist communities. This increasing visibility of "power" means, negatively, that the traditional, overarching community ideas disappear from sight.

Under the assumption that the basic framework of the new community idea becomes increasingly clear and sheds what has remained of the earlier idea, we must now characterize how such a particularist community with a body idea develops through the simultaneous rise of its counterimage. Fichte's idea of the opposition of the divine and satanic kingdoms anticipated the scheme according to which a particularist community shaped in part by a body idea—Aryan, Teutonic, German, Nordic—becomes aware of itself as its counterpart becomes visible. Similarly, every race must have a counterrace or antirace, which is, in fact, what the Jews have occasionally been called.[1] Which group of the population functions as the counterrace depends on the prevailing population structure of the territory in which the race idea gains ground as well as on external circumstances. In the United States the race idea chiefly has *two* counterraces: the Negroes and the immigrants from southern and eastern Europe. These counterrealms have grown out of the importation of certain demographic groups, the African Negroes, and the second so-called bad immigration after 1880. In Europe today this definition of a race through its counterrace takes place in its broadest sphere through the counterimage of the Jews, even though in the last few decades other demographic groups—in Germany especially the Eastern European race [*ostisch*]—have taken on a similar function. We will limit our investigation here chiefly to Germany in an effort to characterize the fundamental traits of the development of the most important counterrace—which is simultaneously the development of the race that creates a counterrace for itself—the Jews.

It is astonishing that the Jews should have become the counteridea of the Germans, and with such extraordinary intensity, considering that in the German Reich they account for only 1 percent of the population. How could a minority of such insignificant number attract so much hatred? Undoubtedly this hate is largely due to a feeling of inferiority on the part of the Germans, to their fear—repeatedly expressed in the anti-Semitic literature—of being dominated by the Jews, to the Germans' belief in a worldwide organization of all Jews directed with diabolical cleverness toward the ultimate, total economic enslavement of the Aryans and, most particularly, of the Germans. There has been much guessing about this riddle—perhaps a completely satisfactory solution is not possible; perhaps peoples are historical entities that cannot be further analyzed or reduced, and *why* some have a closer inner affinity while others hate each other should not, perhaps, be asked. Descriptive analyses of the Jewish type, on the other hand, are frequently presented in order to show why they are incompatible with other

1. See Alfred Rosenberg, *Mythus des 20. Jahrhunderts* (1931), 437.

types, and the most significant attempt in this direction seems to me to be that of Werner Sombart.[2]

According to Sombart, the peculiarity of the Jewish type consists in four basic characteristics, from which the others can be derived: (1) intellectualism, the predominance of intellectual capacities and interests before all others, especially manual skills; (2) an egocentric pragmatism, the clear setting of short-range goals for daily life; (3) energetic determination; (4) great intellectual flexibility. Conflict is inevitable when people of this kind live with others for whom (1) reason is not an independent substance but an instrument, and not a very refined one at that, for the coping with situations determined primarily by the *Lebensraum* and sphere of activity of people in the community; (2) personal status in the community is a guiding principle for the way they lead their lives; (3) who therefore do not possess that energetic determination that serves to expand, change, and improve status; and (4) who therefore do not require great mobility for their way of life, who in fact consider such mobility immoral. However, this characterization merely contrasts two types of people without explaining why permanent conflicts, continuing through decades and centuries, between Germans and Jews have seemed inevitable. After all, the tiny minority would conceivably have adapted to the lifestyle of the majority. To a certain extent, adaptation is clearly possible, since there have always been individual Jews who were able to integrate themselves into the German community.[3]

A complete explanation for why the German-Jewish conflict is so tenacious and refuses to disappear does not, as I noted, exist. The following possibilities might be considered.

(1) The intellectual and ethnic history of the Jews has produced a psychological and physical type that differs markedly from the northern European ethnotypes [*Völkertypen*] and cannot change. The advantage of this explanation is that it emphasizes the distance between an Oriental and a Northern European people; it is unsatisfactory because the Jews would then be the only people in the

2. Werner Sombart, *Die Juden und das Wirtschaftsleben* (1911).

3. On the interpretation of "Jewish traits," see also Arthur Ruppin, *Soziologie der Juden,* Vol. I: *Die soziale Struktur der Juden* (1930), 53–54. These traits are considered to be traits of people of all *ancient* cultures. "The mentality shown by today's Jews is the mentality of tomorrow's non-Jews."

history of nations that have neither perished nor adapted to or blended with other peoples in spite of living in dispersion.

(2) A pariah existence under persecution, lasting for a thousand years, bred the qualities that today appear to be Jewish; a tenacious tradition became established, and it cannot easily be shattered. This explanation, in my opinion, explains nothing at all, since the problem consists precisely in why persecution did not lead to some form of disintegration but resulted instead in the development of an ever more pronounced Jewish type (quite aside from the fact that, as far as we can tell, the type was already firmly established at the beginning of the diaspora).

(3) The type of the Western assimilationist is characterized by a peculiar psychological blindness toward the reality of the peoples among whom he lives. Assimilation is thus hardly possible because he does not see to what he must adapt. This explanation allows us to understand a number of phenomena, but what remains astonishing is the enormous tenacity and vitality with which this unique character has been maintained and preserved. Moreover, this explanation is contradicted by the fact that there are Jews who are in fact quite capable of understanding the foreign character and of bringing themselves into line with it.

(4) The capacity to assimilate exists; the fact that the individual does not assimilate is a personal weakness of character. This interpretation is likewise largely valid, but it does not explain why this personal weakness of character should be so much more widespread among Jews in particular while individuals of other ethnic groups assimilate themselves more easily and completely into their surroundings.

Clearly, much remains unexplained.

Concerning the Jews as the counteridea to the Germans and especially to the Nordic race in Germany, the enigma of the Jews is important only inasmuch as it is the starting point for the formation of the counteridea. Though the creation of the counteridea teaches us a thing or two about the Jews, the extensive political literature we are dealing with here is not primarily interested in *knowing* the Jewish character but aims at *contrasting* it to its own character. The epistemological basis of the personal definition of Jews as a collective in the anti-Semitic literature is therefore quite vague. The designation "Jew" is applied equally to a group whose core consists of people of the Jewish faith and those who, though no longer members of the religious community, are ethnic Jews; to persons who, though not entirely Jewish, are nevertheless of Jewish descent (with vaguer boundaries in those cases where the share of Jewish blood is very small); and finally to some people, regarded as somehow "Jewish" or "Judaicized" ["*verjudet*"], "suspected" of being Jewish on the basis of their membership in certain professional groups and associations (in Germany, for example, certain pacifist organizations, societies for the support of conscientious objectors, the league for human rights, and the like).

Already here, in the mere definition of the collective noun "Jews" for members of the social environment of the Jews, an essential trait of the new particularist community formation becomes noticeable that is fully developed only at the higher levels of the phenomenon, namely, the "scientific" procedure involved in forming the community, which we have shown to be essential in Fichte's thinking. The classification of people as Jews is not left to the needs and acumen of individuals in the social environment of the Jews, but it is organized into a literary pursuit. An extensive literature of periodicals and pamphlets deals with ferreting out Jews and Jewish activities in all social classes and all walks of life in Germany. A *Handbuch der Judenfrage* [Manual on the Jewish Question] (the number of copies in print is approaching 100,000) instructs the reader on the position of Jewry in politics, in theater, music, motion pictures, and radio and informs him about Jews in journalism and book publishing and in economics in general as well as about Jewish organizations, and so forth. That already the definition alone of the groups of people considered members of the counternation requires this very considerable expenditure of tedious detailed labor is due to the social mixture [*Gemenglage*] of the particularist community intent on setting itself apart with the other, which is its counterpart. In the case of Fichte and his opposition between the German and the French people this labor was not needed because the two societies lived in separate territories.[4]

4. See Theodor Fritsch, *Handbuch der Judenfrage* (31st ed.; 1932). On the question of the scientific nature of this stage of community formation, see also Hilaire Belloc, *Die Juden*, trans. Haecker (Munich, 1927), 107–108. "The strength of anti-Semitism was and is based not only on the vehemence of the sentiments but also on diligence—a diligence with very specific methods. The anti-Semitic pamphlets,

When Jews are experienced as members of their own social collective distinct from one's own in the context of the formation of
a particularist community, this experience connects itself to other
emotion- and value-laden experiences setting up the Jews as the
counterrealm to one's own community. The occasions for such experiences are of a very varied sort; here we will content ourselves
with pointing out two fundamentally important types at the opposite extremes of the experience of community and countercommunity: (1) the compulsion to experience the Jews as the counterrealm, based on the historical fact that they themselves are a
particularist community of enormous intensity—perhaps the most
intense in all of history—that views the rest of mankind as counterrealm, and this view is not only felt but also expressed, sometimes with astonishing naïveté; (2) immediate personal financial
damage because of Jews.

The first type of occasion—the proclamation of the experience
of one's own chosenness—seems to me the deepest reason for the
hatred of Jews throughout history. The author of the article "Anti-
Semitism" in the *Jewish Encyclopedia,* speaking of the beginning
of the history of anti-Semitism in classical antiquity, notes simply
that once the Jews came in contact with other nations that did not
acknowledge their claim to superiority, the Jews became the object
of hate and contempt—in context this passage evokes the impression that the author considers himself a member of the community,
approves of the claim to superiority, and finds fault with all other
nations for not acknowledging, as would only be seemly, this claim
to superiority and for responding to it instead with hate and contempt.[5] In the German history of anti-Semitism the more or less
explicit emphasis of Jewish chosenness and superiority serves as
constant ferment for an atmosphere of hate, and as the ever recurring occasion driving the proponents of the German idea to rejection of the Jews, a rejection that runs the gamut from moderate,
contemplative assertions of the evil as incurable to outbursts of

---

journals, and books that are so carefully boycotted by the major daily press offer a
huge amount of information on the entire Jewish problem, an amount that is already
overwhelming and still continues to grow; and all that is hostile to the Jews. Of
course, we will not find in this material any legal presentation of the evidence
against the accused; but as a dossier for persecution it is astonishing in its extent
and specificity and coherence."

5. Gotthard Deutsch, "Antisemitism," in the *Jewish Encyclopedia* (1902).

frenzied rage at Jewish "impertinence," "outrageousness," "presumptuousness," "arrogance," and the like. As an example of an early work that plainly shows the reaction to the proclamation of the Jewish belief in being the chosen people and its comprehensiveness we can look at the book by Friedrich Rühs.[6] Citing specific passages, Rühs lists a number of works propagandizing Jewish superiority: a letter by Moses Mendelssohn concerning Lessing's work on the Jews; Salomon Maimon's autobiography; an apologia of human rights by Moses Hirschel, a work particularly rich in stylistic howlers; a *Germanomanie* by Saul Ascher that propounds the thesis that the victory of the German armies over Napoleon was possible only in 1813–1814 because it was not until then that the Polish and Russian Jews joined the battle; a small pamphlet proposing to shift Sunday to the Sabbath in order to reach an agreement on the question of the holiday since the Jews would never abandon their customs; and the like. I will not even mention the great number of causes for irritation issuing from the Jewish daily press, especially since the middle of the century,[7] and only discuss the case of Heinrich Graetz's *Geschichte der Juden* because it, among others, led to Heinrich von Treitschke's outburst that in turn resulted in a strong increase in the anti-Semitic movement. I will cite a few passages in extenso because we can understand the reaction to this work only if we know its tone as well as the factual contents it asserts. Speaking about Ludwig Börne and Heinrich Heine and their achievement on behalf of Judaism, Graetz writes:

> The conductor of history brought into being for them two angels of vengeance who flayed the Germans with fiery whips, toppled them from their visionary height, and mercilessly exposed their wretchedness. . . . With their lightninglike minds they broke through the medieval mists the Germans had artificially piled around themselves in order to dim the light, and they allowed the pure light to enter again.
> Judaism equipped an apostle of freedom of firm character with a language reminiscent of the prophets and the Roman Catos, and this apostle confused all concepts Germans held about their public-law

6. Friedrich Rühs, *Über die Ansprüche der Juden an das deutsche Bürgerrecht: Mit einem Anhange über die Geschichte der Juden in Spanien* (Berlin, 1816); first printed in *Zeitschrift für die neueste Geschichte, die Völker-, und Staatenkunde* (1815). [Published in English as *The Claims of the Jews for Civil Rights in Germany,* trans. Helen Lederer (Cincinnati, 1977).]

7. On their influence, see Heinrich von Treitschke, *Ein Wort über unser Judentum* (3rd ed.; 1880), 3 (first published in *Preussische Jahrbücher,* November, 1879).

theory [*Staatsrechtslehre*], and it further gave the world a poet with an artistic sensibility and a mixture of profound poetry and bitter irony, and he overturned all their artistic rules. . . .

Instead of exacting revenge for the wounds inflicted on him and the other members of his race by German hatred of Jews, Börne took upon himself the hard task of eliminating this hatred by putting his hand to ennobling the German people. He wished to imbue them with feelings for freedom, human dignity, and self-respect—in a word, to make them mature. . . .

Soon the German people learned that a writer had arisen for them who was reminiscent of Lessing but who was more than Lessing because he transplanted art not to isolated, icy altitudes but to the plains of life. . . .

But more than the Jews, Germany owes thanks to these, its stern tutors. They have emptied a veritable horn of plenty of ideas over Germany, like two kings who open-handedly throw out gold coins on their journey. They have created an elegant, clear-minded, and smoothly turned language for the plain honest German and opened the temple of freedom to him. Young Germany, which brought about the contemporary state of culture and the year of liberation of 1848 in the German nation, is the child of these two Jewish fathers.[8]

The same tone marks Graetz's work throughout in all passages dealing with the relationship between Judaism and the German nation. Discussing Mendelssohn's defense of the Jews, he writes, "All those who had not divested themselves of all reason . . . saw with astonishment that Judaism despite being so utterly despised had such a significant advantage over celebrated orthodox Christianity."[9] Christianity, he claims, has "lectured" ["*gehofmeistert*"] the European nations for almost sixteen centuries on the belief in heavenly things and "almost crammed them to the brim with it." After Christianity had been subverted by the philosophy of the Enlightenment, Mendelssohn's *Phaidon* "lifted up flagging religious

8. Heinrich Graetz, *Volkstümliche Geschichte der Juden* (10th ed.), III, 573–74. Treitschke's outrage was caused by the publication at that time of the *Grosse Geschichte der Juden*, of which the *Volkstümliche Geschichte* is largely, particularly in the selections cited here, a faithful excerpt. After a lengthy enumeration of passages, Treitschke (p. 14) writes: "And to all this is added this indescribably impertinent and spiteful tone: the man shakes with pleasure whenever he finds something truly offensive to say to the German people."

9. *Ibid.*, 479.

courage again." Theologians, philosophers, artists, poets (Herder, Gleim, Goethe in his early years) thanked "the Jewish philosopher" who restored to them the consolation Christianity was no longer able to provide. "Redemption through the Jew Mendelssohn was welcomed by a world become pagan as joyously as the tidings once brought by Jesus of Nazareth and Paul of Tarsus."[10] On various individuals Graetz had the following comments: Lavater was "a Lutheran priest from Zurich, half enthusiast and half hypocritical intriguer, who later entered into an alliance with the Jesuits"; Friedrich von Gentz was "the incarnation of egotism, hedonism, depravity, and unscrupulousness, who cared about nothing but seducing women"; Schleiermacher, "this apostle of the new Christianity, who made new ropes from cobwebs to fetter human minds"; Friedrich Schlegel, "this romantic idealist with a child's fists"; on Rahel Lewin and Goethe: "Their cleverness and their penetrating minds could not protect them from the pollution of the immorality emanating from the elegant Christian world of the time. The seducer . . . was Goethe. His poetry and pagan philosophy of gratifying sensuality, half covered over with flowery garlands, was for Rahel a Bible she learned by heart and applied";[11] and so forth. We can imagine the effect such a book must have had on Prussian-Protestant minds![12]

The second type of cause for outrage concerns the economic damage inflicted by Jews. For this reason after the change of the form of the economy in Germany and the simultaneous shift in the Jewish pattern of settlement, all classes of the population, with the exception of the working class, were seized, to a greater or lesser extent, by anti-Semitism. Well into the 1880s, economic setbacks affected primarily the peasant sector of the population; beginning in 1870, the weight shifted to the cities and the irritation of the middle classes. The difference between these two periods is due externally to a shift in the population. Until 1870, far more Jews lived in the country than in the cities; beginning in 1870 the proportion was reversed. In 1871 only about 24 percent of German Jews

10. *Ibid.*, 476.
11. *Ibid.*, 528ff.
12. On this point, see the passage from Treitschke's work cited in note 8 above. A detailed description of the phenomenon of the proclamation of superiority on both sides is found in Belloc, *Die Juden*, 78–79.

lived in major cities with more than 100,000 inhabitants, but in 1925, about 68 percent were living in the same cities.[13]

In the first period, the constantly renewed criticism of the Jews focused on usury [Bewucherung] practiced at the expense of the rural peasants.[14] The outrage was continuous, increased steadily, and found its most remarkable expression in the "Pomeranian Civil War" of 1881, an uprising against Jews in Pomerania that was quelled with the help of military forces from outside the area. The report of the governor of Pomerania states: "The causes lie in the profound bitterness the Jews have aroused through their usury and reapportionment [Parzellierung] as well as through the fact that these practices brought about the ruin of many small and medium-sized landowners in the province among all levels of the population, from the man in the street to the educated classes and the well-to-do."[15] How serious the situation was became fully clear as the result of the 1881 investigation carried out by the Verein für Sozialpolitik [Association for Social Policy]; its results were published in three volumes in 1883.[16] The investigation revealed that in a large number of rural districts in Germany the peasant farmers had indeed been damaged considerably by the Jewish merchant class. That class took advantage of the farmers' weakness—their inexperience in business matters; the farm businesses lacked organized bookkeeping; it was impossible to set up and carry out a budget plan; for most of the farmers the formalities of land-registry law were an impenetrable wilderness, and they could not rationally conceive of the consequences of taking out loans. To get these farmers mixed up in disastrous business deals was extremely easy.[17]

The second period, beginning with the founding of the Reich, saw

13. Calculated on the basis of the data given in the article "Statistik der Juden" in Jüdisches Lexikon (Berlin, 1930), IV. On the question of Jewish population shifts, see Felix A. Theilhaber, Der Untergang der deutschen Juden (1911), 37, and the literature cited there.

14. See, for example, Karl Streckfuss, Über das Verhältnis der Juden zu den christlichen Staaten (1833), with an appendix, "Die Erklärung der Stände sämtlicher Provinzen der preussischen Monarchie über die bürgerlichen Verhältnisse der Juden."

15. In Walter Frank, Hofprediger Adolf Stoecker und die christlich-soziale Bewegung (Berlin, 1928), 96.

16. Bäuerliche Zustände in Deutschland: Schriften des Vereins für Sozialpolitik (1883), XXII–XXIV.

17. For the details about the business practices used to destroy a farm, see the three volumes of the inquiry cited above, passim.

the Jews advancing into the urban economy in finance, trade, large-scale enterprises, the intellectual professions, and politics. "Anti-Semitism was based in the middle class in the countryside and the cities, in the social classes who encountered exploitative capital primarily in a Jewish guise."[18] Manual laborers saw themselves sac-rificed to competition from the factories and big business, small merchants began to feel the squeeze put on them by department stores, the entire population suffered in the crash of 1873.[19] Since that time, anti-Semitism as a mass phenomenon has taken on the character of a middle-class movement in part due to the fact that the economic revolution of the liberal era, which occurred chiefly at the expense of the middle class, was visibly carried by the mass movement of the rising Jewish people.

In spite of such far-reaching causes, the anti-Semitic movement[20] would hardly have been capable of its decisive contribution to the formation of the community if anti-Semitism had not at that time become "socially acceptable" thanks to the intervention of a scholar of Treitschke's caliber.[21] What is important about the three short articles in the *Preussische Jahrbücher* (the first, of November 1879, which had such a powerful effect, was only six pages long) is that Treitschke wrote them. Compared to the seriousness of the accusations made, the tone of the articles is moderate; in content they do not add anything to what was commonly said in contem-porary discussions of the Jewish question; and their ideas are not very profound. Treitschke mentions some of the typical issues that make the existence of Jews a problem—their economic expansion-ism [*Gründerwesen*], usury in the rural areas, expressions of supe-riority in the Jewish press, Graetz's history of the Jews, irreverence, and hard-hearted criticism of German-Christian institutions and convictions, and the like. Then the author indulges in some out-

18. Frank, *Hofprediger Adolf Stoecker*, 96.

19. On the Jewish part in these events, see Sombart, *Die Juden und das Wirt-schaftsleben*, 123ff.

20. On the history of anti-Semitism, see the long encyclopedia articles on anti-Semitism and the bibliographies given there; the article by Deutsch in the *Jewish Encyclopedia* (1902), the more recent article by Lucien Wolf in the *Encyclopedia Britannica* (1929), and especially the detailed and careful article by Alberto Pincherle in the *Enciclopedia Italiana* (1929). The article in the *Jüdische Lexikon* is far less comprehensive and provides a bibliography going back only to the 1870s.

21. See Kurt Wawrzinek, "Die Entstehung der deutschen Antisemitenparteien, 1873–1890," *Historische Studien*, No. 168, (1917), 28.

bursts that made particularly bad blood: recalling Tacitus' *odium generis humani* and the "crowd of industrious and ambitious trouser-selling youths" who year after year immigrate from Poland, and finally makes the statement, "the Jews are our misfortune"— ending with the suggestion that the contrasts could be less severe if only the Jews would practice the tolerance they mention so freely. These six pages, of no great consequence as far as content is concerned, became so important in the history of anti-Semitism because the fact that Treitschke made the content his own, thus removing the claims presented from the politically and socially not highly respected sphere of squabbles and elevating them to the standing of a judgment pronounced by an esteemed scholar. Thus, the idea of Judaism as the counterrealm to the German community and the wealth of material that served to support this idea received scientific sanction at a time when agitation had psychologically prepared large sections of the population for an intense experience of the particularist community and the countercommunity. Treitschke's public position gave this experience scientific legitimacy in the eyes of wide sections of the population, particularly of academic circles. Through Treitschke this experience gained that tone of absoluteness and legitimacy that is conferred in this time of the decline of Christian truth by "scientific truth." Treitschke's articles contributed to a socially considerable extent to the scientific constitution of the particularist community as the true and right one.[22]

---

22. On the effect of Treitschke's articles, see Theodor Mommsen, "Auch ein Wort über unser Judentum" (Berlin, 1880), in *Reden und Aufsätze* (Berlin, 1905), 419: "This was expressed by Herr v. Treitschke, a man to whom the German nation in its last great crises owes the greatest thanks of all its writers, whose pen was and is one of the best swords in the turning of the not-yet-ended struggle against the old archenemy of the nation, particularism. What he said was thus given respectability. Thus the bombshell effect of those articles that we have all seen with our own eyes. The muzzle of shame was thus removed from this 'deep and strong movement'; and now the waves run high and the foam splashes." On the effect of Treitschke's articles, see further Heinrich Class, *Wider den Strom: Vom Werden und Wachsen der nationalen Opposition im alten Reich* (1932), 157–58:

For me Treitschke was the master who shaped my life. I had been prepared by my parents, and especially by my grandfather, for what this great teacher had to give. Since I fully entrusted my soul to him, I also accepted without reservation the new matter he offered: *the uncompromising condemnation of the Jewish people.* For particular reasons Treitschke dealt in late 1879 and early 1880 with the *Jewish question* in Germany. Although he did so in the distinguished manner typical of him, the Jewish camp flew into a rage, and the more

In assessing Treitschke's contribution we emphasize the *mass effect of scientific legitimation* that occurred all at once as its truth content, insofar as Treitschke worked on it, as we have seen, was not very significant. This "truth" itself, the content filling the counteridea to the German idea, had been created by others; Treitschke merely cleared the way by which this truth could be brought to the community to use as its building material. The counterimage to the German community, the Jewish race, was as-sembled piece by piece in a fairly long process that had already begun several decades before Treitschke. In what follows we will characterize the principal elements of this image.

Our examination must begin with the idea of the Jewish particu-larist community as a whole. Awareness of this idea goes back all the way to the first emergence of a Jewish question, that is, to an-tiquity. It becomes relevant for our consideration when it begins to be filled with ideas that developed out of the transition from the Kingdom of Christ to the secular particularist communities. Fichte already regarded the Jews no longer as primarily as a foreign reli-gious community but viewed this connection between them as only one of the moments making of the Jews a "state within the state." For him, the main reason for their isolation lies in their hate of the rest of humanity, from which they differ as a community of common descent with the ancestral line that goes back farthest. The Jewish people, Fichte claims, represent an aristocracy of blood and confront all other people with feelings of contempt and, where external pressure is added, with hatred.[23]

---

they did so, the more they taught the author about the intolerance, arrogance, and claims to power of the Jewish people. Treitschke, who came from the liberal camp, gained ever deeper insight into the nature of the Jews, and his criticism and rejection of them became ever sharper. The Jews, with few ex-ceptions, countered his superior objectivity with screaming hate. As I sat at Treitschke's feet at the time, he frequently spoke of the Jewish question, and there was no doubt: this man, under whose spell I stood, saw in the Jewish people an enemy, a danger to his people. He, the old liberal, who had had Jewish friends in his youth, had come to this conclusion after much hesitation. I now studied his earlier essays, which had appeared in the *Preussische Jahrbücher*, and I became fully convinced that Treitschke's view was correct. His phrase, "The Jews are our misfortune" became second nature to me at the age of twenty; it has determined an essential part of all my later political work.

These impressions were received in Berlin in the summer of 1887.

23. Fichte, *Beitrag zur Berichtigung der Urteile des Publikums über die fran-zösische Revolution*, ed. Reinhard Strecker (Meiner, 1922), in *Werke*, VI, 149–50.

The entire complex of issues resulting from the existence of several particularist communities was not explored in more detail until Bruno Bauer's essay on the Jewish question.[24] This essay is frequently mentioned in the pertinent literature though its significance is never appreciated. This because, as I believe, understanding it requires clear insight into the idea of the particularist community as it was developed by Fichte, and also because even with such insight, the dense and abstract style of this Hegelian is not exactly easy to penetrate.[25] According to Bauer, none of the efforts for the emancipation of the Jews, for their incorporation as citizens with equal rights into the modern state, addressed the fundamental question of the character of the Jewish community to be incorporated. For Bauer sees it as essentially characterized by its lack of history and finds triple justification for it: (1) in the national character of Orientals; (2) in the special relationship of Jewish religiosity to the possibilities of its historical development; (3) in the resulting difference of the Jewish nationality from that of the historical nations.

1. The first point does not invite any deeper and more detailed discussion. In the East, Bauer argues, a stationary way of life was part of the ethnic character as can be seen from the fact that, in Hegelian terms, the consciousness of human freedom and reason did not develop. As a result the possibility of development is cut off; and intellectual life is limited to irrational and groundless per-

---

24. Bruno Bauer, *Die Judenfrage* (Braunschweig, 1843).

25. The essay in which Marx takes up Bauer's book on the Jewish question deals less with the latter than with the general problem of emancipation. Marx came out strongly against the destructive character of bourgeois democracy, which, in his view, draws a line between the materialism of society and the ideality of the state. Bourgeois emancipation was the casting off of the chains that had fettered the egoistical spirit of bourgeois society. The newly won democratic freedom amounted to the recognition of the *unbridled* movement of the elements forming the life content of *egoistic* man. *Human* emancipation would be complete only "when the real, individual man . . . in his empirical life, in his individual work, and in his individual relationships . . . has become a *species-being*" (Marx, "Bruno Bauer, *Die Judenfrage*" [Braunschweig, 1843]. Krönersche Taschenausgabe: *Der Historische Materialismus*, I, 225–26). If we translate the time-bound terms of "I" and "species" into current terms, this means that democracy is built on an atomistic individualism, and the true human being in the true state comes into being only when he becomes a member of the whole. Marx attempted to develop a new expression for reincorporating the concrete person into the state as opposed to the clamoring for emancipation of his day. Marx sees the emancipation of the Jews as a particular case within the emancipation movement, understood as a privatization of all the concrete life conditions of people.

formance of ceremonies designed by a higher, inscrutable will in the form they now have. Everything else concerning the historical situation of the Jewish people follows from this fundamental structure of the Middle Eastern mind.[26]

2. The opposition between Judaism and Christianity as separate religious communities is in Bauer's view, the result of their different position in the history of religious life. Historically, Judaism is the preparation for Christianity, while the latter is the fulfillment of Judaism. The fulfillment of Judaism is the coming of the Messiah, the end of the sacrificial rite, and the abolition of the external law through ennobling it into the inner law of morality and individual conviction. Judaism has taken the step toward its fulfillment in the Christian community, but at the same time it had persisted in the old form; a part of the Jewish people refused to participate in the development and therefore has increasingly taken on the character that, in succinct terms, distinguishes it today from all historical peoples—its character as a chimerical people. This chimerical character consisted and still consists today of the fact that one people separates itself from all others as the chosen one, the one awaiting the coming of the Messiah and as a people that cannot live historically out of the springs of its national spirit but whose history is suspended until the coming of the Messiah, who will free this people from captivity and make it the ruler over all other peoples. The existence of Judaism through the centuries therefore has not been a historical struggle but suffering without history in expectation of the history to come.

Though Judaism abolished the barriers between peoples in Christianity and founded the universal community, Bauer continues, "particularism" has survived within this universality. The Jewish people only excluded the *other* peoples from chosenness; Christianity, on the other hand, is fundamentally opposed to *all* national identity [*Volkstum*]. "It excludes everyone who relies on himself, on the rights he possesses by virtue of being human—that is, on human rights. It does not want to have the real human being but the man who has been driven out of his true humanity, the born-again man, the wonderful man."[27] The Messiah has come, but only

26. Bauer, *Judenfrage*, 10 ff.
27. *Ibid.*, 47.

in a first revelation; the community is not yet what it should be but still awaits the second revelation, when He will show himself in his true glory and assume world dominion. Christianity has overcome Jewish particularism by expanding the community to include all humanity. It has thus shifted particularism to another plane in that historical national identity, the "real" human being, is outside the Christian idea. Christianity has overcome the chimerical trait of Judaism inasmuch as it has severed the connection between the belief in redemption and a particular people; it has heightened this trait to gigantic dimensions by placing the community in opposition to *all* national identity.[28]

3. As long as these two particularist chimerical communities oppose each other, the author continues, the problem of emancipation cannot be solved. Neither can emancipate, or free, the other, since both are equally imprisoned in their prejudices. Tolerance of one toward the other means merely acknowledgment of the other's privilege in exchange for acknowledgment of one's own. According to Bauer, the genuine union of the two communities into one state is possible only if both overcome their chimerical nature and find their way to "real" humanity, the life of the community based on the natural wellsprings of national identity. For Bauer, humanity in the sense of the theory of human rights, nature, and nation, all mean the same thing—reality as opposed to illusion or chimera. Human rights and thus the true historical reality of nations, have emerged as an idea only in the eighteenth century, and Christian humanity has not yet fully emancipated itself from its chimera.

Here Bauer sees the third aspect of Judaism and its isolation, namely, its insistence on continuing even in the post-Christian era of national development as the chimerical nation it had been in pre-Christian times. Judaism thus is separated from other modern nations by a double barrier: the suspended history of its religion and its nation's lack of history. Compared to the national identity of the other nations around it, which are beginning to attain their own consciousness, Jewish national identity is characterized by the "rootlessness" ["*Bodenlosigkeit*"] of its existence. Mosaic law was meaningful at the historical site where it originated as an imposed

28. See Spengler's theory of the "magical nation" in *Der Untergang des Abendlandes*, II, in the chapter on the problems of Arabic civilization, passim, particularly p. 312.

law, and by its content it was meaningful in the ancestral seats [*Stammsitze*] of Judaism, but, as Bauer puts it, actual compliance with that law in the present day historical and geographical situation is meaningless. The belief of the Jews that they are living in obedience to the law is thus "a self-delusion and illusion that can be maintained only by ignoring the majority of the commandments, which cannot now be followed."[29] A boundless casuistry and sophistry, Bauer continues, busied itself to come up with the means of creating the semblance of obedience since real obedience was impossible in the present situation. "The law becomes the law of a chimerical world and itself takes on chimerical form." "The Talmud is Mosaicism grown rootless." The "rootless and false seriousness" expended on sheer appearance differentiates the Jews from the European nations and the seriousness with which they pursue their affairs.[30] Seen from the vantage point of the new national identity, the rootlessness of the Jews is manifest in the unreality of Jewish existence—unreality in the sense of the lack of that substance that constitutes the reality of a national identity, while the vital union of community consciousness is expressed in a great man who "could have given" the Jews "in their totality as a people a new impulse, new momentum, and a higher—and indeed a universal, pervasive—sense of self."[31] The religious truth of Judaism is rigid; it is not imbued with historical life through permanent criticism and transformation. According to Bauer, however, a truth is true only once, when it becomes apparent to consciousness, is fully taken up by the historical mind, is assimilated, and in its dissolution creates the "roots" [*Boden*] for a new truth. As Bauer puts it, here the natural human sources of the new

29. Bauer, *Judenfrage*, 26.
30. *Ibid.*, 26–27, 43. On the concept of rootlessness [*Bodenlosigkeit*], compare Kierkegaard's doctrine, formulated at the same time. The concept with all its meanings, also found in Bauer, as the contrast to rootedness [*Bodenständigkeit*] in the original sense and as intellectual rootlessness recurs in the writings of Count Paul Yorck von Wartenburg (see *Briefwechsel* with Dilthey, 1923, for example p. 39, especially the letter of May 9, 1881, pp. 19–20, as well as pp. 254). See also Fritz Kaufmann, "Die Philosophie des Grafen Paul Yorck von Wartenburg," *Husserls Jahrbücher*, IX (1928), 41. "Yorck contrasts the groundlessness [*Haltlosigkeit*] and rootlessness of 'presuppositionless' research and its vague evidence with the sure and tested certainty of his own life, which externally was a threefold system of anchoring: in soil, history, and God, but in actuality it extends completely uniformly from the roots to the crown of existence." The topic is taken up again by Heidegger.
31. Bauer, *Judenfrage*, 82.

idea are blocked. We would say that that kind of historicity is lacking that has as its source the person—just as for Fichte, Christ is the human source of the kingdom, just as for Kant, Frederick the Great becomes the guarantor of growth, just as for Schiller, Goethe secured the new community. This assertion concerning the lack of history most deeply touches on the spot from which in the later literature the accusations of the destructive Jewish mind, the insufficient creative force, and the like, pour forth.[32]

The current wealth of books, pamphlets, essays, and the like to describe Judaism as it manifests itself in art, religion, philosophy, politics, and so forth is almost impossible to keep track of, and we do not intend to offer a synopsis of it, since most of the material is significant not so much for what it says than for the sheer amount in which it has appeared. The type of contemporary presenting Judaism as an intellectual phenomenon, namely, as the counterphenomenon to Aryanism, was established in its fundamentals by

32. This idea is already emphasized *ibid.* Bauer saw the dissolution of Christianity not as a splintering into particularist communities, as Fichte described it for the German people; instead he believed that the idea of human rights would bring the further development of Christianity into a natural humanity within which the nationalities would be separated only by conflicts of interest, not by new faith doctrines. Therefore, his work lacks a characterization of the particularist community with regard to the image of the nation. His notion is exclusively guided by the counterimage of the Jewish particularist community. Nevertheless, his remarks on the dialectic and psychology of the particularist community have fundamental significance. On dialectic, see pp. 33–34: "As the Jewish religion was the faith of this particular people in its own uniqueness, its historical development had to result in the people's lack of belief in itself, since it believed that it possessed universal truth and also had to posit the truth as the universal possession of all and thus burst the confines of its nation. As the Jewish people—insofar as it wishes to remain Jewish and the people in whose special possession the truth rests—the people must not arrive at the goal of its historical development and must not admit that the goal has been reached. Its history must not complete itself. Their faith in themselves keeps the Jews from having a history, and if they nevertheless could not escape historical development they must, once it has occurred, deny it. Their faith in themselves, that is, their religion, which must lead them to unbelief in themselves, compels them at the same time to remain what they are." This is the dialectical situation of all communities that live *for* a goal but live *from* the fact that they do not attain it. On psychology see p. 39: "The arrogance and conceit of a people that believes only in itself and wants to be everything as this One People are stimulated and kept alive through the mere existence of other peoples, a fact that also causes it uneasyness and insecurity. The One and Only People is not what it should be, the one and only and universal one, if there are many peoples. It loses its faith in itself if other happy and powerful nations exist, and to avoid total misery and despair it must cling all the more rigidly to the thought of its uniqueness and become intoxicated with its conviction of the injustice of the other peoples—they are unjust through the mere fact of their existence as peoples, that is, their existence in the guise of a people, which by night belongs only to the One, true people."

Joseph-Ernest Renan. With him originated the juxtaposition of Semites and Aryans as a crucial "division du genre humain" [division of the human species], which he derived from his philological studies.[33] Each of the two races has contributed half to the intellectual achievements of mankind, but in such a way that religious genius has been the particular characteristic of the Semitic race, while the Aryans have been just as uniquely talented in all other cultural areas, especially politics, philosophy, the sciences, and the arts. Thus the accomplishments are quantitatively somewhat unevenly distributed; Renan therefore did not hesitate to conclude that the Semitic race is "une combinaison inférieure de la nature humaine" [an inferior blend of human nature],[34] that the Semitic race has declined after the spread of Islam, and that at present the Aryan race was marching "à la tête des destinées du genre humain" [at the spearhead of man's destiny].[35] The dogma of Jewish inferiority has survived ever since down to the most recent present, when race theoreticians are occasionally inclined to consider the "otherness" of Judaism, or of the several races that make up the Jewish people, as on an equal footing with the character of the Aryan or Nordic race. However, this otherness is said to have most detrimental consequences when it comes into too close contact with the Nordic community. Renan's dogma of the inferiority of the Jews stands midway between the view of emancipation literature—which considers the Jews as currently inferior because of their history in the diaspora, as a population group that could, by suitable measures, be raised to the civilizational and moral level of the world around them—and the more recent literature, which explains social harmfulness as resulting from the symbiosis of two very different races without intending a value judgment on the character of the races with this claim of social harmfulness. Renan tries to illuminate the essence of the inferior Semitic race by ref-

33. Ernest Renan, *Histoire générale et système comparé des langues sémitiques* (3rd ed.; Paris, 1863), Pt. 1, p. 2 (1st ed., 1855; first version, 1847). It was Renan's intention to present in his system of Semitic languages a counterpart to Franz Bopp's work on Indo-European languages. The word *Semitic* is said to have been first used by Johann Gottfried Eichhorn in his *Historisch-kritische Einleitung in das Alte Testament* (2nd ed., 1787), 45 (according to Deutsch, "Antisemitism," in the *Jewish Encyclopedia*). In philosophy the word gained ground in the contrast of Semitic and Indo-European languages after Bopp's *Vergleichende Grammatik*.
34. Renan, *Histoire générale*, 4.
35. *Ibid.*, 503.

erence to its monotheism. To the extent that he considers the religious talents and the creation of monotheism positive qualities and achievements, the correctness of Renan's theses has been disputed.

Houston Stewart Chamberlain has denied the Jews' religious genius; in his view, their original form of religion is polytheism, and monotheism is merely a later creation due to external influence. Furthermore, monotheism was not adopted in its spiritual greatness but was corrupted into monolatry[36] by turning the *one* God into the God of the Jewish people. Other authors therefore speak of Jewish henotheism, using the term to indicate that it is not a matter of monotheism in the proper sense of belief in the *one* God of all mankind.[37] Aside from the fact that the Semites' religious genius was later denied, the picture Renan sketched of the Semites as resulting from their religious conviction has been kept alive. According to this view, monotheism leads to intolerance; therefore, freedom of thought and the spirit of free inquiry can be found only among Indo-Europeans, and for the same reason the Semites lack any philosophical and scientific culture. Moreover, concerning poetry, the Semites are capable only of lyrical poetry because of their restricted subjectivism; they also lack creative imagination and have no narrative literature, no drama, and no epics. Their naïve realism, which is useless when faced with products of the imagination which it can interpret only as natural reality, precludes the development of the fine arts;[38] their political life is equally lacking in creativity. The Semites, it is claimed, have no politically aware public, no public spirit, no large kingdoms, no polity, no absolute monarchy; for them the questions of aristocracy, democracy, and monarchy are unimportant, and the Jewish aristocracy is purely patriarchal, without the characteristic military position the aristocracy has among other peoples. Therefore, taken all in all, the

36. According to Friedrich Delitzsch, *Die grosse Täuschung: Kritische Betrachtungen zu den alttestamentlichen Berichten über Israels Eindringen in Kanaan, die Gottesoffenbarung vom Sinai und die Wirksamkeit der Propheten* (1920), Pt. 1, p. 97, the recognition of "monolatry" was already present in Renan (without citation of sources).

37. See, for example, Adolf Wahrmund, *Das Gesetz des Nomadentums* (1887), 37. For a more recent interpretation of the Jewish image of God, see Delitzsch, *Die grosse Täuschung*, especially pp. 70 ff.

38. Compare Chamberlain's thesis that only the Semites had had "idols." *Die Grundlagen des 19. Jahrhunderts* (3rd ed.; 1901), 230–31.

Semitic race can be recognized by its "negativity": it has no my-thology, no epics, no science, no philosophy, no literature, no graphic arts, no political forms—in fact, there is a complete lack of differentiation within the faith in having been chosen by the one God, who is the private God of the people.[39]

The type established by Renan is more broad than deep. His race concept is not very precisely articulated and has more the signifi-cance of an ethnographic group than of a biological unit. The racial differences cited in the first place are not physical traits but cus-toms, languages, attitudes;[40] nor is the character of the race con-stant—it can be destroyed by the power of civilization, which is superior to the race, so that many Jews of our time are nothing more than modern men formed by civilization, "la grande force supé-rieure aux races et destructive des originalités locales."[41] In its con-tent the race concept thus belongs to developmental history, and Renan uses it to designate a population that is still at the beginning of its development and has not yet advanced to a civilized state.[42] The spiritual character of the race is also formulated with little clarity and little depth: monotheism as the principle of explanation is not sufficient, and others, such as subjectivism and egoism, must be introduced to explain the restrictedness of literature to lyrical poetry, and a lack of imagination is used to explain the prohibition of visual arts.

After Renan, the idea of the Jewish people forks in two directions. One is defined by the ruling idea of total essence, the other by the ruling idea of the physical part of man (we will ignore the huge amount that is characterized less by intellectual clarity than by the strength of its hatred[43]). The first must in its classification of ne-

39. See also the similar contemporaneous description in Christian Lassen, *In-dische Altertumskunde* (1867), 494–95 (1st ed., 1847, pp. 414–15).

40. Renan, *Etudes d'histoire religieuse* (3rd ed.; Paris, 1858), 84–85.

41. Renan, *Langues sémitiques*, I, 15. See also Renan, *Le Judaïsme comme race et comme religion* (Paris, 1883).

42. See also the division into "races inférieures," "premières races civilisées," and "grandes races nobles" (Aryans and Semites) in Renan, *Le Judaisme*, 501–502.

43. In this category I include, for example, the writings of Eugen Dühring, *Die Judenfrage als Rassen-, Sitten-, und Culturfrage: Mit einer weltgeschichtlichen Ant-wort* (1st ed.; 1880). The sixth edition was published in 1930 under the title *Die Judenfrage als Frage des Rassencharakters und seiner Schädlichkeiten für Existenz und Kultur der Völker: Mit einer gemeinverständlichen und denkerisch freiheit-lichen Antwort*. Note should be taken of the fine nuances of the titles; the fourth edition, for example, is entitled *Die Judenfrage als Frage der Rassenschädlichkeit*

cessity try repeatedly to find the central point for understanding the Jews in their spiritual structure; the other takes its point of departure from the physical type and treats, in rhapsodic overview, the intellectual "traits" as concomitants of the *somata* lacking any interrelationships among themselves.

The doctrine of the Jewish character as an intellectual style pervading the total human being revolves around the problem of Jewish rootlessness, as Bruno Bauer already formulated it. Richard Wagner's now famous essay, *Judaism in Music*, concentrates on describing the Jews' twofold rootlessness and its consequences for music. For one, the Jews are "rootless" as such, splintered, incapable of development, aroused not by higher "heart-glowing passion" but only by personal interest, dominated by "repulsive circumspection" that makes naive feeling impossible, and therefore they are incapable of a great and immediate expression of personal emotions. Second, the Jews are thus incapable because they cannot gain new ground for their spiritual life in the surrounding community, since the latter is accessible to them only by way of its intellectual circles but not through the sections of the population rooted to the soil [*urwüchsig*].[44]

Chamberlain understood the question of "rootlessness" on a deeper level even though it was not he but, later, Otto Weininger who discussed it under this title. Chamberlain rejected Renan's concept of monotheism and replaced it once and for all with that of monolatry;[45] it retreats from the center of the discussion, thus making room for nomocracy. The rule of law, according to Chamberlain is the ultimate cause of the Jews' creative incapacity. For the Jews there is no "inner need" out of which a particular behavior

---

für Existenz, Sitte, und Kultur der Völker: Mit einer weltgeschichtlichen, religionsbezüglich, social, und politisch freiheitlichen Antwort (1892). See further Dühring, *Die Überschätzung Lessings und dessen Anwaltschaft für die Juden* (1881), in which the author hints that Lessing was a Jew—a suspicion that has been picked up again by Josef Nadler in his *Literaturgeschichte der deutschen Stämme und Landschaften* (1928), IV, 7. Here we have an excellent example of somebody being included among the Jews on the basis of an intellectual position that does not fit into the national program.

For the same reason I will here mention only in passing the respected and effective writings by Paul de Lagarde, now collected in *Schriften für das deutsche Volk* (2 vols., 1924). See especially Point 10 of the program for the Conservative Party in Prussia (*Schriften*, I, 420 ff); further, the passage on Judaism in Vol. II.

44. Richard Wagner, *Das Judentum in der Musik* (1850).

45. Chamberlain, *Grundlagen*, 403.

becomes the rule. The ethical commandments are heteronomous, imposed from the outside at a particular time in history and alterable and revocable by God; they "do not emerge with inner necessity from the depths of the human heart."[46] The opposite to the guidance of the will by the moral law is therefore "arbitrariness" of the Jews, a complete indeterminacy of the will in all questions not concerning obedience to the "law" and lack of obligation in the entire area of human actions that lies outside the stipulations of the law.[47]

With his precise description of the Jewish "idea,"[48] the author severs its connection to the physical basis of the Jews as race. The Jewish nation, on this view, has become one in race and idea and, in principle, can therefore be dissolved again. In addition to the concept of the Jew by race, Chamberlain develops that of the "inner Jew,"[49] a person who is a Jew not by racial descent but by allowing himself to be imbued with the Jewish "idea." "It is not necessary to bear the authentic Hittite nose to be a Jew; rather the word mainly defines a special way of feeling and thinking; a man may, even without being an Israelite, very quickly become a Jew; many need only assiduously cultivate Jewish acquaintances, read Jewish newspapers, and become accustomed to the Jewish way of life, to Jewish literature and art."[50] We will discuss the significance of this theory in the context of race theory in the following chapter; here we will merely note it as a doctrine grounded in a systematic context that has had further repercussions, still making itself felt in political practice wherever people are included among the Jews by virtue of having become "Judaicized."

Building on Chamberlain's theory, Weininger carried the isolation of the Jews to its conclusion. For him, Jewishness is a psychological constitution that is potentially present in all people but has found its most grandiose realization in historical Jewry. The central point of his analysis—quite extensive and with detailed classifications—of this psychological constitution is once again moral heteronomy, as in Chamberlain, but Weininger proceeds further in the

46. *Ibid.*, 234.
47. *Ibid.*, 244–45.
48. *Ibid.*, 348, 449.
49. *Ibid.*, 457–58.
50. *Ibid.*, 457.

Kantian conceptual world to the radical consequences: where moral autonomy is absent, that is, where the rational substance [*Vernunftsubstanz*] is not the dominating principle of intellectual life, there personality is lacking. The Jew is a person without spiritual personality, an individual without individuality, he is primarily a species-being. According to Weininger, the Jew lacks an attachment to the higher being and, therefore, on this plane of being, he is nothing. "The Jew is nothing because, at bottom, he believes in nothing."[51] He lacks faith, that is, the action by which man enters into relationship to his own being. The Jew, however, believes neither in God, nor in himself, nor can he take root in another person since he does not believe in anybody else either. "The Jew believes in nothing, neither inside nor outside himself; nor does he find a foothold in the stranger, he cannot take root even there. And his lack of any rootedness whatever appears symbolically, as it were, in his lack of understanding for all ownership of land and his preference for movable capital."[52] This rootlessness, then, this spiritual unreality, serves to explain the individual characteristics cited by Weininger and others: the Jews' "adaptability" and readiness to enter into a form developed out of a foreign substance without committing themselves; their "nomadic character";[53] the absence of "*verecundia*" before the spirit, which Schopenhauer had stressed;[54] their characteristic of being "an effective ferment of cosmopolitanism and national decomposition," which Theodor Mommsen mentions;[55] the demonic aspect of realism; their efficiency in the sphere of personal interest, which comes into play unhampered by concern for the mind and which is dealt with at length by Wilhelm Marr, the man who is credited with coining the word "anti-Semitism."[56]

When the criterion of classification is not the total human being, culminating in the mind, but the physical type, psychological

51. Otto Weininger, *Geschlecht und Character* (1903), 430.

52. *Ibid.*, 431.

53. Adolf Wahrmund, *Das Gesetz des Nomadentums und die heutige Judenherrschaft* (1887).

54. Arthur Schopenhauer, *Parerga und Paralipomena*, II, §133.

55. Theodor Mommsen, *Römische Geschichte*, III, 550; see also his essay "Auch ein Wort über unser Judentum," in *Reden und Aufsätze* (1905), 416–17.

56. Wilhelm Marr, *Der Sieg des Judentums über das Germanentum: Vom nicht-konfessionellen Standpunkt aus betrachtet* (1879), 16. See also his pamphlet *Vom jüdischen Kriegsschauplatz* (1879).

[*geistespsychologisch*] and characterological types become less important. Though such analyses list a few mental or psychical "traits," as the terminology already suggests, these traits have little connection to each other; they come together more by accident to form a picture. The racial components of Jewry are the raw material for these analyses, primarily the Near Eastern and Oriental races. Günther analyzes the composition in more detail as follows: for Sephardic Jews: Oriental–Near Eastern–Mediterranean–Hamitic–Nordic–Negroid; for Ashkenazic Jews: Near Eastern–Oriental–East Baltic–Central Asian–Nordic–Hamitic–Negroid.[57] Thus the Jews are not a "race" but a highly disparate mixture of races. The fact that nevertheless a comparatively clear physical and psychical type has developed is due, according to Günther, to selective inbreeding over many generations, so that the Jews have become a "race of the second order." Lenz believes that Jewishness is more clearly recognizable as a psychical rather than a physical race, and the core of the Jewish soul is formed by Near Eastern traits.[58] He lists such traits as: a high degree of cleverness; the ability to empathize with the souls of other people and to act accordingly; skill in commerce and trade; breeding for the exploitation not of nature but of human beings; little capacity for the formation of states; fermenting decay and progress when in community with other races; capability for abstraction, formal logic, and dialectic; eloquence and a talent for expression; a tendency toward optimistic monism in worldview; and so on.[59] It requires no critical discussion to point out the theoretical simplicity of this listing compared to the analyses carried out by Bauer, Chamberlain, and Weininger.

Even the most recent rhapsodic recitations of "traits" originate in the same experience of community as the older, more profound studies of Judaism. These attempts to understand the essence of Jewry are not made in a vacuum but receive ever new impetus from the opposition of particularist communities. The names of these communities and the persons constituting them may change, the

57. Günther, *Rassenkunde Europas* (3rd ed.; 1929), 104. Further, Günther, *Rassenkunde des jüdischen Volkes* (1929).

58. Lenz, *"Die Erblichkeit der geistigen Begabung,"* in Baur, Fischer, and Lenz, *Menschliche Erblichkeitslehre* (3rd ed.; 1927), I, 537ff. On the soul type of Judaism, see also Clauss, *Von Seele und Antlitz der Rassen und Völker: Eine Einführung in die vergleichende Ausdrucksforschung* (1929), 84ff.

59. Lenz, "Erblichkeit," 537ff.

theory on which the analysis is based may alter, but the idea of opposition remains the same. We see this same idea in the opposition of Christianity and Judaism as the chimerical communities, the chimerical nation, and the natural national identity; we see it gradually fill up more and more with body ideas in the "races" of the philologists Renan and Lassen; we find it again in Chamberlain's philosophy of history, in which the Semites and the Teutons take the stage as the warring fundamental races of post-classical history; and finally we see a high degree of spiritualization of the opposition in Weininger's characterization of Jewishness. The driving force of the differentiation was the desire to present the image of the positive particularist community by setting it off from its counterimage—rootedness versus rootlessness, history versus the lack of history, moral autonomy versus external law, spiritual substance versus insubstantiality, personality versus nothingness.

In order to preclude even the slightest possibility of a misunderstanding, let us again point out emphatically that the contrasting descriptions of the Semitic and the Aryan, the Jewish and the German character, even in the best work of Bauer, Chamberlain, and Weininger, contain little that is true about the nature of Jewishness. Those psychological efforts are not motivated by the desire to understand the Jews but by the desire to elaborate one's own idea of community and personality; the juxtaposition to the Jews is here only a means to an end. That the Jewish idea is only a means, its instrumentality as a counteridea, is evident in its negativity. Judaism is chimerical, unreal, its mind has no roots in the "heart" or "inner necessity"; it is devoid of "personality," it is a "nothing." And it must appear as a nothingness when the opposition focuses on the German antithesis of moral autonomy and heteronomy, for in the context of Jewish religious ethics, where divine will and the will of the community are experienced as coinciding directly, without the intermediary problem of autonomy and heteronomy, this antithesis is simply meaningless.[60] The psychological description

60. At times the absurdity becomes evident in the literature on the Jewish question without the particular author's intention. So, for example, in a passage in Wahrmund, pp. 36–37: "Supposing some naive thinker, in a passionate burst of feeling, places his desires as one with those of his God, and defines everything opposing this God, the personification of his own right to exist, which he perceives as unique, and the 'Furies of his own mind' as nonhumans, who must be destroyed or forced into servitude; if this view is subsequently raised to the level of a scholarly theory, sup-

of Jews as presented in this idea tells us nothing about Jews but a great deal about the community regarded as positive in contrast to which the Jews are simply nothing. The uniquely German struggle for intellectual roots and for the idea of intellectual rootedness, its sharp contrast with Jewish rootlessness, goes to show less the latter than the problem of German "rootedness" itself. This is such a burning question in the German formation of ideas because there is no natural and immediately sure political rootedness in reality [*Wirklichkeitsboden*] for the German ideas of community as there is for the world of ideas of France, England, and America.[61] Here we cannot point out all the details of the great problem arising when philosophy of the person coincides with philosophy of political man in the Western nation states, or when the two are separated by a wide chasm, as in German intellectual history; we must be content with simply referring to it. The following chapter will have something more to say on the special question of the body idea.

---

ported by literary means, as happens to this day in Jewish and Moslem religious writings."

The passionate identification of personal with divine will touched upon here has nothing to do with the question of subjective and objective ethics.

A more recent attempt fueled by a desire to understand is that of Clauss, *Von Seele und Antlitz der Rassen und Völker*, 84ff.

For another effort, about whose value I am unable to say anything, see further Friedrich Muckle, *Der Geist der jüdischen Kultur und das Abendland* (1923).

61. That the inner uncertainty of the Germans is one of the reasons for the severity of the German-Jewish conflict is very vigorously stressed in Wilhelm Stapel, *Antisemitismus und Antigermanismus: Über das seelische Problem der Symbiose des deutschen und des jüdischen Volkes* (1928), 108. Stapel calls for a "strengthening of national consciousness" for the Germans.

This has nothing to do with the clamorous patriotism of the petit bourgeois [*Spiessbürger*], nor is any arrogance involved; it is instead the calm self-assurance of one's own nature, loyal steadfastness in what is German [*Deutschtum*]. With honest self-knowledge, one will neither overestimate German values nor let them be devalued by Jewish agitation. Quiet, tenacious self-assurance, provoking no one, is *the* protection under which what is purest and best in us can develop unspoiled and undistorted. That such an indigenous and strong German national identity [*Volkstum*] banishes the dangers of anti-Germanism from its own sphere may be seen in Schleswig-Holstein. In that province there is no "Jewish danger," since the people of Lower Saxony and Friesland are so firm in themselves that what is alien find those doors closed that are only too open to him in the west and southwest, and even more so in the east of Germany. To help achieve this *internal security* is the purpose of this work.

8

The Nordic Idea

After the investigations in the preceding chapters, the concluding classification of the body ideas contributing to the formation of today's particularist communities has become almost a problem of deduction. I will sum up the premises:

1. The ideas differ depending on whether they are (a) primarily ideas of the animal sphere or (b) primarily ideas of the human being as a whole.

2. In the case of 1(a), they either relate (a) to more specific animal contexts or (b) to races.

3. In the case of 2(b), they differ depending on whether they (a) take up the theory of pure races and claim the superiority of a pure race or (b) presuppose that mixed races must be the carriers of particularist communities.

4. For the formation of community on the basis of the race idea, the rural and urban middle class has been defined as the political force field. Consequently, the counterrealm is designated as the totality of all the forces that politically and socially jeopardize the status of the middle class, that is, social democracy and communism as political mass phenomena on the one hand, and capitalist big enterprise on the other, as well as Jewry, which appears in leading positions among both of the opponents.

5. The formation of ideas makes use of the scientific form; that is, though it relies on real-political oppositions and ethical convictions for its impact, it does so not directly but by way of theories about social structure, social hygiene, race, and the like, that claim to be scientific.

6. The mood of this idea formation ranges from the pessimism handed down in race theory since Gobineau and fueled by the threatened status of the middle class to the optimism arising from the awareness of scientific insight into the workings of the social

processes and thus the control of rational means to correct the current imperiled situation.

From these premises follow several types of body ideas, depending on which traits and groups of traits are combined, as well as correspondingly more or less vehement feuds between the representatives of one or another type. The supporters of pure race treat the supporters of race mixture sometimes as scientific dilettantes, sometimes as traitors to the great tradition of Gobineau, and other times they simply silently ignore them. Theoreticians who believe in selection in the Darwinian sense *within* a race consider the others, who are convinced of the superiority of one race over another in the contemporary social structure, fantastic ideologues. Within the theory of selection, the camps are split by whether the selection theory is seen as having democratic character, thus supporting social democracy, or as an aristocratic theory and thus useful as a weapon in the fight against social democracy. Concerning the question of how the races within the German people should be evaluated, matters come to a head, on the one hand, in a Prussian-Bavarian race conflict, and, on the other hand, efforts were made to accept the Phalian [*fälisch*] and Alpine [*dinarisch*] races alongside the Nordic race so as not to overly incense the South German population.

The theoretical level of these disputes is quite modest; fundamental problems are not addressed and these disputes are therefore of little interest to us. Below I will only summarize the principal historical facts.

The politically relevant beginnings of the formation of the community, like those of the concurrent anti-Semitic movement, are found in the late 1870s. At the fiftieth conference of German scientists and physicians in Munich in 1877, Rudolf Virchow gave a powerful address, entitled "Die Freiheit der Wissenschaft im modernen Staat" [The Freedom of Science in the Modern State], condemning Darwinian theory. The scientific-factual content was not very significant since Virchow apparently was not familiar with the details of either Darwin's theory or its underlying material. Virchow's talk culminated in the argument that only experiments could furnish a precise basis for science and that the theory of the origin of species must be rejected, because no experiments could prove the transition of one species into another. On the basis of this scientific rejection, Virchow propagandized against the theory (doctrine of man's descent from the apes) because it could not be reconciled with Christian dogma, because it undermined the Christian basis of community ethics, and most particularly, because it served the enemy of the state, social democracy, as a weapon in its fight. Only proven scientific results should be allowed to be taught in schools, not problematic theories, and the theory of descent was by no means assured. In 1878 Ernst Haeckel responded with an essay, entitled "Freie Wissenschaft und freie Lehre" [Free Science and Free Teaching], impelled by the reception Virchow's address got from conservative journalism and by Hödel's and Nobiling's assassination attempts—for which the *Kreuzzeitung* ultimately held the theory of the origin of species responsible.[1] After addressing the scientific questions, Haeckel in his essay also opposed the political arguments advanced by Virchow. According to Haeckel, if this theory can be said to have any political tendency, it could only be an aristocratic one.[2]

As it happened that Treitschke's entry into the discussion made the Jewish question more respectable, so the quarrel between two learned men of the rank of Virchow and Haeckel seems to have given the question of the political significance of Darwinism for Germany scientific approval. We must emphasize the qualifier: for Germany—because Francis Galton's work on the heredity of dominant traits, published in 1869, already contained all the elements necessary for the further political development of social hygiene on a Darwinian basis. Galton had established that exceptional mental abilities within a family are hereditary; a famous man was thus not an accidental phenomenon but was predetermined by the combination of inherited gifts and external influences, and in his family other individuals with exceptional talents will appear more frequently. From these statements, supported by extensive factual material, Galton drew conclusions for the social structure. The achievements of a society in terms of civilization, Galton argued, are determined by the existence of a number of families with superior genes, and depending on the relative size and quality of this

1. Ernst Haeckel, *Freie Wissenschaft und freie Lehre: Eine Entgegnung auf Rudolf Virchows Münchener Rede über "Freiheit der Wissenschaft im modernen Staat"* (1878), 4.
2. *Ibid.*, 74.

group, nations and races differ in their historical significance. In modern society, the situation of this group so important for civilization is not good because the late marriage age and low birth rate greatly diminish its numbers compared to those of the lower classes and because through the social rise out of the lower classes the good hereditary factors [*Erbwerte*] still present there are gradually brought into the same disadvantageous situation that will have to end with their extinction by degrees. The conditions of the struggle for existence in human society are different from those in nature for an animal species, and social selection does not always result in the survival of the fittest; rather, given the conditions of civilized society, the result tends to be the gradual displacement of the fittest. Galton gave his conclusions a political turn: "I wish to emphasize the fact that the improvement of the natural gifts of future generations of the human race is largely, though indirectly, under our control."[3]

Applied to the political scene in Germany, these statements, which Galton did not elaborate in detail, break apart along cracks that had not been evident until then. The struggle for existence and the selection of the fittest in society could be interpreted to mean (1) that the organization of society is a result of the struggle and that the fittest have in fact risen to the top; the leading social group would then also be the one entitled to leadership because of its qualities. The "egalitarianism" advocated by social democracy, in this view, contradicts the natural inequality of human beings, and if it is politically successful, society would decline because those capable of social leadership have been eradicated. (2) The theory of the struggle for survival can be interpreted to mean that while the struggle and selection of animals takes its course in nature, the struggle and selection of man takes place in an artificial environment, which raises the question whether the contemporary social environment is so constituted that the fittest can indeed rise socially or whether it is not primarily people with questionable moral and intellectual traits who are best adapted to the contemporary environment, so that consequently the environment is in need of thoroughgoing change. In Germany the first interpretation has al-

3. Francis Galton, *Hereditary Genius* (2nd ed., 1892, 1st ed., 1869), xxvi.

ways been that of the middle class and national socialism, the second that of the social-democrats.[4]

One of the chief proponents of the first interpretation, Otto Ammon, declared that he wrote his book on the natural foundations of the social order for the "broadest strata of the educated bourgeoisie" and was therefore selling it for two Marks; he hoped it would "become a handbook and guide for our middle classes."[5] This select reading public, according to his view, should be conscious of being a "social aristocracy," an "educated aristocracy" of culture, and as the responsible section of the population it should be "German-national," for "only in the *national* context can the *social* tasks that occupy our era be pursued." "For a German social aristocracy there is only *one* supreme principle, and it is, 'Deutschland, Deutschland, über Alles!' This aristocracy must fight for the fatherland not only on the battle fields, if necessary, but also internally to spread national thinking and oppose emphatically all unpatriotic doings."[6]

The relationship of social democracy to the idea of selection was more tenuous than that of the middle-class, national-socialist movement. The lively interest of the social-democrat movement in the Darwinian ideas in the 1890s must be seen rather as an effort not to miss a scientific value of Darwin's standing for their own cause. The assumed natural inequality of human beings is nevertheless too alarming to a democratic political doctrine intent on creating a new societal form to give the good predispositions distributed equally among the lower and the upper social classes room to develop. Today a connection between socialist ideas and the theses of social hygiene is more rejected than sought, though it has not been completely severed.[7]

4. For a literal interpretation of competition as rivalry under the conditions of the order of private property, see Mises, *Die Gemeinwirtschaft: Untersuchungen über den Sozialismus* (2nd ed.; 1932), 287–88.

5. Otto Ammon, *Die Gesellschaftsordnung und ihre natürlichen Grundlagen: Entwurf einer Sozialanthropologie zum Gebrauch für alle Gebildeten, die sich mit sozialen Fragen befassen* (3rd ed., 1900, 1st ed., 1895), iv.

6. *Ibid.*, 284 (italics in the original). See also Ammon, *Der Darwinismus gegen die Sozialdemokratie: Anthropologische Plaudereien* (1891). Galton's works, mentioned above, are not the only immediate precursors in intellectual history for German theoreticians; a significant role was also played by the studies of Ribot and de Candolle; for materials further required, see Otto Ammon, *Die natürliche Auslese beim Menschen: Auf Grund der Ergebnisse der anthropologischen Untersuchungen der Wehrpflichtigen in Baden und anderer Materialien* (Jena, 1893).

7. On this problem during the 1890s, see Enrico Ferri, *Sozialismus und moderne*

The first interpretation of Galton's theories subdivides further, depending on whether the selected group whose hereditary traits are endangered is identified as a "race" or not. For Galton, this was not a burning question because he used the word *race* without a clearly defined meaning—he speaks of the human race, of the Anglo-Saxon race, of the Greek race; for him *race* can also be synonymous with *nation*. In German theory, the meanings become distinct, and we find a sheerly "selectorial" [*"selektorisch"*][8] theory of social structure alongside one that has social selection and organization coincide with the selection of a particularly excellent race in the scientific sense of the word. Occasionally these two views conflict, as in the debate between Schallmayer and Ludwig Woltmann;[9] as a rule, their interests run parallel to each other, so that the proponents of eugenics are also adherents of the race idea, as in the case of Lenz and Günther. The idea of race hygiene passes over completely into that of a treatment of history in terms of the race idea when, as in Ammon's case, social selection is synonymous with race selection, when superior talents regularly occur in connection with the physical type of a race in the scientific sense

---

Wissenschaft (1895), Bibliothek der Sozialwissenschaft, Vol. V; also the earlier works by Ludwig Woltmann, especially *Die Darwinsche Theorie und der Sozialismus: Ein Beitrag zur Naturgeschichte der menschlichen Gesellschaft* (1899). On the latest developments, see Oda Olberg, *Nationalsozialismus* (1932), where, among other things, the author attempts to salvage those elements of social hygiene that can be reconciled with socialism (especially pp. 27–28). See also the party reprimand by Paul Stein, "Das biologische System der nationalsozialen Reaktion—und das Proletariat," in *Der Kampf*, XXV (October, 1932), 414: "Let us take care lest, for the sake of genuine and real but narrowly limited eugenics, we stray into the ideological neighborhood of the race hygienicists who derive the most reactionary monstrosities from the concept of 'hereditary values,' which is quite unassailable, incomprehensible for concrete measures."

8. The concept of "selectorial view of history" was developed in opposition to the geographic (Buckle), economic (Marx, Engels), and race-theoretical one (Gobineau) by Schallmayer, *Beiträge zu einer Nationalbiologie: Nebst einer Kritik der methodologischen Einwände und einem Anhang über wissenschaftliches Kritikerwesen* (1905), 42–43.

9. Schallmayer, *Nationalbiologie*, in the appendix on the nature of critics. See also Schallmayer, *Vererbung und Auslese: Grundriss der Gesellschaftsbiologie und der Lehre vom Rassedienst* (3rd ed.; 1918) (*Natur und Staat*, Vol. III), 1: "This ambiguity of 'race hygiene' has led to the attempt to link the idea of race service [*Rassedienst*], which applies to every race and every nation, no matter what racial mixture created it, with efforts based on the assumption—more naive than scientific— that of the various races that make up the population of Germany, the 'Nordic race' is the most noble and therefore to be preferred to the others."

of the word.[10] Galton's theses are completely subsumed into the wider complex of the race idea.

The complex of race ideas itself is a confused web of all the lines of construction that can be drawn from the material. I will point out only the most important ones. The principal line is the Nordic idea—the idea, historically, that a race exists that stands out above all others, the Nordic race, to which we owe the cultural achievements of all Western and much of Oriental humanity, and the idea, politically, that the Nordic race elements of the population must be encouraged by social-political measures. The concept of the Nordic race can be traced back as far as Linnaeus; its scope varies depending on how much is known about the material and which classifying principle the individual scholar uses. Linnaeus focused on the more narrowly zoological concept of *Homo europaeus*; Johann Blumenbach, drawing on his investigations of the cranium, spoke of the broader group of the Caucasian race; within his active race, Klemm differentiated between a lighter and a darker race; Gobineau distinguishes the white race and, within it, the prototype of the tall, blond, dolichocephalic, blue-eyed race; Schlegel's linguistic studies created the concept of the Indo-Germans; Renan chose the Aryans as the opposites of the Semites; Chamberlain preferred the Teutons, as did Woltmann; Georges Vacher de Lapouge fell back on Linnaeus' *Homo europaeus* but used the term *Aryan* as a synonym; more recent scholars have adopted Joseph Deniker's term and speak of the Nordic race.[11]

Opinions vary widely on the nature of the chosen race, which is the bearer of European culture. Vacher de Lapouge, for example, believed that in general races do not differ in their essence. He argued that there are a number of psychological types with varying capacities for civilized achievement and that these types were distributed among all races. Races were to be distinguished according to the percentage of their members belonging to the better or the worse psychical types. The Aryan race has the largest percentage of people of the best type. But next to the superior blond dolicho-

10. See especially Ammon, *Natürliche Auslese beim Menschen.*
11. Wilser in particular was concerned to prove that the Nordic race did in fact originally live in the north.

cephalic people, there are those who are on a level with the most inferior Negroes.[12]

In sharpest contrast to these arguments, we find the theories that see in each race a particular mental nature [*Geistwesenheit*] from which no member of the race is exempt. In Germany, the type of theory of social hygiene that Schallmayer propounds comes closest to Vacher de Lapouge's theory. However, for the formation of particularist communities, the second is decisive.

Similarly, the advantages of the chosen race have also been assessed very differently. For Galton, the ideal of selection was the human type that is maximally adapted to the conditions of modern civilization. He deplored painfully the counterselection of the Middle Ages, when the celibacy of monks practically excluded almost all literary, scientific, and morally valuable hereditary factors from transmission. The selection carried out by the church had the effect of breeding "ferocious, currish, and stupid natures"—causing irreparable damage to civilization.[13] Galton believed that contemporary selection must eradicate the type of nomadic and hunting peoples because the adventurer does not fit into our age; instead, we need steady workers, with inner contentment and insensitivity to external impressions that are not relevant to their work. The type of the "Norman" has become meaningless; the adventure-loving, daring, rash spirit has been displaced by the more solid, more profound, genuine force.[14] The German idea of Nordic man, however, tends in the opposite direction and takes its inspiration from the Old Norse sagas, the deeds of the Vikings, the Norman founders of states, the early Germanic aristocracy.

And finally, the race idea is deeply divided on how to evaluate the achievements of the Nordic race in history. In the tradition of Gobineau, the great cultural achievements are presented as products of racially mixed peoples. According to one theory, carefully elaborated by Albert Reibmayr, the precondition for any cultural achievements of genius is a period of inbreeding of talents within a society followed by an advantageous mixture with other inbred bloodlines. This advantageous mixture of inbred lines then pro-

12. Georges Vacher de Lapouge, *Les sélections sociales* (1896), 78–79; *L'Aryen: Son rôle social* (1899), 399ff.
13. Galton, *Hereditary Genius*, 344.
14. *Ibid.*, 335.

vides fertile soil for cultural achievements of genius.[15] Chamberlain's thinking runs along the same lines: a major race emerges as the result of a quick, one-time addition of blood from a related type to an inbred community.[16] According to Reibmayr's theory, supported by a wealth of data, both blood components are equally important for the emergence of accomplishments of genius. According to the theory that has become politically effective and that draws essentially on the same data as Reibmayr, we owe all major cultural achievements to the Nordic race. Both theories—Reibmayr's and that advocated by Woltmann, Günther, and Lenz—particularly like supporting their thesis by citing the counterexample of the achievements of the Nordic race in the areas where it has remained relatively pure—in Sweden. For the one theory, the case of Sweden shows that the cultural achievement of the unmixed race lags behind the great cultural areas populated by mixed races (Attic and Ionic Greece, the southern and northern Alpine foothills, the Bohemian-Saxon border, and so on); for the other theory, the case of the northern countries proves that even under such unfavorable external conditions, the Nordic race has already attained such outstanding achievements although its full, latent capacity could unfold only while in the southern regions.[17]

This brief survey points up the great difficulties confronting the race idea in its contribution to the building of a particularist community in the concrete German political situation. A mass democracy, where the political community is formed by way of forming a mass party, for the simple reasons of political propaganda,

15. Albert Reibmayr, *Inzucht und Vermischung beim Menschen* (1897). Also Reibmayr, *Die Entwicklungsgeschichte des Talentes und Genies*, Vol. I: *Die Züchtung des individuellen Talentes und Genies in Familien und Kasten* (1908), 503, a polemic directed against Gobineau and Woltmann. The second volume contains the historical, genealogical, and statistical references. Ernst Kretschmer bases his psychology of men of genius (Kretschmer, *Geniale Menschen* [Berlin, 1929]) on Reibmayr's theory; it is Kretschmer's claim that genius grows out of talents by the cross-breeding of dissimilar aptitudes. These are processes similar to those of the "heterosis" of hybrids in the animal and plant world, p. 69: "In any case the theory of the pure race [*Reinrassigkeit*], the belief that any one talented race, such as the Nordic race, is in itself the source of superior talent, completely contradicts the accumulated historical and geographic-statistical facts."

16. Chamberlain, *Die Grundlagen des 19. Jahrhunderts* (3rd ed.; 1901), 277ff. The five basic laws of race formation.

17. I will not go into the details of the arguments because what is important here is not the correctness of the very problematic studies of racial mixture and purity but the political effect of the ideas connected to one or the other subject.

can make use only of a body idea that establishes a numerically large community and excludes only numerically small groups as "counterrealm." Therefore, the race idea appears in everyday politics only in a form that eschews any clear-cut elaboration of the details that would lead to political difficulties. The connection between the racial contrast and the political opposition of social democracy and middle-class national socialism, as Ammon has established it, must be extremely flexible in the practice of political propaganda. The Communist is a red subhuman creature only as long as he follows international socialism; when he converts to national socialism, he becomes a nation-building element. There is only a small percentage of people of the pure Nordic race in Germany; the concept of the good race must therefore be extended to people of "predominantly Nordic" race, and other races—such as the Phalian and the Alpine—are also elevated to the status of good races, so that only the numerically small group of purely Baltic and Sudetic peoples remain as the counterrealm.[18] Under these circumstances, the crucial function of the counterrealm is transferred to the Jews as a people of Oriental racial descent. The practical-political race idea is less positively defined through a race ideal than negatively through the opposition to the Jews.

The idea of the Nordic race, such as Günther advocates in a typical way, is, interestingly, only loosely connected to the race idea in concrete politics, and that is precisely what makes this connection so characteristic of Germany. The race idea relevant for party politics lacks definition except as the negation of Jewry; its background, from which it draws effective forces, is the clearly defined Nordic idea. However, it can draw from the latter only because this pure and sharply defined idea forms its background, which is never clearly and directly visible to the acting masses in the foreground. The Nordic idea can be the source of the real-political idea only because and only as long as it flows into the foreground idea in a pale and diluted form. For in its pure form it stands in sharpest contrast to the concrete political situation. Today's Nordic idea is

18. See Hans Rudolf, *Nationalsozialismus und Rasse* (Nationalsozialistische Bibliothek, No. 31), 43ff and especially 47. The breeding of a "German Race" out of *all* the elements present in the German area, including the Baltic, was rejected. Hildebrandt's race idea (see *Norm und Entartung des Menschen*, 223–24; *Staat und Rasse*, 16–17) goes further in this direction. Mommsen went even further, since he included Jews in forming the nation (*Auch ein Wort über unser Judentum*, 417).

the type of race idea that Gobineau created, with all the concomitant contents and emotions of that time. On the basis of a wealth of historical material, the Nordic race is acknowledged as the one that contributed to all the great cultural creations of the Indo-European peoples; the rise and fall of these cultural creations are seen as paralleling the advance and waning of the Nordic racial elements in the culture-creating populations. The "decline of the great race" mentioned by Madison Grant is a historical reality, and it goes hand in hand with (according to the race idea, caused by) phenomena of culture and national life that followers of the Nordic idea regard as decline. The Nordic, value-creating race, is threatened with decline, and to stop the decline of culture, according to this idea, requires an increase of the Nordic proportion of the total population or *Aufnordung* (upping the Nordic factor).

Politically, these propositions lead to the idea of a Nordic elite, which must assert itself through the tenacious fight against a large, surging mass of other racial elements and, if possible, strengthen its position. This is a struggle of a weak minority against a large majority, and it remains hopeless under the conditions of mass-democratic politics. Günther sees very clearly that the current political order of the European-American world of nations makes it impossible for the Nordic idea to prevail in the political struggle. A national policy of *Aufnordung* would have to be preceded by a radical internal change that eliminates all institutions of mass democracy. Günther does not explain in detail the new constitutional forms that would have to take the place of those institutions, but occasionally he mentions the idea of popular representation based on professions and trades as replacing meaningless partisan activity. In his opinion in a nation with a new political order "on the one hand, there would no longer be 'voting masses,' that alarming phenomenon of politics, and, on the other, there would no longer be professional 'agitators,' that other alarming phenomenon."[19] The Nordic idea cannot be helped by a new political direction within the prevailing political system but only by removing the mass-democratic elements from politics altogether. The Nordic elite can prevail nationally only in a privileged political position; it cannot prevail as long as it depends on the mood of the masses.

19. Hans F. K. Günther, *Rassenkunde des deutschen Volkes* (15th ed.; 1930), 466.

The rift between the concrete political situation in the modern mass state and the Nordic idea is deepened by the content of the latter. This contrast is absent from English and American eugenics and race theory because there the ideal image of the Nordic character, or of the select and superior race elements in general, coincides with the image of socially fit man obedient to the prevailing political order. I have already referred to Galton's political views. His selected families, the vessels of excellent hereditary traits in terms of civilization, represent the type of the English civilized person. The type of the daring, enterprising man who breaks the established order and is exemplified by the "Norman," is regarded as inferior. The warlike virtues were considered less valuable than those of the peaceful progress of civilization. The goals of Galton's eugenics do not diverge from Spencer's idea of development from the warlike to the industrial-peaceful society.

The case is similar in the United States. Grant and Stoddard[20] find the Nordic ideal fulfilled by the type of immigrants from northern and northwestern Europe; typically, it is not fulfilled by immigrants from southern and eastern Europe and by Negroes. The American Nordic idea mirrors in the sphere of the body idea the great internal problem of a threat to the idea of the frontier that had been created by the pioneers of English, German, and Scandinavian descent, a threat posed by urban democracy, which is supported by the "bad" immigration wave. This opposition has not yet erupted fully because until very recently the American political idea of the pioneer period has been virtually unquestioned and because the urban democracy has not yet become relevant to federal politics. Though American democracy with its sources in the experience of the frontier is visibly endangered, it lives on quite vigorously. The Nordic idea coincides in America with the classical democratic idea as a mass phenomenon. English and American democracy is conservative; it aims to preserve a lifestyle and human type that is politically dominant, or still dominant.

The German Nordic idea, in contrast, is revolutionary. It is not based on the mass phenomenon of a political human type; it does not coincide with the prevailing ideal image of political man, for

20. Lothrop Stoddard, *The Rising Tide of Colour Against White World-Supremacy* (1920). See the racial map following p. 228 (1930 edition). Also *Der Kulturumsturz* (1925; English, 1922).

the section of the population that could embody this Nordic idea politically, namely, the rural and urban middle class, is not the one that has given the nation its political form, as the aristocracy did in England, the bourgeoisie in France, and the pioneers in America. The German middle class did not create any political form; it has no political form today, nor has it ever had one, and its position as a factor of political power cannot be characterized as ruling but only as a desperate revolt against total proletarianization, against being drowned in a mass without status. Therefore, Günther is unable to name a socially relevant group in which the Nordic idea has a political basis in reality. In fact, he notes explicitly: "Almost every German, whether he is of pure Nordic racial descent or not, has been swamped by the racially rootless [*artlos*], often destructive, and distorting views of the present time. Whether physically or mentally, all people of our time have in some way become half-breeds and are daily exposed to confusing influences."[21] Thus the task of the Nordic idea is not the preservation of a currently real image of man but the shaping of people in accordance with a mental image. Since this mental image does not exist in the present, it is taken from the Nordic past.

> To salvage the Nordic soul through understanding the Nordic character and, primarily, to strengthen the mind and feeling, Germans with a Nordic orientation will make use of everything that has come down to us from the earliest (that is, the most strongly Nordic oriented) history of the Indo-European peoples. He will especially celebrate the experience the wealth of testimony of ancient Teutonic life. The Icelandic sagas, the *Edda,* the *Nibelungenlied,* all the heroic epics of the early Germanic period that have been handed down to us will show him the Nordic way of life. Along with the earliest literature, he will seek to understand the nature and orientation of the early architecture of the Teutons, their original beliefs [*Urschau*] (myths), their laws and customs, and he will be at pains to understand the nature of Teutonic piety.[22]

The figures of ancient Teutonic life are to serve as models guiding the lives of present-day Germans. In his studies of the Nordic soul, Clauss showed at length that the Nordic character, the Nordic figure-idea, is not visible among present-day Germans. He argued that while the "German soul" has a Nordic character, it has become

21. Günther, *Rassenkunde,* 474.
22. *Ibid.*

separated from the Teutonic element by incorporating alien powers
of soul, Baltic, Alpine, and Mediterranean ones. "The German character, then, reveals itself as determined through the interplay of
effect and countereffect between the Nordic core figure and its mar-
ginal figures."[23] The Nordic core that is to serve as the model, however, can be clearly grasped in the "German beginnings," in the
tradition of "the closely related early Nordic life and activity."[24]
The Nordic hero, as he appears in early Germanic legends and poetry, the pugnacious and courageous hero, who finds his "high
point [Hochgezeit] in his downfall," who experiences as his most
sublime moment the one that still contains "distance," the moment of reaching for victory—this is the purest expression of Nordic man.[25]

The distance between the Nordic idea and the political reality of
our time is also evident when its advocates revert to the community idea of German classicism, to Schiller's idea of the beautiful
life and the living figure, to Hölderlin's idea of the rebirth of the
German community out of the genius that inspired Greece.[26] The
"Archipelago" and its critique of the contemporary division of labor
and the consequent meaninglessness of the individual's life are
evoked; the idea of the perfect community that grows out of the
unanimous striving after the same model of humanity is once more
proposed; the "festival," the highest expression of community, is
recalled,[27] as are the "great poets" who rouse the people from their
slumber and lay down their "laws."[28] Nietzsche's "great health"
and "new aristocracy" are presented as guiding ideas.[29] And above
all of this rises the image of Plato's polity with its strict eugenic
breeding.[30]

The Nordic idea is in its nature not a national idea. The Nordic

23. Ludwig Ferdinand Clauss, *Die nordische Seele: Artung, Prägung, Ausdruck*
(1923), 174.
24. *Ibid.*, 175.
25. *Ibid.*, 191. On the effect of the idea of the early Teutonic aristocracy, see also
Richard Walter Darré, *Das Bauerntum als Lebensquell der nordischen Rasse,* and
Neuadel aus Blut und Boden (1930). See also Günther, *Adel und Rasse* (1926).
26. Günther, *Der nordische Gedanke unter den Deutschen* (1925), 12, 17.
27. Friedrich Hölderlin, "Gesang des Deutschen."
28. Hölderlin, "An unsre grossen Dichter."
29. Günther, *Der nordische Gedanke,* 20.
30. Günther, *Platon als Hüter des Lebens: Platons Zucht- und Erziehungsge-
danken und deren Bedeutung für die Gegenwart* (1928). Oddly, Stefan George's
name does not, as far as I can see, appear anywhere in Günther's work. Clauss in

elite that is endangered today is viewed as the elite of *all* the great cultures of Europe. In some, the argument goes, this elite has been eradicated to such an extent that the formerly culturally creative nations have sunk into insignificance—Eugen Fischer counts Italy, Spain, and Portugal among these and considers France the next nation that has to die. After that it will be Germany's turn unless the nation fights against this development.[31] The remaining great civilized nations shaped by the Nordic element are Germany, England, the United States, and the Scandinavian countries. Accordingly, wars between these nations will only accelerate the decline of this great race. "From the point of view of race the world war was essentially a civil war, and nearly all the officers and a large portion of the personnel on both sides were members of the Nordic race. It was a replay of the same old tragedy of mutual butchery and mutual destruction among the Nordic people, just as the Nordic aristocracy of Renaissance Italy seems to have been possessed by blood lust to kill each other off. It was the contemporary version of the old berserker blood rage and represented class suicide on a gigantic scale."[32] A more favorable development for the Nordic idea is, according to this view, the trend toward a new internationalism[33] that will prevent further "civil wars" and thus help preserve the race. In this question the German Nordic idea once again reacts characteristically differently than those of the other nations. The conservative character of the American race idea is clear from the fact that while it opposes egalitarian democracy and melting-pot politics and, in fact, has put a stop to the immigration of "undesirables,"[34] it has done so in the name of that democratic idea that still forms the basis of the nation to this day; thus, it is na-

one passage (*Nordische Seele,* 191) quotes one verse. George's idea of aristocracy seems to have no significance in race theory except in the works of his friend Kurt Hildebrandt.

31. Eugen Fischer, *Sozialanthropologie und ihre Bedeutung für den Staat* (1910), quoted in Günther, *Rassenkunde Europas* (3rd ed.; 1929), 332, *Rassenkunde des deutschen Volkes* (15th ed.; 1930), 473.

32. Madison Grant, *Der Untergang der grossen Rasse: Die Rassen als Grundlage der Geschichte Europas,* trans. Rudolf Polland (1925), 141. English edition, *The Passing of the Great Race* (1916).

33. The "blonde Internationale." Lenz, *Menschliche Auslese und Rassenhygiene* (2nd ed.; 1923), 273.

34. The effect of race-hygienic theories and federal measures in the United States are discussed by Géza von Hoffmann in *Die Rassenhygiene in den Vereinigten Staaten von Nordamerika.*

tional. The thought of civil war does not keep Grant from formulating his idea in such a way that the national policy of going to
war against Germany is justified. At the beginning of the war, he
believes, it had been difficult to decide which side had the greater
component of Nordic blood; Flanders and northern France were
more Nordic than southern Germany, and the English armies
were almost purely Nordic, and a majority of the Russian troops
were Nordic. With North America's entry into the war, it had become a war of the larger segment of the Nordics of the world against
Germany. But Germany's Nordic character was doubtful. "The
contemporary inhabitants of the German Reich, not to mention
Austria, are only to a limited degree descendants of the old Teutonic tribes, since for the most part they are Alpines, especially in
the east and the south. To leave to the Germans and Austrians the
exclusive right to the name of Teutons would be to acknowledge
one of their greatest presumptions."[35]

In contrast, the German Nordic idea tends to yield to the movement toward internationalism. Günther emphasizes that the "all-
Nordic idea" was genuinely an idea of peace. The circles with a
Nordic outlook in the major Nordic countries must come to an
agreement, and—even if only in the far distant future—they must
make possible a propaganda for the all-Nordic idea among the various nations, in the sense of an all-Nordic community, in order to
influence foreign-policy events and measures from the Nordic
standpoint. Finally, the possibility must be anticipated "that, for
example, a combination of warring powers that inevitably has such
a destructive effect as the world war had, on the Nordic race in
particular, will henceforth no longer be possible. . . . But today such
a thought is still much closer to the fantasies of a visionary than
to the sober reflection on the present."[36] Nevertheless, that thought
is being voiced in Germany, and it points in the same direction as
the other German internationalist movements, those of the social-
ists and the liberal-pacifists, all of whom leave behind the ground
of the nation-state's political reality, while parallel ideas among
other nations are subordinated to the national idea. The German
tension between cosmopolitanism and the nation-state is reflected
in the sphere of body ideas.

35. Grant, *Untergang der grossen Rasse,* 142.
36. Günther, *Rassenkunde des deutschen Volkes,* 472.

Index